THE
END
OF THE
DAYS

EDWARD L. RHODES

Acknowledgments

I wish to express a very sincere "thank you" to my family and friends who have shared in my life and inspired me to write this book. Margie, my wife, has a full share in my 60 years of ministry and has been an ongoing encouragement to me. Tamara and Tarissa, daughter and granddaughter, have been especially helpful with editing and publishing of this effort.

Many other friends, both ministers and laypeople, have encouraged and inspired me as to a need for such as "The End of the Days".

Table of Contents

Preface

Many Christians are interested in end time events, and rightfully so, because there are many wonderful events coming for those who are prepared for the end times. A lot of these Christians, including some pastors, have uncertainties about the end time and uncertainties about studying it. Part of the problem is a simple lack of study, possibly brought on by a lack of dedication to the Lord. Another part of the problem is the use of symbolic language by the prophets in their presentation of prophecies regarding the end time. No doubt there are other things that enter the picture as hinderances to studying God's word.

The purpose for writing this book from the author's viewpoint is to help some, even one of the Christians who feel a desire for a better understanding of end time events and for drawing nearer to the Lord. The author's hope extends even further that some who have never accepted the Lord will come to realize they truly need to do so. There, no doubt, will be some readers who differ with the viewpoints expressed here and that is to be expected, and we are not here to debate these issues. This information is not presented with a know-it-all attitude because the author still has many unanswered questions. Hopefully the reader will receive answers to some of his/her questions.

The internet can be a very helpful tool, but one must be very careful in going there because there is a lot of questionable information found on the internet, along with that which is helpful. What is needed before anyone should begin such a study is a truly born-again experience with a real desire to draw nearer to God, along with the Holy Spirit's presence so that He can guide one in such a search.

The author entered into this endeavor keenly aware of what the Lord said in Rv 22:18-19, so this information is presented carefully and prayerfully.

Rv 22:18-19 *For I testify unto every man that heareth the words of the prophecy of this book, If any man shall add unto these things, God shall add unto him the plagues that are written in this book: 19 And if any man shall take away from the words of the book of this prophecy, God shall take away his part out of the book of life, and out of the holy city, and from the things which are written in this book.*

In the chapter entitled "The Seven Churches of Asia," mention is made of the enormous number of Christians in the world today and the Lord promises to spew out of his mouth any who are not living a fiery and zealous life for Him.

Rv 3:16-21 *So then because thou art lukewarm, and neither cold nor hot, I will spue thee out of my mouth. 17 Because thou sayest, I am rich, and increased with goods, and have need of nothing; and knowest not that thou art wretched, and miserable, and poor, and blind, and naked: 18 I counsel thee to buy of me gold tried in the fire, that thou mayest be rich; and white raiment, that thou mayest be clothed, and that the shame of thy nakedness do not appear; and anoint thine eyes with eyesalve, that thou mayest see. 19 As many as I love, I rebuke and chasten: be zealous therefore, and repent. 20 Behold, I stand at the door, and knock: if any man hear my voice, and open the door, I will come in to him, and will sup with him, and he with me. 21 To him that overcometh will I grant to sit with me in my throne, even as I also overcame, and am set down with my Father in his throne.*

These words of Jesus are spoken to the Laodicean church, the church that will be present when the Rapture occurs. Add to these words a question Jesus once asked.

Lk 18:8   *... Nevertheless when the Son of man cometh, shall he find faith on the earth?*

It is the hope of the author that all who read will be challenged to draw closer to the Lord in readiness for the Rapture so that we may sit with Jesus in His throne.

Introduction

"The End of the Days" gives details of where we are in relationship to the end time, what is next, the many events that unfold in the coming times, and the order in which to expect them. In the last verse in the book of Daniel, Daniel is told he will rest and stand in his lot, and have a part in "the end of the days". As well, each of us will have a part in "the end of the days".

This book is about end time prophecies from the pre-tribulation point of view.

The King James Version is used unless otherwise noted.

For references to the quotes, see the numbered "Notes" at the end of the chapters involved.

Some common standards have not been used, such as listing scripture location only. Plenty of scripture has been included, so as to sufficiently prove the points being made and to have direct input from the Lord. God's word tells us many things, His words speak for Him better than we ever can. Another variation from common standards is: some characters and events show up repeatedly because there is an intermingling of subjects, such as the Antichrist who is involved in nearly every situation, so he shows up repeatedly in each of the chapters in which he is involved, and many of the other subjects show up in turn repeatedly because they are so intermingled.

The chapter on the Revelation gives a full overview of the end times so it is presented first, and the prophet Daniel adds a lot to what the Revelation presents so Daniel follows next. After these two introductory chapters, the other chapters follow in a somewhat chronological order.

Throughout all of scripture especially those related to the end times, the Lord offers encouragement to all who are interested to be alert and ready for His return so that we can be accounted worthy to escape the years of the Tribulation, so those encouragements are repeatedly included. The warnings are just as strong from the Lord to all who are not Christians that they should choose to live for the Lord or they will suffer not only the years of the Tribulation, but the fires of hell forever.

Rv 22:10-12,20 *And he saith unto me, Seal not the sayings of the prophecy of this book: for the time is at hand. 11 He that is unjust, let him be unjust still: and he which is filthy, let him be filthy still: and he that is righteous, let him be righteous still: and he that is holy, let him be holy still. 12 And, behold, I come quickly; and my reward is with me, to give every man according as his work shall be. ... 20 He which testifieth these things saith, Surely I come quickly. Amen. Even so, come, Lord Jesus.*

1
Overview of the Revelation

Separate events:

The book of Revelation has much to say about what will happen in the end time, during the Tribulation after the Rapture occurs. In the Revelation, we are reminded that Jesus will return, both in the Rapture and in His Second Coming, as two separate events. For those who love the Lord, both of those appearances will be laden with abundant blessings. For those who have denied His name, the Tribulation and the Lord's Second Coming will bring great horrors. In the scripture below the Second coming is mentioned.

Rv 1:1,5-8   *The Revelation of Jesus Christ, ... 5-8 And from Jesus Christ, who is the faithful witness, and the first begotten of the dead, and the prince of the kings of the earth. Unto him that loved us, and washed us from our sins in his own blood, 6 And hath made us kings and priests unto God and his Father; to him be glory and dominion for ever and ever. Amen. 7 Behold, he cometh with clouds; and every eye shall see him, and they also which pierced him: and all kindreds of the earth shall wail because of him. Even so, Amen. 8 I am Alpha and Omega, the beginning and the ending, saith the Lord, which is, and which was, and which is to come, the Almighty.*

Jesus expresses His love for the churches:

Rv 1:10-20   *I was in the Spirit on the Lord's day, and heard behind me a great voice, as of a trumpet, 11 Saying, I am Alpha and Omega, the first and the last: and, What thou seest, write in a book, and send it unto the seven churches which are in Asia; unto Ephesus, and unto Smyrna, and unto Pergamos, and unto Thyatira, and unto Sardis, and unto Philadelphia, and unto Laodicea. 12 And I turned to see the voice that spake with me. And being turned, I saw seven golden candlesticks; 13 And in the midst of the seven candlesticks one like unto the Son of man, clothed with a garment down to the foot, and girt about the paps with a golden girdle. 14 His head and his hairs were white like wool, as white as snow; and his eyes were as a flame of fire; 15 And his feet like unto fine brass, as if they burned in a furnace; and his voice as the sound of many waters. 16 And he had in his right hand seven stars: and out of his mouth went a sharp twoedged sword: and his countenance was as the sun shineth in his strength. 17 And when I saw him, I fell at his feet as dead. And he laid his right hand upon me, saying unto me, Fear not; I am the first and the last: 18 I am he that liveth, and was dead; and, behold, I am alive for evermore, Amen; and have the keys of hell and of death. 19 Write the things which thou hast seen, and the things which are,*

*and the things which shall be hereafter; 20 The
mystery of the seven stars which thou sawest in
my right hand, and the seven golden candlesticks.
The seven stars are the angels of the seven
churches: and the seven candlesticks which thou
sawest are the seven churches.*

Jesus warns and encourages the churches:

In Rv 2:1-3:22, John records the letters from
the Lord Jesus, to the seven churches of Asia.
Each of these seven churches represents a real
individual church in Asia Minor (modern day
Turkey) and each represents a church age during
church history from the time Jesus declared, "I will
build my church...", until the present time. These
church characteristics are found in each age and
every individual believer finds his own character in
the character of one or more of these churches.
Notice that the Lord points out the weaknesses
and/or strengths of each of the churches and
church ages. Scripture indicates that the Laodicean
church, the Church present when the Rapture
occurs, will be largely unprepared, as can be seen
in:

Rv 3:16-17 ... *So then because thou art
lukewarm, and neither cold nor hot, I will spue thee
out of my mouth. 17 Because thou sayest, I am
rich, and increased with goods, and have need of
nothing; and knowest not that thou art wretched,
and miserable, and poor, and blind, and naked: ...*

So, rather than being taken in the Rapture,
many at that time will be spewed (rejected) out of

the mouth of the Lord. Even so the remaining verses show the Lord standing at the door of every person's heart, asking to be let in. The Lord offers forgiveness to everyone who truly repents of sin in their lives. Many believe and teach that every person who claims, for any reason, to be a Christian will go in the Rapture, with no regard to whether or not a person has actually been born again. In actuality, every person who has been truly born again and is continuing to live in obedience to the Lord will go in the Rapture.

The chapter entitled "Seven Churches of Asia" addresses the messages that Jesus sent through John to the seven churches. We are presently in the Church age. When the Rapture occurs the Church age is over and the Tribulation begins.

The Rapture occurs:

The Rapture is shown to us in:

Rv 4:1   *After this I looked, and, behold, a door was opened in heaven: and the first voice which I heard was as it were of a trumpet talking with me; which said, Come up hither, and I will shew thee things which must be hereafter.*

Here, John is miraculously transported to heaven, either in the body or perhaps in spirit only, as a type of one being taken in the Rapture. From the viewpoint of the book of Revelation, Rv 4:1 is where THE RAPTURE occurs. THE RAPTURE is the first of several events in the end time where people are taken to heaven.

John begins to describe the scenes he sees in heaven:

Rv 4:2-6   *And immediately I was in the spirit: and, behold, a throne was set in heaven, and one sat on the throne. 3 And he that sat was to look upon like a jasper and a sardine stone: and there was a rainbow round about the throne, in sight like unto an emerald. 4 And round about the throne were four and twenty seats: and upon the seats I saw four and twenty elders sitting, clothed in white raiment; and they had on their heads crowns of gold. 5 And out of the throne proceeded lightnings and thunderings and voices: and there were seven lamps of fire burning before the throne, which are the seven Spirits of God. 6 And before the throne there was a sea of glass like unto crystal: and in the midst of the throne, and round about the throne, were four beasts full of eyes before and behind. ...*

These are all redeemed ones "out of every tribe and tongue and people and nation" and are representative groups of the redeemed. John describes what is obviously the throne of God surrounded by 24 lesser thrones on which are seated 24 elders. The 24 elders may well be representative of the 12 tribes of Israel from the Old Testament and the 12 apostles from the New Testament Church. John also mentions (King James version) four beasts who had access to the throne of God. Several other versions use the words "living ones" rather than "beasts".

Rv 4:7-8   *And the first beast was like a lion, and the second beast like a calf, and the third beast had a face as a man, and the fourth beast was like a flying eagle. 8 And the four beasts had each of them six wings about him; and they were full of eyes within: and they rest not day and night, saying, Holy, holy, holy, Lord God Almighty, which was, and is, and is to come.*

Before the throne was a sea of glass. In and around the throne were four living creatures; the first was like a lion (bravery), the second like an ox (strength), the third like a man (intelligence), and the fourth was like a flying eagle (swiftness). These characteristics are exemplary of Christians who are brave, strong, intelligent, and swift in serving the Lord and watchful for the Lord's coming. The four living ones had access to the throne of God along with Jesus Christ; this sounds very much like the promise that Jesus made to the overcomers of the Laodicean church in:

Rv 3:21   *To him that overcometh will I grant to sit with me in my throne, even as I also overcame, and am set down with my Father in his throne.*

All of these twenty-four elders and the four living ones are human beings who have been redeemed by the blood of Jesus, Rv 5:8-10 and Rv 7:11. They are not Seraphim or some other order of angels, as some scholars declare. On several occasions the word "vials" is used; a vial is "a large shallow cup" or "bowl."

Rv 5:8-10   And *when he had taken the book, the four beasts and four and twenty elders fell down before the Lamb, having every one of them harps, and golden vials full of odours, which are the prayers of saints. 9 And they sung a new song, saying, Thou art worthy to take the book, and to open the seals thereof: for thou wast slain, and hast redeemed us to God by thy blood out of every kindred, and tongue, and people, and nation; 10 And hast made us unto our God kings and priests: and we shall reign on the earth.*

Yes, angelic beings are present, standing around the throne and the elders and four beasts.

Rv 7:11 *And all the angels stood round about the throne, and about the elders and the four beasts, and fell before the throne on their faces, and worshipped God, ...*

The seven sealed book:

The seven sealed book and only the slain Lamb, our kinsman redeemer, Jesus, was found worthy to open it and release the righteous judgments of God on the nations. Those in heaven begin to rejoice and praise the Lord Jesus, when He takes the book to begin opening the seals. The opening of the seals in heaven is the beginning of judgments in the Tribulation on those on the earth who are sinners against God.

Rv 5:2-7 *And I saw a strong angel proclaiming with a loud voice, Who is worthy to open the book, and to loose the seals thereof? 3 And no man in heaven, nor in earth, neither under the earth, was able to open the book, neither to look thereon. 4 And I wept much, because no man was found worthy to open and to read the book, neither to look thereon. 5 And one of the elders saith unto me, Weep not: behold, the Lion of the tribe of Juda, the Root of David, hath prevailed to open the book, and to loose the seven seals thereof. 6 And I beheld, and, lo, in the midst of the throne and of the four beasts, and in the midst of the elders, stood a Lamb as it had been slain, having seven horns and seven eyes, which are the seven Spirits of God sent forth into all the earth. 7 And he came and took the book out of the right hand of him that sat upon the throne.*

With the opening of the seals, and throughout the rest of the book, much of what happens in the Book of "The Revelation" is the judgments of God against the ungodly. These judgments come about under the opening of the seven seals from Rv 6:1 to 8:1, and the sounding of the seven trumpets found in Rv 8:6 to 11:19, followed by the pouring out of the seven vials as seen in Rv 16:1-21. Of course, there are many other things going on while God's judgments are being poured out, such as all that the Antichrist is doing with his mark of the beast and all of his deception of individuals and nations. While these judgments are going on, there will be many turning to God in repentance, and many others continuing in their lives of sin and wickedness.

Opening of the seals:
• **First Seal:**   The opening of the first seal and the going forth of the white horse is the appearance of the Antichrist and the beginning of the Tribulation on the earth, Rv 6:1-2. One of the first acts of the Antichrist, after his initial appearance, as the supposed messiah, is to make a

seven-year covenant, Da 9:27, with the people of Israel, many of which will believe him to be the Messiah; at the midpoint of the covenant, he will break the agreement and defile the Temple. The Jews will then recognize him for who he is and begin to turn to Jesus the true Messiah. At this first appearance, the Antichrist is a friendly fellow, intent on securing his position to begin taking power over the whole earth. The Antichrist will succeed in establishing his position and go on to become the tyrant of all history; at his hands hundreds of millions will die. Compare the Antichrist, rider of the white horse under the first seal, Rv 6:2, with the true Christ, Rv 19:11-16.

Rv 6:1-2   *And I saw when the Lamb opened one of the seals, and I heard, as it were the noise of thunder, one of the four beasts saying, Come and see. 2 And I saw, and behold a white horse: and he that sat on him had a bow; and a crown was given unto him: and he went forth conquering, and to conquer.*

• **Second Seal:**   As the red horse goes forth under the second seal, Rv 6:4, war and killing breaks out all over; peace is taken from the earth. Red is the symbol of blood; the sword is the symbol of war. Compare Rv 6:4 to Mt 24:6-7.

Rv 6:3-4   *And when he had opened the second seal, I heard the second beast say, Come and see. 4 And there went out another horse that was red: and power was given to him that sat thereon to take peace from the earth, and that they should kill one another: and there was given unto him a great sword.*

• **Third Seal:**   The black horse under the third seal, Rv 6:5-6, brings forth worldwide, devastating, famine; famine follows war. Lack of food brought on by the famine will result in many deaths and pressure people to consider taking the mark of the beast to be able to survive. Any who take the mark have no further chance to accept the Lord, they are doomed to an eternity in the fires of hell (Rv 14:9-11).

Rv 6:5-6   *And when he had opened the third seal, I heard the third beast say, Come and see. And I beheld, and lo a black horse; and he that sat on him had a pair of balances in his hand. 6 And I heard a voice in the midst of the four beasts say, A measure of wheat for a penny, and three measures of barley for a penny; and see thou hurt not the oil and the wine.*

• **Fourth Seal:**   Under the fourth seal the pale horse rider, "Death", rides forth and "Hell" followed with him; the fourth part of men are killed with sword, hunger, death, (possibly some great pestilence) and beasts of the earth. Death on earth, is on an unbelievable scale, all slain as a result of the work of these two riders. According to the U. S. Census Bureau[1], in July 2019 earth's population was about 7,583,315,000. One fourth of that number is 1,895,828,750 slain, or 267,857,142 per year, or 733,855 per day for 7 years. In the first six months of 2018 there were 30,153,000 deaths worldwide from all causes, as a comparison of what occurs under the opening of the fourth seal. These deaths under the fourth seal judgment may not take seven years for fulfillment;

this judgment could be fulfilled in a few months to a year or two, therefore, unimaginable numbers will be slain per day. These figures do not take into account all of the deaths by other means.

Rv 6:7-8 *And when he had opened the fourth seal, I heard the voice of the fourth beast say, Come and see. 8 And I looked, and behold a pale horse: and his name that sat on him was Death, and Hell followed with him. And power was given unto them over the fourth part of the earth, to kill with sword, and with hunger, and with death, and with the beasts of the earth.*

• **Fifth Seal:** When the fifth seal is opened, "... under the altar the souls of them that were slain for the word of God and for their testimony;" they are crying out for God to avenge them; they are given white robes and are told to rest a little longer until those yet to be martyred join them. This is a picture of persecution and martyrdom, through fire and blood. The Tribulation has barely started and here is evidence of much persecution and bloodshed of Christians. The persecution is against the Jews but will also include Gentile Christians from all other nations. These all have been martyred during the Tribulation, having missed the Rapture. This doubtlessly is the work of Antichrist and other evil persons during the early stages of the Tribulation. The souls under the altar (Rv 6:9-11) seem to be bodyless souls who were found in heaven as a result of having been slain; their bodies are still in the graves on earth; they have not yet been resurrected and raptured, but will be in a subsequent rapture event.

Rv 6:9-11   And when he had opened the fifth seal, I saw under the altar the souls of them that were slain for the word of God, and for the testimony which they held: 10 And they cried with a loud voice, saying, How long, O Lord, holy and true, dost thou not judge and avenge our blood on them that dwell on the earth? 11 And white robes were given unto every one of them; and it was said unto them, that they should rest yet for a little season, until their fellowservants also and their brethren, that should be killed as they were, should be fulfilled.

• **Sixth Seal:**   As the sixth seal is opened, a series of horrifying events takes place on the earth, such as a great earthquake, the sun becomes black and the moon blood, stars (meteors?) fall from heaven, the sky recedes (possibly some event never before seen in history) and every mountain and island are moved out of place. These events are so violent and horrendous that the people on earth plead with the rocks and mountains to fall on them, to hide them from the face of God and the wrath of the Lamb.

Rv 6:12-17   And I beheld when he had opened the sixth seal, and, lo, there was a great earthquake; and the sun became black as sackcloth of hair, and the moon became as blood; 13 And the stars of heaven fell unto the earth, even as a fig tree casteth her untimely figs, when she is shaken of a mighty wind. 14 And the heaven departed as a scroll when it is rolled together; and every mountain and island were moved out of their places. 15 And the kings of the earth, and the great men, and the rich men, and the chief captains, and the mighty men, and every bondman, and every free man, hid themselves in the dens and in the rocks of the mountains; 16 And said to the mountains and rocks, Fall on us, and hide us from the face of him that sitteth on the throne, and from the wrath of the Lamb: 17 For the great day of his wrath is come; and who shall be able to stand?

With all that is taking place, along with many recognizing that this is the wrath of the Lamb being poured out in judgment, still, many are refusing to repent and turn to God.

An interlude occurs here in the telling of what John saw; the first six seals have been opened. John tells some other things he saw both in heaven and on earth.

The appearance of the 144,000 Jews:

Rv 7:1-8   On earth, the 144,000 Israelis are sealed; 12,000 from each of the 12 tribes. These are the first of a great turning of the Jews to accept Jesus as the Christ, the Messiah; these 144,000 will evangelize the remainder of the Jews. It is good to know that in the midst of all the horrors of the Tribulation, the gospel will be preached, bringing many to the Lord. Please notice, all of the tribes of Israel are present in this list except the tribe of Dan. (Manasseh, son of Joseph, takes Dan's place.) Taking note of this, some scholars teach that the Antichrist will come as a Jew himself from the tribe of Dan, perhaps rightfully so.

13

Rv 7:1-8   *And after these things I saw four angles standing on the four corners of the earth, holding the four winds of the earth, that the wind should not blow on the earth, nor on the sea, nor on any tree. 2 And I saw another angel ascending from the east, having the seal of the living God: and he cried with a loud voice to the four angels, to whom it was given to hurt the earth and the sea, 3 Saying, Hurt not the earth, neither the sea, nor the trees, till we have sealed the servants of our God in their foreheads. 4 And I heard the number of them which were sealed: and there were sealed an hundred and forty and four thousand of all the tribes of the children of Israel. 5 Of the tribe of Juda were sealed twelve thousand. Of the tribe of Reuben were sealed twelve thousand. Of the tribe of Gad were sealed twelve thousand. 6 Of the tribe of Aser were sealed twelve thousand. Of the tribe of Nepthali were sealed twelve thousand. Of the tribe of Manasses were sealed twelve thousand. 7 Of the tribe of Simeon were sealed twelve thousand. Of the tribe of Levi were sealed twelve thousand. Of the tribe of Issachar were sealed twelve thousand. 8 Of the tribe of Zabulon were sealed twelve thousand. Of the tribe of Joseph were sealed twelve thousand. Of the tribe of Benjamin were sealed twelve thousand.*

A great multitude, which no man could number:

In heaven, John sees a vast multitude of Tribulation saints; they did not go in the Rapture which occurred before the Tribulation started, but they now appear in heaven having come out of the Tribulation as a result of having died for their stand for Christ. "This great multitude which no man could number" are in heaven as a result of being taken to heaven from this world during the Tribulation.

Rv 7:9-17 *After this I beheld, and, lo, a great multitude, which no man could number, of all nations, and kindreds, and people, and tongues, stood before the throne, and before the Lamb, clothed with white robes, and palms in their hands; 10 And cried with a loud voice, saying, Salvation to our God which sitteth upon the throne, and unto the Lamb. 11 And all the angels stood round about the throne, and about the elders and the four beasts, and fell before the throne on their faces, and worshipped God, 12 Saying, Amen: Blessing, and glory, and wisdom, and thanksgiving, and honour, and power, and might, be unto our God for ever and ever. Amen. 13 And one of the elders answered, saying unto me, What are these which are arrayed in white robes? and whence came they? 14 And I said unto him, Sir, thou knowest. And he said to me, These are they which came out of great tribulation, and have washed their robes, and made them white in the blood of the Lamb. 15 Therefore are they before the throne of God, and serve him day and night in his temple: and he that sitteth on the throne shall dwell among them. 16 They shall hunger no more, neither thirst any more; neither shall the sun light on them, nor any heat. 17 For the Lamb which is in the midst of the throne shall feed them, and shall lead them unto*

living fountains of waters: and God shall wipe away
all tears from their eyes.

Sounding of the Seven Trumpets:
• **Seventh Seal:**   Rv 8:1-6   The opening of the
seventh seal is a prelude to the sounding of the
seven trumpets. The sounding of the first four
trumpets affects one third of certain things on the
earth, having tragic and overwhelming
consequences.

• **First Trumpet:**   Affects vegetation, hail and fire
mingled with blood are thrown to the earth. One
third of trees and all green grass are burned.
Doubtlessly the storm of hail, fire, and blood are
going to be like something nightmares are made of,
only this nightmare will be all too real; and the
devastation left behind will leave the earth a very
undesirable place compared to what it has been
through history.

Rv 8:7   *The first angel sounded, and there*
followed hail and fire mingled with blood, and they
were cast upon the earth: and the third part of
trees was burnt up, and all green grass was burnt
up.

• **Second Trumpet:**   Affects seas. The
"something like a great burning mountain" could be
a huge meteor coming from outer space and
landing in one of the oceans, destroying one third
of sea life and one third of ships on those seas.
There very well may be worldwide tsunamis or
other calamities associated with this event.   God is
not limited to our imaginations, so, this "great

burning mountain" may be something other than a meteor. At any rate the effects will be awesome.

Rv 8:8-9   *And the second angel sounded, and as it were a great mountain burning with fire was cast into the sea: and the third part of the sea became blood; 9 And the third part of the creatures which were in the sea, and had life, died; and the third part of the ships were destroyed.*

• **Third Trumpet:**   Affects waters. A great star, burning like a torch, falls from heaven. Again, we want to say a meteor, but the description is different and the consequences are different. One third of the drinking water sources are made virtually undrinkable and possibly poisonous for those who do drink.

Rv 8:10-11   *And the third angel sounded, and there fell a great star from heaven, burning as it were a lamp, and it fell upon the third part of the rivers, and upon the fountains of waters; 11 And the name of the star is called Wormwood: and the third part of the waters became wormwood; and many men died of the waters, because they were made bitter.*

• **Fourth Trumpet:**   Sun and moon both are darkened by one third, affecting both day and night by one third. An angel flies through the heavens declaring "Woe, Woe, Woe" because of the three remaining trumpets. All that has occurred already has had devastating effects on the earth; hundreds of millions have been slain, world economies are in a shamble, all production, including food, has slowed, perhaps stopped altogether. Life as we presently know it is turned upside down, and now there is the announcement that it is going to get radically worse. This is at or near the midpoint of the Tribulation; the remaining time of three-and-one-half years is called the Great Tribulation. The demon world plays a heavy role in the remaining time, all orchestrated by God Himself.

Rv 8:12-13   *And the fourth angel sounded, and the third part of the sun was smitten, and the third part of the moon, and the third part of the stars; so as the third part of them was darkened, and the day shone not for a third part of it, and the night likewise. 13 And I beheld, and heard an angel flying through the midst of heaven, saying with a loud voice, Woe, woe, woe, to the inhabiters of the earth by reason of the other voices of the trumpet of the three angels, which are yet to sound!*

As bad as the judgments under the first four trumpets were, the judgments under the last three trumpets will be much worse. The last three trumpets are referred to as woes because of the horrible results.

The three woes, last three trumpets:
• **Fifth Trumpet:**   First woe sounds. Demonic creatures are released from the bottomless pit (Hell) onto the Earth; these creatures have an appearance of locusts with a scorpion like tail, with which they inflict agonizing pain on the godless inhabitants of the Earth. These creatures have a terrifying appearance and the pain endures unabated for five months; those who are smitten by these demonic scorpions long in vain for death to take them. Death will not come. The king over

these locusts/scorpions from the bottomless pit is called Abaddon (Hebrew) and Apollyon (Greek) meaning destroyer or destroying angel. The first Woe is past; it seems that this Woe endures at least five months; two more woes are coming.

Rv 9:1-12 *And the fifth angel sounded, and I saw a star fall from heaven unto the earth: and to him was given the key of the bottomless pit. 2 And he opened the bottomless pit; and there arose a smoke out of the pit, as the smoke of a great furnace; and the sun and the air were darkened by reason of the smoke of the pit. 3 And there came out of the smoke locusts upon the earth: and unto them was given power, as the scorpions of the earth have power. 4 And it was commanded them that they should not hurt the grass of the earth, neither any green thing, neither any tree; but only those men which have not the seal of God in their foreheads. 5 And to them it was given that they should not kill them, but that they should be tormented five months: and their torment was as the torment of a scorpion, when he striketh a man. 6 And in those days shall men seek death, and shall not find it; and shall desire to die, and death shall flee from them. 7 And the shapes of the locusts were like unto horses prepared unto battle; and on their heads were as it were crowns like gold, and their faces were as the faces of men. 8 And they had hair as the hair of women, and their teeth were as the teeth of lions. And they had breastplates, as it were breastplates of iron; and the sound of their wings was as the sound of chariots of many horses running to battle. 10 And they had tails like unto scorpions, and there were stings in their tails: and their power was to hurt men five months. 11 And they had a king over them, which is the angel of the bottomless pit, whose name in the Hebrew tongue is Abaddon, but in the Greek tongue hath his name Apollyon. 12 One woe is past; and, behold, there come two woes more hereafter.*

• **Sixth Trumpet:**   Second woe. There are four Angels (evil) that have been bound in the Euphrates River, to be released at this exact time to kill one third of mankind. They will accomplish this by using an army of 200,000,000 horsemen, presumably from hell, (this is not clearly stated in scripture). One third of mankind is killed by the fire, smoke, and brimstone that came from the mouths of the horses of these two hundred million horsemen. At the opening of the Tribulation, world population will probably exceed 7,583,315,000; perhaps hundreds of millions will be slain under the opening salvo, the first three seals. At the opening of the fourth seal, one fourth of the world's population was killed; now another one third are killed under the second Woe (sixth trumpet). Giving no consideration to the other deaths, the deaths of the one fourth and the one third alone will amount to: 7,583,315,000 x 25% = 1,895,828,750 slain, leaving 5,687,486,250 x 33%, = 1,876,870,462 slain under sixth trumpet, leaving the world's population at 3,810,615,788. Approximately one half of Earth's population will be killed as a result of the opening of the fourth seal and the release of the demonic beings under the sixth trumpet which is the second woe. These two and other judgments of God will have reduced the earth's population by well more than half; this does not take into account all of the deaths by the Antichrist and other godless beings taking the lives of countless Christians. This sixth trumpet judgment does not occur until near or even after the midpoint of the tribulation. We know that the time for this judgment is a year, a month, a day, an hour, so, therefore the daily death rate is going to be near 4,800,180 for that year, month, day, time period. God's whole purpose in all of this is to bring men to repentance, yet most of those left alive after this incomprehensible slaughter still refuse to repent and turn from their godlessness.

Rv 9:13-21 *And the sixth angel sounded, and I heard a voice from the four horns of the golden altar which is before God, 14 Saying to the sixth angel which had the trumpet, Loose the four angels which are bound in the great river Euphrates. 15 And the four angels were loosed, which were prepared for an hour, and a day, and a month, and a year, for to slay the third part of men. 16 And the number of the army of the horsemen were two hundred thousand thousand: and I heard the number of them. 17 And thus I saw the horses in the vision, and them that sat on them, having breastplates of fire, and of jacinth, and brimstone: and the heads of the horses were as the heads of lions; and out of their mouths issued fire and smoke and brimstone. 18 By these three was the third part of men killed, by the fire, and by the smoke, and by the brimstone, which issued out of their mouths. 19 For their power is in their mouth, and in their tails: for their tails were like unto serpents, and had heads, and with them they do hurt. 20 And the rest of the men which were not killed by these plagues yet repented not of the works of their hands, that they should not worship devils, and idols of gold, and silver, and brass, and stone, and of wood: which neither can see, nor hear, nor walk: 21 Neither repented they of their murders, nor of their sorceries, nor of their fornication, nor of their thefts.*

The little book:

Between the sixth and seventh trumpets John presents the "little book," which speaks of great bitterness ahead for Israel. John was told to take the little book and eat it. It will be sweet in your mouth but bitter in your belly. In other words, what is spoken of in the book will seem good but the results will be bad.

Rv 10:1-11   The Little Book, an angel declares, "time no longer", or no more delay.

Rv 10:3-4   Seven thunders uttered their voice, for some unknown reason John was told not to write what the seven thunders said.

Rv 10:7   "The mystery of God should be finished" ...

Rv 11:1-6   The events introduced here seem to begin at or near the midpoint of the Tribulation, which is the beginning of the Great Tribulation; these events run concurrently with all else that is going on during the last three-and-one-half years before the Lord returns to reign as King over the whole earth during the Millennium; we, truly born again Christians, will be reigning with Him as kings and priests.

The two witnesses:

At the end of three-and-one-half years of ministry, these two witnesses (possibly Enoch and Elijah, or Moses and Elijah) will be killed by the Antichrist; their bodies will lie in the streets of Jerusalem for three-and-one-half days with the people of the world looking on and rejoicing "because these two prophets tormented those who dwell on the earth". Besides bringing famine and plagues and other miracles, these "two olive trees and the two lampstands standing before the God of the earth" (see Zec 4:1-14), will surely be proclaiming the Gospel. So, the 144,000 Jews are preaching the gospel and the two witnesses are preaching the gospel; both groups are warning everyone concerning the Antichrist and judgment; most of the world are not repentant and only see the ministry of the two witnesses as torment.

Rv 11:3-10 *And I will give power unto my two witnesses, and they shall prophesy a thousand two hundred and threescore days, clothed in sackcloth. 4 These are the two olive trees, and the two candlesticks standing before the God of the earth. 5 And if any man will hurt them, fire proceedeth out of their mouth, and devoureth their enemies: and if any man will hurt them, he must in this manner be killed. 6 These have power to shut heaven, that it rain not in the days of their prophecy: and have power over waters to turn them to blood, and to smite the earth with all plagues, as often as they will. 7 And when they shall have finished their testimony, the beast that ascendeth out of the bottomless pit shall make war against them, and shall overcome them, and kill them. 8 And their dead bodies shall lie in the street of the great city, which spiritually is called Sodom and Egypt, where also our Lord was crucified. 9 And they of the people and kindreds and tongues and nations shall see their dead bodies three days and an half, and shall not suffer their dead bodies to be put in graves. 10 And they that dwell upon the earth shall rejoice over them, and make merry, and shall send gifts one to another; because these two prophets tormented them that dwelt on the earth.*

After three-and-one-half days their bodies will be resurrected and then caught up into heaven, all accompanied by an earthquake; the people of earth are filled with fear, 7000 inhabitants of Jerusalem will be killed in the earthquake, the remainder (in Jerusalem) will give glory to the God of heaven.

Rv 11:11-13   *And after three days and an half the Spirit of life from God entered into them, and they stood upon their feet; and great fear fell upon them which saw them. 12 And they heard a great voice from heaven saying unto them, Come up hither. And they ascended up to heaven in a cloud; and their enemies beheld them. 13 And the same hour was there a great earthquake, and the tenth part of the city fell, and in the earthquake were slain of men seven thousand: and the remnant were affrighted, and gave glory to the God of heaven.*

In Rv 11:14, we are told the second woe is past; the third woe is coming.

• **Seventh Trumpet:** Brings the third woe, which brings in the pouring out of the seven vials. The third woe seems to include everything all the way to, and including, the return of Christ, and Him fighting the battle of Armageddon. Note in Rv 11:15-19, the seventh angel sounded and all of heaven pauses.

The woman clothed with the sun:

Rv 12:1-17   As a parenthetical statement, we are told of the woman in childbirth confronted by the dragon. The woman is Israel, the people of God; the child is Jesus the Savior; the dragon is Satan who is intent on destroying the child. The child is caught up into heaven (the ascension of Jesus). There is war in heaven; Satan is cast out of heaven; Satan then turns to pursue the woman who then flees to the wilderness. We know that the child has already been born and ascended to heaven. The rest of this story actually occurs during the time of the Tribulation. In reality during the Tribulation, Christian Jews will actually flee and hide from Antichrist and Satan. When Satan sees he cannot persecute the woman, then he will turn to persecute all of the remaining Christians throughout the world. What we see here is a spiritual battle going on with Satan manifesting himself through the Antichrist.

The Antichrist and his False Prophet present the mark of the beast:

Rv 13:1-18 shows the appearance of the Antichrist and False Prophet. This depiction of the Antichrist is at the midpoint of the Tribulation. He is no longer that friendly fellow who appeared riding a white horse at the opening of the first seal, Rv 6:1-2. At this point Antichrist is fully possessed of the devil. He received a deadly head wound, then was healed; this really impressed the people of the world to worship him. He continues for 42 months blaspheming God and warring against the saints.

Rv 13:1-10   *And I stood upon the sand of the sea, and saw a beast rise up out of the sea, having seven heads and ten horns, and upon his horns ten crowns, and upon his heads the name of blasphemy. 2 And the beast which I saw was like unto a leopard, and his feet were as the feet of a bear, and his mouth as the mouth of a lion: and the dragon gave him his power, and his seat, and great authority. 3 And I saw one of his heads as it were wounded to death; and his deadly wound was healed: and all the world wondered after the beast. 4 And they worshipped the dragon which gave power unto the beast: and they worshipped the beast, saying, Who is like unto the beast? who is able to make war with him? 5 And there was given unto him a mouth speaking great things and blasphemies; and power was given unto him to continue forty and two months. 6 And he opened his mouth in blasphemy against God, to blaspheme his name, and his tabernacle, and them that dwell in heaven. 7 And it was given unto him to make war with the saints, and to overcome them: and power was given him over all kindreds, and tongues, and nations. 8 And all that dwell upon the earth shall worship him, whose names are not written in the book of life of the Lamb slain from the foundation of the world. 9 If any man have an ear, let him hear. 10 He that leadeth into captivity shall go into captivity: he that killeth with the sword must be killed with the sword. Here is the patience and the faith of the saints.*

The Antichrist is joined by his companion the False Prophet, who goes all out, performing great miracles calling fire down from heaven deceiving the whole world, all to support the Antichrist and promote his mark of the beast program, the number of which is 666.

Rv 13:11-18   *And I beheld another beast coming up out of the earth; and he had two horns like a lamb, and he spake as a dragon. 12 And he exerciseth all the power of the first beast before him, and causeth the earth and them which dwell therein to worship the first beast, whose deadly wound was healed. 13 And he doeth great wonders, so that he maketh fire come down from heaven on the earth in the sight of men, 14 And deceiveth them that dwell on the earth by the means of those miracles which he had power to do in the sight of the beast; saying to them that dwell on the earth, that they should make an image to the beast, which had the wound by a sword, and did live. 15 And he had power to give life unto the image of the beast, that the image of the beast should both speak, and cause that as many as would not worship the image of the beast should be killed. 16 And he causeth all, both small and great, rich and poor, free and bond, to receive a mark in their right hand, or in their foreheads: 17 And that no man might buy or sell, save he that had the mark, or the name of the beast, or the number of his name. 18 Here is wisdom. Let him that hath understanding count the number of the beast: for it is the number of a man; and his number is Six hundred threescore and six.*

The 144,000 first fruits of the Jews are taken to heaven:

This group of 144,000 now appears in heaven having evangelized the Jews and the rest of the world.

Rv 14:1,4   *And I looked, and, lo, a Lamb stood on the mount Sion, and with him an hundred forty and four thousand, having his Father's name written in their foreheads. ... 4 ... These are they which follow the Lamb whithersoever he goeth. These were redeemed from among men, being the firstfruits unto God and to the Lamb.*   (These are the 144,000 of chapter seven.)

The gospel is preached:

Some of this preaching is done by angels who are untouchable by Satan and the Antichrist. And even though the two witnesses are human, they are, also, untouchable until they have finished their testimony after three-and-one-half years. Not only is the gospel being preached, but these preachers are also warning all the inhabitants of the world not to accept the deception of the Antichrist and his False Prophet. At this point in the Tribulation, probably well along toward the end, we have seen at least three massive efforts at world evangelization. Rv 7:1-8 tells of the efforts of the 144,000 Jews to win the rest of the Jews, and no doubt the whole world is watching and hears the gospel story. Then Rv 11:7-10 gives the story of the two witnesses who give their testimony, then are ultimately killed by the Antichrist. They resurrect after three-and-one-half days and ascend into heaven to add to their testimony. The whole world watches all of this in awe and fear, only to continue to reject the Lord. Rv 14:6 speaks of an angel flying in the midst of heaven "having the everlasting gospel to preach unto them that dwell on the earth, apparently to every nation and tongue and people group on earth". This angel and two others that follow make it clear to all that they should follow after the Lord and reject the Antichrist and all that he stands for, else they will suffer the torments of fire and brimstone. In Rv 14:8 another angel followed saying "Babylon the great is fallen". In Rv 14:9 a third angel followed saying, "If any shall worship the beast ...The same shall drink of the wine of the wrath of God poured out without mixture into the cup of his indignation;". Add to this the testimony of the angel mentioned in Rv 8:13 who was flying through the midst of heaven saying "Woe, Woe, Woe" to the inhabitants of the earth because of the three trumpets which are yet to sound. Presumably this angel is flying in the airspace above the earth giving the inhabitants of the earth fair warning about what is yet to come. Rejection of the Lord by the inhabitants of the earth after all of this warning simply points out the determined evil in the hearts of the people left on the earth and the righteous justice of the judgment brought against them by the Lord.

Armageddon is coming:

Rv 14:20 *The wine press was trodden without the city, blood flowed to the depth of the horse's bridles, for a length of 1600 furlongs.* (From Megiddo to Bozrah, about 200 miles.)

This is a preview of the battle of Armageddon; the actual Battle of Armageddon takes place in Rv 19:11-21. This much bloodshed is beyond imagination, but God's word declares it, and it will happen.

Preparation for the seven bowl judgments:

Rv 15:1-2 *And I saw another sign in heaven, great and marvelous, seven angels having the seven last plagues; for in them is filled up the wrath of God. 2 And I saw as it were a sea of glass mingled with fire: and them that had gotten the victory over the beast, and over his image, and over his mark, and over the number of his name, stand on the sea of glass, having the harps of God.* (This appears to be another group taken to heaven, Although, these could be from groups already accounted for.)

Seven Vials (seven last plagues):

These are the seven last direct actions of judgments of God during the time of the Tribulation until the Second Coming occurs to end it all. Under the first bowl (vial), a severe plague of sores breaks out on those who have taken the mark of the beast. Second bowl, the sea becomes as the blood of a dead man, everything in the sea dies. Third bowl, rivers and other fresh water sources become blood. Fourth bowl, fierce heat from the sun scorches men with fire; rather than repent, they blaspheme God. Fifth bowl, darkness comes over the kingdom of the Antichrist; pain is associated with this darkness; again, blasphemy against God.

- **First Vial:** Rv 16:1-2 *And I heard a great voice out of the temple saying to the seven angels, Go your ways, and pour out the vials of the wrath of God upon the earth. 2 And the first went, and poured out his vial upon the earth; and there fell a noisome and grievous sore upon the men which had the mark of the beast, and upon them which worshipped his image.*
- **Second Vial:** Rv 16:3 *And the second angel poured out his vial upon the sea; and it became as the blood of a dead man: and every living soul died in the sea.*
- **Third Vial:** Rv 16:4-6 *And the third angel poured out his vial upon the rivers and fountains of waters; and they became blood. 5 And I heard the angel of the waters say, Thou art righteous, O Lord, which art, and wast, and shalt be, because thou hast judged thus. 6 For they have shed the*

blood of saints and prophets, and thou hast given them blood to drink; for they are worthy.

● **Fourth Vial:** Rv 16:8-9 *And the fourth angel poured out his vial upon the sun; and power was given unto him to scorch men with fire. 9 And men were scorched with great heat, and blasphemed the name of God, which hath power over these plagues: and they repented not to give him glory.*

● **Fifth Vial:** Rv 16:10-11 *And the fifth angel poured out his vial upon the seat of the beast; and his kingdom was full of darkness; and they gnawed their tongues for pain, 11 And blasphemed the God of heaven because of their pains and their sores, and repented not of their deeds.*

When the sixth bowl is poured out, the Euphrates river is dried up to prepare the way for the kings of the east to gather at Armageddon. Demonic spirits from the mouths of Satan, Antichrist, and the False Prophet go out to all the kings of the world to gather them to Armageddon.

● **Sixth Vial:** Rv 16:12-16 *And the sixth angel poured out his vial upon the great river Euphrates; and the water thereof was dried up, that the way of the kings of the east might be prepared. 13 And I saw three unclean spirits like frogs come out of the mouth of the dragon, and out of the mouth of the beast, and out of the mouth of the false prophet. 14 For they are the spirits of devils, working miracles, which go forth unto the kings of the earth and of the whole world, to gather them to the battle of that great day of God Almighty. 15 Behold, I come as a thief. Blessed is he that watcheth, and keepeth his garments, lest he walk* *naked, and they see his shame. 16 And he gathered them together into a place called in the Hebrew tongue Armageddon.*

Notice that the Lord Jesus speaks out, even this late in the Tribulation, in the middle of the pouring out of the bowls of wrath and just before the battle of Armageddon; in verse 15 He says, *"Behold, I come as a thief. Blessed is he that watcheth, and keepeth his garments, lest he walk naked, and they see his shame."*

Verses 15 and 16 refer to the second stage of the Lord's coming (the actual Second Coming) when He touches down on the earth to fight the great battle of Armageddon, then to be established as King of Kings and Lord of Lords over the whole earth for 1000 years, and His faithful people will rule and reign with Him.

Events leading the whole world to Armageddon:

When the seventh vial (bowl) is poured out, God brings justice in His righteous wrath and the whole world is shaken nearly to destruction. The cities of the nations fall. Scripture doesn't make clear how many cities are involved, but we may well assume that quite possibly every city on earth is destroyed. Great Babylon came in remembrance before God. In July of 2020 there is no city of Babylon, but there is a large city called Al Hillah where the ancient city of Babylon once stood. It only needs to be renamed to become the Babylon that God will pour out His wrath upon.

• **Seventh Vial:** Rv 16:17-21   *And the seventh angle poured out his vial into the air; and there came a great voice out of the temple of heaven, from the throne, saying, It is done. 18 And there were voices, and thunders, and lightnings; and there was a great earthquake, such as was not since men were upon the earth, so mighty an earthquake, and so great. 19 And the great city was divided into three parts, and the cities of the nations fell: and great Babylon came in remembrance before God, to give unto her the cup of the wine of the fierceness of his wrath. 20 And every island fled away, and the mountains were not found. 21 And there fell upon men a great hail out of heaven, every stone about the weight of a talent: and men blasphemed God because of the plague of the hail; for the plague thereof was exceeding great.*

Joseph Seiss[2] says, the great city divided into three parts (v. 19) is Jerusalem. Different Bible study resources give different weights for the talent, according to different times and places. Apparently, the talent could range anywhere from 60 pounds to 120 pounds. Consider the damage from hailstones of this size and weight striking a human being or even a house or other similar building. This is another preview of a part of Armageddon.

Mystery Babylon destroyed:

The woman in this passage of scripture represents false religion, of all ages, including the false church of all the Church ages. She appears here riding on the authority, power, and support of the Antichrist and his supporting ten nation federation. She rides over all the peoples, multitudes, nations, and tongues in the earth. She is guilty of the shed blood of saints and martyrs of all ages.

Rv 17:3-6 *So he carried me away in the spirit into the wilderness: and I saw a woman sit upon a scarlet coloured beast, full of names of blasphemy, having seven heads and ten horns. 4 And the woman was arrayed in purple and scarlet colour, and decked with gold and precious stones and pearls, having a golden cup in her hand full of abominations and filthiness of her fornication: 5 And upon her forehead was a name written, MYSTERY, BABYLON THE GREAT, THE MOTHER OF HARLOTS AND ABOMINATIONS OF THE EARTH. 6 And I saw the woman drunken with the blood of the saints, and with the blood of the martyrs of Jesus: and when I saw her, I wondered with great admiration.*

Even though the woman at first has the support of the Antichrist and the ten-nation federation, they eventually destroy her, so that the Antichrist may be exalted and worshipped as god alone, but only for a short time.

Rv 17:15-18 *And he saith unto me, The waters which thou sawest, where the whore sitteth, are peoples, and multitudes, and nations, and tongues. 16 And the ten horns which thou sawest upon the beast, these shall hate the whore, and shall make her desolate and naked, and shall eat her flesh, and burn her with fire. 17 For God hath put in their hearts to fulfil his will, and to agree, and give their kingdom unto the beast, until the words of God shall be fulfilled. 18 And the woman which thou sawest is that great city, which reigneth over the kings of the earth.*

The destruction of commercial Babylon:

Revelation 18 speaks of the destruction of Babylon. The language used sounds like the destruction of an actual city; as of August 2020, there still is no city of Babylon that would answer to this city, if there proves to be no destruction of an actual city of Babylon, then the references are to the destruction of the world's commercial system.

Rv 18:1-8   *And he cried mightily with a strong voice, saying, Babylon the great is fallen, is fallen, and is become the habitation of devils, and the hold of every foul spirit, and a cage of every unclean and hateful bird. 3 For all nations have drunk of the wine of the wrath of her fornication, and the kings of the earth have committed fornication with her, and the merchants of the earth are waxed rich through the abundance of her delicacies. 4 And I heard another voice from heaven, saying, Come out of her, my people, that ye be not partakers of her sins, and that ye receive not of her plagues. 5 For her sins have reached unto heaven, and God hath remembered her iniquities. 6 Reward her even as she rewarded you, and double unto her double according to her works: in the cup which she hath filled fill to her double. 7 How much she hath glorified herself, and lived deliciously, so much torment and sorrow give her: for she saith in her heart, I sit a queen, and am no widow, and shall see no sorrow. 8 Therefore shall her plagues come in one day, death, and mourning, and famine; and she shall be utterly burned with fire: for strong is the Lord God who judgeth her.*

It makes sense that the kings of the earth would bewail a major city or the world's commercial system or both.

Rv 18:9-10   *And the kings of the earth, who have committed fornication and lived deliciously with her, shall bewail her, and lament for her, when they shall see the smoke of her burning, 10 Standing afar off for the fear of her torment, saying, Alas, alas, that great city Babylon, that mighty city! for in one hour is thy judgment come.* (Another preview of a part of Armageddon)

Rv 18:21   *And a mighty angel took up a stone like a great millstone, and cast it into the sea, saying, Thus with violence shall that great city Babylon be thrown down, and shall be found no more at all.*

The marriage of the Lamb:

Meanwhile in heaven the marriage of the Lamb takes place. Within the scripture in Revelation this event is presented with only three verses, yet the marriage of the Lamb is a truly great event. If this marriage follows normal biblical marriage procedures, seven days of feasting, then there may very well be a feast and celebration, lasting seven years. As the scripture says, "Blessed are they which are called unto the marriage supper of the Lamb."

Rv 19:7-9   *Let us be glad and rejoice, and give honour to him: for the marriage of the Lamb is come, and his wife hath made herself ready. 8 And to her was granted that she should be arrayed in fine linen, clean and white: for the fine linen is the righteousness of saints. 9 And he saith unto me, Write, Blessed are they which are called unto the marriage supper of the Lamb. And he saith unto me, These are the true sayings of God.*

Armageddon:

A description of Jesus is given as he arrives on earth in the Second Coming to destroy the evil forces at Armageddon. Those who went in the Rapture to heaven will return with Him. This view of Armageddon is when the event actually occurs. The Lord has come in what is referred to as His Second Coming. He comes at this time to judge and make war. He will smite the nations with the sword of His mouth. He is accompanied by the armies of heaven, but there is no fighting between the armies of heaven and the armies of the nations on earth. The Lord Jesus uses the sword of his mouth, He simply speaks, and the sinful armies are destroyed.

Rv 19:11-16   *And I saw heaven opened, and behold a white horse; and he that sat upon him was called Faithful and True, and in righteousness he doth judge and make war. 12 His eyes were as a flame of fire, and on his head were many crowns; and he had a name written, that no*

*man knew, but he himself. 13 And he was clothed
with a vesture dipped in blood: and his name is
called The Word of God. 14 And the armies which
were in heaven followed him upon white horses,
clothed in fine linen, white and clean. 15 And out
of his mouth goeth a sharp sword, that with it he
should smite the nations: and he shall rule them
with a rod of iron: and he treadeth the winepress of
the fierceness and wrath of Almighty God. 16 And
he hath on his vesture and on his thigh a name
written, KING OF KINGS, AND LORD OF LORDS.*

The birds are invited to a great supper. The
Beast and the kings of the earth gather to make
war against Him that sat on the horse. The Beast
and the False Prophet are taken and cast alive into
the lake of fire. The remnant (their armies) are
slain with the sword. The Tribulation is ended,
probably with no sinners left alive on earth.

Rv 19:17-21 *And I saw an angel standing in
the sun; and he cried with a loud voice, saying to
all the fowls that fly in the midst of heaven, Come
and gather yourselves together unto the supper of
the great God; 18 That ye may eat the flesh of
kings, and the flesh of captains, and the flesh of
mighty men, and the flesh of horses, and of them
that sit on them, and the flesh of all men, both free
and bond, both small and great. 19 And I saw the
beast, and the kings of the earth, and their armies,
gathered together to make war against him that
sat on the horse, and against his army. 20 And the
beast was taken, and with him the false prophet
that wrought miracles before him, with which he
deceived them that had received the mark of the*

beast, and them that worshipped his image. These both were cast alive into a lake of fire burning with brimstone. 21 And the remnant were slain with the sword of him that sat upon the horse, which sword proceeded out of his mouth: and all the fowls were filled with their flesh.

After the Tribulation:

Immediately following the battle of Armageddon, Satan is bound and cast into the bottomless pit for 1000 years.

Rv 20:1-3   *And I saw an angel come down from heaven, having the key of the bottomless pit and a great chain in his hand. 2 And he laid hold on the dragon, that old serpent, which is the Devil, and Satan, and bound him a thousand years, 3 And cast him into the bottomless pit, and shut him up, and set a seal upon him, that he should deceive the nations no more, till the thousand years should be fulfilled: and after that he must be loosed a little season.*

The Millennial Kingdom of Christ:

The faithful saints are established as kings and priests to reign with Christ for a thousand years.

Rv 20:4-6   *And I saw thrones, and they sat upon them, and judgment was given unto them: and I saw the souls of them that were beheaded for the witness of Jesus, and for the word of God, and which had not worshipped the beast, neither his image, neither had received his mark upon their foreheads, or in their hands; and they lived and reigned with Christ a thousand years. 5 But the rest of the dead lived not again until the thousand years were finished. This is the first resurrection. 6 Blessed and holy is he that hath part in the first resurrection: on such the second death hath no power, but they shall be priests of God and of Christ, and shall reign with him a thousand years.*

Satan's last effort:

Notice that Satan is loosed from the pit for a short time to try those who have been born during the Millennium and have never been tried. Apparently, millions believe Satan's deceit and they go to surround the camp of the saints to perhaps destroy them. But they proceed no further, for, fire comes down from God in heaven and devours them.

Rv 20:7-10   *And when the thousand years are expired, Satan shall be loosed out of his prison, 8 And shall go out to deceive the nations which are in the four quarters of the earth, Gog and Magog, to gather them together to battle: the number of whom is as the sand of the sea. 9 And they went up on the breadth of the earth, and compassed the camp of the saints about, and the beloved city: and fire came down from God out of heaven, and devoured them. 10 And the devil that deceived them was cast into the lake of fire and brimstone, where the beast and the false prophet are, and shall be tormented day and night forever and ever.*

The Great White Throne Judgment follows:

The Great White Throne is the judgment of all of the sinners, of all ages, forever separated from God, lost forever and cast into the lake of fire.

Rv 20:11-15   *And I saw a great white throne, and him that sat on it, from whose face the earth and the heaven fled away; and there was found no place for them. 12 And I saw the dead, small and great, stand before God; and the books were opened: and another book was opened, which is the book of life: and the dead were judged out of those things which were written in the books, according to their works. 13 And the sea gave up the dead which were in it; and death and hell delivered up the dead which were in them: and they were judged every man according to their works. 14 And death and hell were cast into the lake of fire. This is the second death. 15 And whosoever was not found written in the book of life was cast into the lake of fire.*

A new heaven and a new earth created:

God creates a new heaven and earth, with no more sea. Whether this is a new creation or a renewal is not clear, see the chapter on New heaven and Earth. This, like many other things going on in the last days of this present world, will be an awesome event.

Rv 21:1-4   *And I saw a new heaven and a new earth: for the first heaven and the first earth were passed away; and there was no more sea. 2 And I John saw the holy city, new Jerusalem,* coming down from God out of heaven, prepared as a bride adorned for her husband. 3 And I heard a great voice out of heaven saying, Behold, the tabernacle of God is with men, and he will dwell with them, and they shall be his people, and God himself shall be with them, and be their God. 4 And God shall wipe away all tears from their eyes; and there shall be no more death, neither sorrow, nor crying, neither shall there be any more pain: for the former things are passed away.

The holy Jerusalem:

Some scholars teach that the holy Jerusalem descends from God out of heaven and perhaps hovers over the new earth. Scripture never states clearly that the new holy city settles onto the earth. Let's not be surprised if we find it either way; however it is, it will be beautiful, and it will be home to all who are faithful.

Rv 21:9-11   And there came unto me one of the seven angels which had the seven vials full of the seven last plagues, and talked with me, saying, Come hither, I will shew thee the bride, the Lamb's wife. 10 And he carried me away in the spirit to a great and high mountain, and shewed me that great city, the holy Jerusalem, descending out of heaven from God. 11 Having the glory of God: and her light was like unto a stone most precious, even like a jasper stone, clear as crystal; ...

The Lord God Almighty and the Lamb are the temple and the light:

This beautiful city is lightened by the glory of God. Nothing evil will ever be allowed there throughout eternity. This is the city that Abraham looked for, Heb 11:10. This is the city we are looking for.

Rv 21:22-27   *And I saw no temple therein: for the Lord God Almighty and the Lamb are the temple of it. 23 And the city had no need of the sun, neither of the moon, to shine in it: for the glory of God did lighten it, and the Lamb is the light thereof. 24 And the nations of them which are saved shall walk in the light of it: and the kings of the earth do bring their glory and honour into it. 25 And the gates of it shall not be shut at all by day: for there shall be no night there. 26 And they shall bring the glory and honour of the nations into it. 27 And there shall in no wise enter into it anything that defileth, neither whatsoever worketh abomination, or maketh a lie: but they which are written in the Lamb's book of life.*

Conclusion:

In the four gospels, and here in this book of Revelation, the Lord Jesus tells us again and again that He is coming quickly and that we all need to be alert and obedient for a very great moment, The Rapture, and for all else involved in the end of this age.

Rv 22:7,12,17   *Behold, I come quickly: blessed is he that keepeth the sayings of the prophecy of this book. ... 12 And, behold, I come quickly; and my reward is with me, to give every man according as his work shall be. ... 17 And the Spirit and the bride say, Come. And let him that heareth say, Come. And let him that is athirst come. And whosoever will, let him take the water of life freely.*

We go now to look at the supporting prophecies of that great prophet Daniel, who showed us some of these things long before John came on the scene.

Notes:
1. U. S. Census Bureau, World Population. Link: http://www.census.gov/popclock/
2. Joseph A. Seiss, The Apocalypse (Grand Rapids, MI: Kregel Publications, 1987), p. 381.

2
Overview of Daniel's Revelations

Behold a great image:

Nebuchadnezzar is probably the best known of the kings of Babylon. He was the king in power when Israel was carried away to Babylon in exile. He had a dream but could not remember what the dream was. God revealed the dream and interpretation to Daniel, who then gave that information to Nebuchadnezzar. Obviously, this dream was from God to Nebuchadnezzar. We, who are living in the time of the end, view this information as prophecy yet to be fulfilled. Why would God pass that information through an ungodly king rather than through Daniel? One reason for God passing this information through a heathen king of this world, is because that king was one of the principal players. The dream was of a great image, its head was gold, chest and arms were silver, belly and thighs were brass, legs of iron, and feet and toes were mixed of iron and clay. Daniel said the form of this image was terrible. The various parts in a descending order, were nations that had a relationship with Israel; the head was Babylon, chest and arms was Medo-Persia, belly was Greece, legs were Roman Empire, feet and toes were the Eastern and Western divisions of Roman Empire. The western division of the Roman Empire was made up of western European nations. The eastern division was made up of Greece and other nations in the middle east (Asia). In the end of days there will arise a ten-nation federation which is represented by the ten toes of the great image in Nebuchadnezzar's dream. Part clay and part iron (Verses 41-43 of Da 2); therefore, the kingdom will be partly strong and partly broken. They will mingle together, but they will not like each other. They will come together for political and economic reasons. Therefore, this ten-nation federation in the end time may be made up of five European nations and five middle eastern nations. This is the kingdom that the Antichrist will be using to rule the world. God will bring this all to an end by setting up a kingdom that will "break in pieces and consume all these kingdoms." God's kingdom will stand forever.

Da 2:36-44 *This is the dream; and we will tell the interpretation thereof before the king. 37 Thou, O king, art a king of kings: for the God of heaven hath given thee a kingdom, power, and strength, and glory. 38 And wheresoever the children of men dwell, the beasts of the field and the fowls of the heaven hath he given into thine hand, and hath made thee ruler over them all. Thou art this head of gold. 39 And after thee shall arise another kingdom inferior to thee, and another third kingdom of brass, which shall bear rule over all the earth. 40 And the fourth kingdom shall be strong as iron: forasmuch as iron breaketh in pieces and subdueth all things: and as iron that breaketh all these, shall it break in pieces and bruise. 41 And whereas thou sawest the feet and toes, part of potters' clay, and part of iron, the kingdom shall be divided; but there shall be in it of the strength of the iron, forasmuch as thou sawest the iron mixed with miry clay. 42 And as the toes of the feet were part of iron, and part of clay, so the kingdom shall be partly strong, and partly broken. 43 And whereas thou sawest iron mixed with miry clay, they shall mingle themselves with the seed of men: but they shall not cleave one to another, even as iron is not mixed with clay. 44 And in the days of these kings shall the God of heaven set up a kingdom, which shall never be destroyed: and the kingdom shall not be left to other people, but it shall break in pieces and consume all these kingdoms, and it shall stand for ever.*

Daniel's Dream:

Daniel's dream in chapter 7 reveals some of the same things as are shown in Nebuchadnezzar's dream in chapter 2, although there are some differences. Chapter 2 uses a great image to show four different empires, each of which have a relationship with Israel. Those empires are Babylonian, Medo-Persian, Grecian, and Roman. Chapter 7 shows the same thing via four beasts. Chapter 7 goes further showing the Antichrist arising out of the fourth empire, the Roman Empire. Both chapters conclude by showing that the kingdom of God will arise and destroy all of these other kingdoms. God's kingdom will last forever, ruled over by Christ and His saints; Christ's kingdom will last forever.

Behold a fourth beast, Rome, dreadful and terrible, and strong exceedingly:

Daniel had a dream, in which he saw four beasts rise up out of the sea; he was told these are four kings which will arise out of the earth, but the saints of the most High will take and possess the kingdom forever and ever. These kingdoms all arose in the past and it is encouraging to know that the saints' time is coming and will endure for eternity. Elements of the fourth beast, Roman Empire, are yet to arise, and soon, in the form of the ten horns, this is, today, commonly referred to as the revived Roman Empire. These ten horns will appear as a ten-nation federation, yet in the future. All of these things are told to us in verses 23-24; we are told further that from that fourth beast ten kings will arise, and among them an eleventh king will arise and subdue three of the original ten. That being is the Antichrist, who will be boastful and deceitful; as well, he will speak great words against God. He will wear out the saints and change laws. After the allotted time his dominion will be destroyed and the saints will rule with the Lord whose kingdom will endure forever.

Da 7:16-27 *I came near unto one of them that stood by, and asked him the truth of all this. So he told me, and made me know the interpretation of the things. 17 These great beasts, which are four, are four kings, which shall arise out*

50

of the earth. 18 But the saints of the most High shall take the kingdom, and possess the kingdom for ever, even for ever and ever. 19 Then I would know the truth of the fourth beast, which was diverse from all the others, exceeding dreadful, whose teeth were of iron, and his nails of brass; which devoured, brake in pieces, and stamped the residue with his feet; 20 And of the ten horns that were in his head, and of the other which came up, and before whom three fell; even of that horn that had eyes, and a mouth that spake very great things, whose look was more stout than his fellows. 21 I beheld, and the same horn made war with the saints, and prevailed against them; 22 Until the Ancient of days came, and judgment was given to the saints of the most High; and the time came that the saints possessed the kingdom. 23 Thus he said, The fourth beast shall be the fourth kingdom upon earth, which shall be diverse from all kingdoms, and shall devour the whole earth, and shall tread it down, and break it in pieces. 24 And the ten horns out of this kingdom are ten kings that shall arise: and another shall rise after them; and he shall be diverse from the first, and he shall subdue three kings. 25 And he shall speak great words against the most High, and shall wear out the saints of the most High, and think to change times and laws: and they shall be given into his hand until a time and times and the dividing of time. 26 But the judgment shall sit, and they shall take away his dominion, to consume and to destroy it unto the end. 27 And the kingdom and dominion, and the greatness of the kingdom under the whole heaven, shall be given to the people of the saints of the most High, whose kingdom is an everlasting kingdom, and all dominions shall serve and obey him.

A king of a fierce countenance:

In Da 8:19, Gabriel begins his explanation by telling Daniel that he has come to help Daniel (and you and I) understand what will be in the latter time of the indignation (Tribulation), for the end will come at an appointed time. Gabriel continues by making it clear that the two kingdoms under consideration are the Medo-Persian and Greek Empires. He says that the large horn between the eyes of the goat is the first king of Greece. We know that to be Alexander the Great. When this large horn is broken off, four other horns grow up to take his place; these are four of Alexander the Great's generals who divide his kingdom; they became the rulers over these four lesser kingdoms, when Alexander the Great died. Verse 23 makes it clear that in the latter times from one of these kingdoms will arise a king (the Antichrist) of a fierce countenance and demeanor; he understands sinister schemes. His power will be mighty, but from another source outside of himself. We know that source to be from Satan. Destruction and deceit will be main features of his kingdom. He will destroy people. He will exalt himself in his pride, presuming to destroy even the Prince of princes (Jesus, the King of Kings). Even though Antichrist is powerful and beyond human abilities to stop him,

52

his allotted time will run out, he will be broken without human means, but by God's hand.

Da 8:19-26 *And he said, Behold, I will make thee know what shall be in the last end of the indignation: for at the time appointed the end shall be. 20 The ram which thou sawest having two horns are the kings of Media and Persia. 21 And the rough goat is the king of Grecia: and the great horn that is between his eyes is the first king. 22 Now that being broken, whereas four stood up for it, four kingdoms shall stand up out of the nation, but not in his power. 23 And in the latter time of their kingdom, when the transgressors are come to the full, a king of fierce countenance, and understanding dark sentences, shall stand up. 24 And his power shall be mighty, but not by his own power: and he shall destroy wonderfully, and shall prosper, and practise, and shall destroy the mighty and the holy people. 25 And through his policy also he shall cause craft to prosper in his hand; and he shall magnify himself in his heart, and by peace shall destroy many: he shall also stand up against the Prince of princes; but he shall be broken without hand. 26 And the vision of the evening and the morning which was told is true: wherefore shut thou up the vision; for it shall be for many days.*

In chapters 2 and 7 of Daniel, we see four world empires: Babylonian, Medo-Persian, Greek, and Roman, with concentration on the Roman Empire. We see that the Antichrist comes out of the Revived Roman Empire, but the fact that the other three empires are included, shows some relationship between them and the Antichrist as well. Daniel 8 makes a different presentation; only two empires are shown, and yet we see the Antichrist appearing on this scene. Any study of maps of each of the empires in question will show sufficient overlap of all these empires to easily see how the Antichrist could come from any one of them. The two empires considered in Daniel's vision in chapter 8 are the Medo-Persian and the Greek Empires, with the Antichrist coming from out of the Grecian Empire. In chapter 8, Daniel sees his vision, then Gabriel appears to tell him what the vision means. We see that Daniel 7 says the Antichrist will arise out of the Roman Empire, and chapter 8 says he will arise out of the Grecian Empire. To simplify and clarify: take a map of each of these two empires, place one over the other, where they overlap is the area from which the Antichrist will arise.

Unto two thousand and three hundred days:

Within the vision, we are made to understand that the Antichrist will defile and desecrate the temple and take away the daily sacrifice.

Da 8:13-14 *Then I heard one saint speaking, and another saint said unto that certain saint which spake, How long shall be the vision concerning the daily sacrifice, and the transgression of desolation, to give both the sanctuary and the host to be trodden under foot? 14 And he said unto me, Unto two thousand and three hundred days; then shall the sanctuary be cleansed.*

From some heavenly being, Daniel learns that from the time of the desecration of the temple until the cleansing and restoration of the temple, it will be 2300 days; Gabriel does not comment on the desecration and cleansing of the temple with the 2300 days in between.

There are a lot of different ideas about the meaning of the two thousand and three hundred days, and only a few who come up with sensible answers. One of the things that complicates the question is that there are many different versions of the Bible. Two examples are the King James Version and the American Standard Version. The King James version says the sanctuary will be cleansed in two thousand three hundred days, but the American Standard Version says the sanctuary will be cleansed in two thousand three hundred evenings and mornings. This is referring to the Old Testament morning and evening sacrifices, see Ex 29:38-42.

Da 8:14   And *he said unto me, Unto two thousand and three hundred days; then shall the sanctuary be cleansed. [KJV]*

Da 8:14   *And he said unto me, Unto two thousand and three hundred evenings (and) mornings; then shall the sanctuary be cleansed. [ASV]*

The sanctuary will be desecrated at, or shortly after, the midpoint of the Tribulation, meaning there will be three-and-one-half years or 1260 days left in the tribulation, Da 12:7. Da 12:11 brings the subject up again where it says the abomination that makes desolate will continue for

1290 days; verse 12 says blessed is he that waits to the 1335 days.

Da 12:11-12   And from the time that the daily sacrifice shall be taken away, and the abomination that maketh desolate set up, there shall be a thousand two hundred and ninety days. 12 Blessed is he that waiteth, and cometh to the thousand three hundred and five and thirty days. [KJV]

Da 12:11-12   *And from the time that the continual (burnt-offering) shall be taken away, and the abomination that maketh desolate set up, there shall be a thousand and two hundred and ninety days. 12 Blessed is he that waiteth, and cometh to the thousand three hundred and five and thirty days. [ASV]*

It appears from all that we are told in these scripture locations that the Antichrist will begin and continue the abomination of desolation through the entire last half of the Tribulation, which is three-and-one-half years or 1260 days. At the Second Coming of Jesus this abomination will be stopped. In the following 30 days the sanctuary will be cleansed. A blessing is pronounced on he that waits another 45 days. The purpose for waiting another 45 days is not clear.

Seventy weeks are determined upon thy people and upon thy holy city, to finish the transgression:

The angel Gabriel tells Daniel that seventy weeks are determined on Daniel's people, the Jews, because of their history of sin and disbelief towards

God. God had chosen Abraham and his descendants as a special people to bring all of the other nations to Him. As far back as the exodus from Egypt, God brought them out of Egypt and showed them miracle after miracle and they seemingly only doubted Him in the centuries that followed, even to rejecting the long-promised Messiah, Jesus. These seventy weeks are like punishment, to catch their attention; it is "to finish the transgression, and to make an end of sins, and to make reconciliation for iniquity, and to bring in everlasting righteousness, and to seal up the vision and prophecy, and to anoint the most Holy." Even though evil persons and nations are involved, this is God at work to bring the Jews back to him in a right relationship. These seventy weeks are actually seventy periods of seven years, or a total of 490 years. The first sixty-nine periods were from the time when the commandment was given to restore and build Jerusalem (Neh 2:1-8) until Messiah was cut off (slain): somewhere near 449 BC to AD 33. When Jesus the Messiah died, the counting of weeks was stopped. The last week begins counting again and goes through the seven years of the Tribulation. All of the first 483 years that have already passed were troublesome times for the Jews. But, this last week, the seven years of the Tribulation, will be much worse.

Da 9:24-27 *Seventy weeks are determined upon thy people and upon thy holy city, to finish the transgression, and to make an end of sins, and to make reconciliation for iniquity, and to bring in everlasting righteousness, and to seal up the vision*

*and prophecy, and to anoint the most Holy. 25
Know therefore and understand, that from the
going forth of the commandment to restore and to
build Jerusalem unto the Messiah the Prince shall
be seven weeks, and threescore and two weeks:
the street shall be built again, and the wall, even in
troublous times. 26 And after threescore and two
weeks shall Messiah be cut off, but not for himself:
and the people of the prince that shall come shall
destroy the city and the sanctuary; and the end
thereof shall be with a flood, and unto the end of
the war desolations are determined. 27 And he
shall confirm the covenant with many for one
week: and in the midst of the week he shall cause
the sacrifice and the oblation to cease, and for the
overspreading of abominations he shall make it
desolate, even until the consummation, and that
determined shall be poured upon the desolate.*

Rise of the Antichrist:

Da 11:21-45. In verse 3 of Da 11, Daniel is
talking about the rise of Alexander the Great, the
first king in the Greek Empire. When Alexander
died, four of his generals rose up in his place and
divided the Greek Empire into four lesser
kingdoms. From verse 5 on, Daniel talks about two
of these kingdoms, referring to them as the king of
the North and the king of the South. These two
kingdoms, which where lesser divisions of the
Greek Empire: are the Seleucid Empire (the king of
the North) and the Ptolemaic Empire (the king of
the South). The Seleucid Empire reached from Asia
Minor (present day Turkey) eastward through

Syria, Mesopotamia (including present day Iraq), Persia and beyond, reaching to the Indus River (India). The kings of both of these empires were Greek; and both empires continued for several generations, until the Roman Empire began to rise. After centuries of interaction between the king of the North and the king of the South, the Antichrist appears as the king of the North. The Antichrist appears in Daniel 11:21. He will probably appear somewhere within the territory of the ancient Seleucid Empire (which is also within the Ancient Greek Empire); that same place needs to be somewhere within the Ancient Roman Empire (Da 7:20). We should say his origin will be within these locations; where he will actually make his appearance, may be another story. He will be a despised nobody, who will not have been recognized as royalty. He will come in peaceably and seize the kingdom by intrigue (treachery); all who oppose him will be overcome. He shall arise from a small (or small number of) people. This seems to be speaking of a small nation or province or some other entity.

Verses 25-28 show us that the Antichrist will be involved in negotiations with the king of the South; the two of them, bent on evil, deceiving each other, even going to war, with the King of the South (Egypt) being defeated. The Antichrist will return to his own land, probably Babylon, with the spoils of war; he will pass through Israel on the way, leaving a path of destruction as he goes.

There are a lot of scriptures that indicate that Babylon may very well prove to be where the

Antichrist is headquartered in the beginning of his reign of terror. He later moves to Jerusalem. See the following scripture locations that lend some support to the idea that Babylon is his land, headquarters: Zech 5:5-11, Rv 17 and 18, Isa 13 and 14, Jer 50 and 51. There is no place in scripture that plainly states that the Antichrist will be headquartered in Babylon, but it seems likely. Babylon will certainly play a big part in the Tribulation.

Again, he turns toward the south, but is deterred by ships from Cyprus (the West, possibly Europe or the USA). So, enraged by this hindrance he goes again to Israel and does more damage. At this time, he defiles the sanctuary, taking away the daily sacrifice, and places the abomination of desolation. This is the midpoint of the Tribulation, and it is at this time when the Jews realize he is not the Messiah; they turn from him and, finally, begin to turn to the true Messiah. All of this time, many other things have been going on during this first half of the Tribulation; hundreds of millions have died from natural disasters and war; with one of those wars possibly being the Battle of Gog/Magog. It will be near this time when the two witnesses will appear; the mark of the beast will be forced on the world. From this point on, the world, and especially Israel, will be a place of chaos, torment, and destruction with demonic beings coming to take part in all of this evil. Some who are godly during this time will stand up strongly and do great exploits; with many of them being slain in the process. The Antichrist will have no desire for women, meaning he may be a homosexual. He will not regard the god of his fathers, nor any god, and will present himself as god. Although, he will honor the god of fortresses, a god his fathers did not know.

Toward the end of the Tribulation, Egypt will attack him, and the Antichrist will strike back viciously with a massive force including help from Libya and Ethiopia. Many countries will be overthrown including Israel and Egypt. Egypt may be hit with a nuclear bomb in the middle of this rampage of war and destruction. The Antichrist will receive disturbing news from the east and the north, which will enrage him to even more destruction. In all of this process he will be found somewhere between the Mediterranean Sea to the west, and the Dead Sea to the east, presumably in Jerusalem; suddenly, he will come to his end with no one to help him. We know that when his end comes, it will be during the battle of Armageddon. He and the False Prophet will be captured and thrown alive into the Lake of Fire (Rv 19:20). All in the scriptures below is about the Antichrist, beginning with the vile person in verse 21.

Da 11:21-45 *And in his estate shall stand up a vile person, to whom they shall not give the honour of the kingdom: but he shall come in peaceably, and obtain the kingdom by flatteries. 22 And with the arms of a flood shall they be overflown from before him, and shall be broken; yea, also the prince of the covenant. 23 And after the league made with him he shall work deceitfully: for he shall come up, and shall become strong with* a small people. 24 He shall enter peaceably even upon the fattest places of the province; and he shall do that which his fathers have not done, nor his fathers' fathers; he shall scatter among them the prey, and spoil, and riches: yea, and he shall forecast his devices against the strong holds, even for a time. 25 And he shall stir up his power and his courage against the king of the south with a great army; and the king of the south shall be stirred up to battle with a very great and mighty army; but he shall not stand: for they shall forecast devices against him. 26 Yea, they that feed of the portion of his meat shall destroy him, and his army shall overflow: and many shall fall down slain. 27 And both these kings' hearts shall be to do mischief, and they shall speak lies at one table; but it shall not prosper: for yet the end shall be at the time appointed. 28 Then shall he return into his land with great riches; and his heart shall be against the holy covenant; and he shall do exploits, and return to his own land. 29 At the time appointed he shall return, and come toward the south; but it shall not be as the former, or as the latter. 30 For the ships of Chittim shall come against him: therefore he shall be grieved, and return, and have indignation against the holy covenant: so shall he do; he shall even return, and have intelligence with them that forsake the holy covenant. 31 And arms shall stand on his part, and they shall pollute the sanctuary of strength, and shall take away the daily sacrifice, and they shall place the abomination that maketh desolate. 32 And such as do wickedly against the covenant shall he corrupt by flatteries: but the *people that do know their God shall be strong, and do exploits. 33 And they that understand among the people shall instruct many: yet they shall fall by the sword, and by flame, by captivity, and by spoil, many days. 34 Now when they shall fall, they shall be holpen with a little help: but many shall cleave to them with flatteries. 35 And some of them of understanding shall fall, to try them, and to purge, and to make them white, even to the time of the end: because it is yet for a time appointed. 36 And the king shall do according to his will; and he shall exalt himself, and magnify himself above every god, and shall speak marvellous things against the God of gods, and shall prosper till the indignation be accomplished: for that that is determined shall be done. 37 Neither shall he regard the God of his fathers, nor the desire of women, nor regard any god: for he shall magnify himself above all. 38 But in his estate shall he honour the God of forces: and a god whom his fathers knew not shall he honour with gold, and silver, and with precious stones, and pleasant things. 39 Thus shall he do in the most strong holds with a strange god, whom he shall acknowledge and increase with glory: and he shall cause them to rule over many, and shall divide the land for gain. 40 And at the time of the end shall the king of the south push at him: and the king of the north shall come against him like a whirlwind, with chariots, and with horsemen, and with many ships; and he shall enter into the countries, and shall overflow and pass over. 41 He shall enter also into the glorious land, and many countries shall be overthrown: but these shall escape out of his hand, even Edom, and Moab, and the chief of the children of Ammon. 42 He shall stretch forth his hand also upon the countries: and the land of Egypt shall not escape. 43 But he shall have power over the treasures of gold and of silver, and over all the precious things of Egypt: and the Libyans and the Ethiopians shall be at his steps. 44 But tidings out of the east and out of the north shall trouble him: therefore he shall go forth with great fury to destroy, and utterly to make away many. 45 And he shall plant the tabernacles of his palace between the seas in the glorious holy mountain; yet he shall come to his end, and none shall help him.*

There shall be a time of trouble, such as never was:

The angel Michael makes it clear that there is coming a greater trouble for Israel then has ever been, but when Israel is shattered it will be over, then Israel will be delivered; Jer 30:7 supports this. As was observed in paragraphs above, Daniel is told that from the time the daily sacrifice is taken away and the abomination of desolation is set up, there will be 1290 days. Blessed are those who come to 1335 days. Daniel is assured that at "the end of the days" he will arise to his inheritance and have his full share in these things.

Daniel 12:1-13 *And at that time shall Michael stand up, the great prince which standeth for the children of thy people: and there shall be a time of trouble, such as never was since there was a nation even to that same time: and at that time thy people shall be delivered, every one that shall be found written in the book. 2 And many of them that sleep in the dust of the earth shall awake, some to everlasting life, and some to shame and everlasting contempt. 3 And they that be wise shall shine as the brightness of the firmament; and they that turn many to righteousness as the stars for ever and ever. ... 6 And one said to the man clothed in linen, which was upon the waters of the river, How long shall it be to the end of these wonders? 7 And I heard the man clothed in linen, which was upon the waters of the river, when he held up his right hand and his left hand unto heaven, and sware by him that liveth for ever that it shall be for a time, times, and an half; and when he shall have accomplished to scatter the power of the holy people, all these things shall be finished. ... 11 And from the time that the daily sacrifice shall be taken away, and the abomination that maketh desolate set up, there shall be a thousand two hundred and ninety days. 12 Blessed is he that waiteth, and cometh to the thousand three hundred and five and thirty days. 13 But go thou thy way till the end be: for thou shalt rest, and stand in thy lot at the end of the days.*

Daniel's prophecies, added to those in the Revelation, and several others of the prophets, help us to understand better what is coming in the days of the Tribulation. Let us be careful and alert so that we are ready when the Lord comes for us, that we may be accounted worthy to escape all of these things.

Rv 16:15   *Behold, I come as a thief. Blessed is he that watcheth, and keepeth his garments, lest he walk naked, and they see his shame.*

Jesus expounded at length on the end times in answer to the disciples' question: "When shall these things be?" Let us now consider His answer.

3
When Shall These Things Be?

Not one stone upon another:

On one occasion, Jesus' disciples were admiring the beauty of the temple in Jerusalem, and they drew Jesus' attention to the grandeur of the temple. Jesus told them there would come the time when there would not be left one stone upon another. The disciples then asked Jesus: when will this happen? And what will be the signs of your coming and of the end of the world? Jesus then began a considerable discourse on the end time events as recorded in three of the four gospels: Matthew 24, Mark 13, and Luke 21. The destruction of the temple occurred about forty years later, in AD 70 by the Roman Army. The temple has never been rebuilt, even though Israel has been re-established as a nation now for 72 years as of May 14, 2020. Plans and preparations are all in place for rebuilding the temple, and according to Bible prophesies, it will be built before the Tribulation begins or early on during the Tribulation.

Mt 24:1-2   *And Jesus went out, and departed from the temple: and his disciples came to him for to shew him the buildings of the temple.*

2 And Jesus said unto them, See ye not all these things? verily I say unto you, There shall not be left here one stone upon another, that shall not be thrown down. (Mark and Luke record their versions of this same event in Mk 13:1-2; Lk 21:5-6.) In Lk 18:20-37, Jesus gave answer to the Pharisees who had asked a similar question that His disciples had asked, the question being, "When will the kingdom of God come?"

The Beginning of Sorrows:
Jesus began a long discourse on the end times by warning of deceivers coming and claiming to be Christ; don't be deceived. He warned of troubles coming, such as war, earthquakes, etc., saying, these are the beginning of sorrows. The beginning of sorrows can refer to two different times, the time before the Tribulation begins when troubles really begin to come about, or the beginning of sorrows may be when the Tribulation begins. There are already many of these signs and the Tribulation has not yet begun. So, it seems we may already be in the beginning of sorrows. The Covid-19 virus is a very good illustration of the beginning of sorrows. Once the Tribulation begins, the signs Jesus mentioned will rapidly pick up in numbers and violence, so then we will be in the beginnings of sorrows for sure. The entire time of the Tribulation is an awful time of trouble and sorrow, and these things Jesus mentions are the beginnings of these sorrows. Then the end begins, and what a terrible end it will be.

68

Mt 24:3-8   *And as he sat upon the mount of Olives, the disciples came unto him privately, saying, Tell us, when shall these things be? and what shall be the sign of thy coming, and of the end of the world? 4 And Jesus answered and said unto them, Take heed that no man deceive you. 5 For many shall come in my name, saying, I am Christ; and shall deceive many. 6 And ye shall hear of wars and rumours of wars: see that ye be not troubled: for all these things must come to pass, but the end is not yet. 7 For nation shall rise against nation, and kingdom against kingdom: and there shall be famines, and pestilences, and earthquakes, in divers places. 8 All these are the beginning of sorrows.*   (See also Mk 13:3-8; Lk 21:7-11)

Then shall the end come:

Jesus continued telling us, we will be afflicted, murdered, and hated by all nations, and many will be offended and will betray each other. The implication here is that often times it will be family and friends who betray each other during these awful times. Because sin becomes so overwhelming, many will turn cold in their stand for Christ. We should give serious thought to the idea that sin can actually become overwhelming unless we maintain a strong hold on the Lord and His Word. When the gospel has been preached to the whole world, then shall the end come. These things will be going on during the first half of the Tribulation; the great Tribulation, the second half, is far worse.

Mt 24:9-14   *Then shall they deliver you up to be afflicted, and shall kill you: and ye shall be hated of all nations for my name's sake. 10 And then shall many be offended, and shall betray one another, and shall hate one another. 11 And many false prophets shall rise, and shall deceive many. 12 And because iniquity shall abound, the love of many shall wax cold. 13 But he that shall endure unto the end, the same shall be saved. 14 And this gospel of the kingdom shall be preached in all the world for a witness unto all nations; and then shall the end come.*   (Mk 13:9-13; Lk 21:12-19)

The abomination of desolation:

The abomination of desolation occurs at the midpoint of the Tribulation. At the beginning of the Tribulation the Antichrist makes a seven-year agreement with the Jews, but after only three-and-one-half years, the Antichrist breaks his agreement. He goes into the newly built temple and stops the daily sacrifice and offers some other abominable, vile and evil sacrifice promoting himself and declaring that he alone is God. There is a lot of confusion as to exactly what does happen at this occasion. No doubt it will be so awful and evil that anyone who is truly concerned about it will see it for exactly what it is. It is at this point when Jesus says: when you see the abomination of desolation (in Jerusalem), flee to the mountains; it is possible that God might well honor that same thing in other parts of the world; scripture is silent on that subject. In Luke's gospel, Jesus says "when you see Jerusalem surrounded with armies then flee to the mountains." Jesus is speaking expressly to the Jews and He literally means flee to the mountains. If a Gentile is concerned, he should flee with the Jews trusting in the Lord, for all who flee to the mountains at that time will be hidden and fed miraculously for the next three-and-one-half years. God has always honored any Gentiles who have joined the Jewish people while trusting in the Lord. Jesus states that the Tribulation at that time will be worse than anything ever before, and there never will be such tribulation afterwards.

Mt 24:15-22   *When ye therefore shall see the abomination of desolation, spoken of by Daniel the prophet, stand in the holy place, (whoso readeth, let him understand:) 16 Then let them which be in Judaea flee into the mountains: 17 Let him which is on the housetop not come down to take any thing out of his house: 18 Neither let him which is in the field return back to take his clothes. 19 And woe unto them that are with child, and to them that give suck in those days! 20 But pray ye that your flight be not in the winter, neither on the sabbath day: 21 For then shall be great tribulation, such as was not since the beginning of the world to this time, no, nor ever shall be. 22 And except those days should be shortened, there should no flesh be saved: but for the elect's sake those days shall be shortened.*   (Mk 13:14-20; Lk 21:20-24)

False christs and false prophets:

Throughout his ministry, Jesus often encouraged us to remain firm and strong in our commitment to Him as a Christian. As well, He here as other times warns us to be alert and very careful not to be deceived by false christs and false prophets. Remember the Antichrist will be present and active at that time, and he will be pretending to be the Christ, but he is not the Christ; he is a pretender and a liar, don't give him a second thought if you should find yourself in this world at that time. Besides the Antichrist, there will be other pretenders and liars. Jesus the true Christ can be identified by the fact that He will appear in the clouds, as lightening from east to west.

Mt 24:23-28   *Then if any man shall say unto you, Lo, here is Christ, or there; believe it not. 24 For there shall arise false Christs, and false prophets, and shall shew great signs and wonders; insomuch that, if it were possible, they shall deceive the very elect. 25 Behold, I have told you before. 26 Wherefore if they shall say unto you, Behold, he is in the desert; go not forth: behold, he is in the secret chambers; believe it not. 27 For as the lightning cometh out of the east, and shineth even unto the west; so shall also the coming of the Son of man be. 28 For wheresoever the carcase is, there will the eagles be gathered together.*   (Mk 13:21-23)

The Son of man coming in the clouds:

When Jesus comes to rapture his people, only those who are ready will hear his call and go to be with Him. The ungodly people of the earth will not understand that anything has happened, only that suddenly a lot of people have disappeared. Of course, there will be many people who have had some understanding of these things to know what has happened, but for various reasons they just were not living in readiness, so they missed going in the Rapture. Many of those will immediately get right with God and then die as martyrs. When Jesus then comes at the end of the Tribulation in what is called the Second Coming, He will come visible to the whole world. Again, He will come in the clouds. He will come to bring judgment on the remaining world of ungodly sinners. That is why the tribes of the earth shall mourn. He will gather to Himself all of the ones who have made themselves ready; all of the rest, as sinner people who have continued to reject Him, will be slain in the battle of Armageddon or in some other way. There will be no sinners left alive as the one-thousand-year reign of peace begins. (Reference Psa 104:35, Isa 1:28, and Isa 13:9.)

Mt 24:29-31   *Immediately after the tribulation of those days shall the sun be darkened, and the moon shall not give her light, and the stars shall fall from heaven, and the powers of the heavens shall be shaken: 30 And then shall appear the sign of the Son of man in heaven: and then shall all the tribes of the earth mourn, and they shall see the Son of man coming in the clouds of heaven with power and great glory. 31 And he shall send his angels with a great sound of a trumpet, and they shall gather together his elect from the four winds, from one end of heaven to the other.* (Mk 13:24-27; Lk 21:25-28)

Know that it is near, even at the doors:

Many believe the fig tree represents Israel being restored in 1948, which was 72 years ago. That is a generation, but all of that generation has not passed away. Jesus went on to say: when you see these signs you can know that the end is near, even at the doors. All of these things will be fulfilled in one generation. You don't know the day or the hour, only my Father knows that, but you can know the season when it is coming, we are in the season now.

Mt 24:32-36   *Now learn a parable of the fig tree; When his branch is yet tender, and putteth forth leaves, ye know that summer is nigh: 33 So likewise ye, when ye shall see all these things, know that it is near, even at the doors. 34 Verily I say unto you, This generation shall not pass, till all these things be fulfilled. 35 Heaven and earth shall pass away, but my words shall not pass away. 36 But of that day and hour knoweth no man, no, not the angels of heaven, but my Father only.*   (Mk 13:28-32; Lk 21:29-33)

Therefore, be ye also ready:

In reading Jesus' words, it is obvious that He is seriously concerned that all will be ready for His coming. He reminds us that, as in the days of Noah, it is easy to be so involved in living, partying, and all the other stuff in life, that we can easily lose touch with the Lord and miss out when He comes. He illustrates the lives of Christians as like two working in the field or grinding at the mill, one taken and one left. That is fifty percent. Jesus is not mandating, but He might well be suggesting that if we are not careful, fifty percent of Christians could easily not be ready. Remember, He has cautioned us many times, since we don't know the day or hour, be ready at all times of the day and night, all day, every day.

Mt 24:37-44   *But as the days of Noe were, so shall also the coming of the Son of man be. 38 For as in the days that were before the flood they were eating and drinking, marrying and giving in marriage, until the day that Noe entered into the ark, 39 And knew not until the flood came, and took them all away; so shall also the coming of the Son of man be. 40 Then shall two be in the field; the one shall be taken, and the other left. 41 Two women shall be grinding at the mill; the one shall be taken, and the other left. 42 Watch therefore: for ye know not what hour your Lord doth come. 43 But know this, that if the goodman of the house had known in what watch the thief would come, he would have watched, and would not have suffered his house to be broken up. 44 Therefore be ye also ready: for in such an hour as ye think not the Son of man cometh.*

A faithful and wise servant:

Again, Jesus is admonishing us to be tending to our calling. It is clear from this discourse and lots of other scripture that all of us have a work to do for the Lord and He fully expects us to be busy at that while we are waiting for Him to come for us. If we prove to be obedient to our calling, He assures us we will be richly rewarded, and all who fail in their appointments face a terrible future.

Mt 24:45-51   *Who then is a faithful and wise servant, whom his lord hath made ruler over his household, to give them meat in due season? 46 Blessed is that servant, whom his lord when he cometh shall find so doing. 47 Verily I say unto you, That he shall make him ruler over all his goods. 48 But and if that evil servant shall say in his heart, My lord delayeth his coming; 49 And shall begin to smite his fellowservants, and to eat and drink with the drunken; 50 The lord of that servant shall come in a day when he looketh not for him, and in an hour that he is not aware of, 51 And shall cut him asunder, and appoint him his portion with the hypocrites: there shall be weeping and gnashing of teeth.*

Behold, the bridegroom cometh; go ye out to meet him:

Jesus often spoke in parables. He once told the parable of ten virgins who went to meet the bridegroom. Notice that they all were virgins, meaning that they were pure, and they all slumbered and slept as they waited. All had burning lamps. The one difference, five were wise and five were foolish. What seems to be the reason that five were foolish was that they took no extra oil with them, so as to have an ongoing supply of oil. When the bridegroom came the foolish could not go in to the marriage because their lamps had gone out, they had to go get a fresh supply of oil. When they returned and knocked on the closed

door for entrance, the Lord said, "I know you not."
The whole problem was caused by a lack of oil. The
oil represents the presence of God in our lives in
the form of the Holy Spirit. Jesus promised us that
the Father would send the Holy Spirit so that we
would have a supply of oil so that our lamps will
always burn brightly and never go out.

Jn 14:26   *But the Comforter, which is the*
Holy Ghost, whom the Father will send in my name,
he shall teach you all things, and bring all things to
your remembrance, whatsoever I have said unto
you.

Every Christian, who is waiting for the Lord to
come to rapture us, should live so that the Holy
Spirit is always present in our lives, and our lamps
are always burning.

Mt 25:1-13   *Then shall the kingdom of*
heaven be likened unto ten virgins, which took
their lamps, and went forth to meet the
bridegroom. 2 And five of them were wise, and five
were foolish. 3 They that were foolish took their
lamps, and took no oil with them: 4 But the wise
took oil in their vessels with their lamps. 5 While
the bridegroom tarried, they all slumbered and
slept. 6 And at midnight there was a cry made,
Behold, the bridegroom cometh; go ye out to meet
him. 7 Then all those virgins arose, and trimmed
their lamps. 8 And the foolish said unto the wise,
Give us of your oil; for our lamps are gone out. 9
But the wise answered, saying, Not so; lest there
be not enough for us and you: but go ye rather to
them that sell, and buy for yourselves. 10 And
while they went to buy, the bridegroom came; and

they that were ready went in with him to the marriage: and the door was shut. 11 Afterward came also the other virgins, saying, Lord, Lord, open to us. 12 But he answered and said, Verily I say unto you, I know you not. 13 Watch therefore, for ye know neither the day nor the hour wherein the Son of man cometh.

Well done, thou good and faithful servant:

Jesus speaks of a man, who speaking of Himself, who travelled to a far country and left goods and gifts with each of his servants; it is obvious from the story that the man expected the servants to trade with the talents given them. Some of them did so and doubled their talents. One servant made excuses and hid his talent in the earth, in other words he buried his talent and did nothing. Those who worked with their talents were rewarded with: "Well done, thou good and faithful servant: thou hast been faithful over a few things, I will make thee ruler over many things: enter thou into the joy of thy lord." The servant who did nothing was "cast into outer darkness."

Mt 25:14-30   *For the kingdom of heaven is as a man travelling into a far country, who called his own servants, and delivered unto them his goods. 15 And unto one he gave five talents, to another two, and to another one; to every man according to his several ability; and straightway took his journey. 16 Then he that had received the five talents went and traded with the same, and made them other five talents. 17 And likewise he that had received two, he also gained other two. 18 But he that had received one went and digged in the earth, and hid his lord's money. 19 After a long time the lord of those servants cometh, and reckoneth with them. 20 And so he that had received five talents came and brought other five talents, saying, Lord, thou deliveredst unto me five talents: behold, I have gained beside them five talents more. 21 His lord said unto him, Well done, thou good and faithful servant: thou hast been faithful over a few things, I will make thee ruler over many things: enter thou into the joy of thy lord. 22 He also that had received two talents came and said, Lord, thou deliveredst unto me two talents: behold, I have gained two other talents beside them. 23 His lord said unto him, Well done, good and faithful servant; thou hast been faithful over a few things, I will make thee ruler over many things: enter thou into the joy of thy lord. 24 Then he which had received the one talent came and said, Lord, I knew thee that thou art an hard man, reaping where thou hast not sown, and gathering where thou hast not strawed: 25 And I was afraid, and went and hid thy talent in the earth: lo, there thou hast that is thine. 26 His lord answered and said unto him, Thou wicked and slothful servant, thou knewest that I reap where I sowed not, and gather where I have not strawed: 27 Thou oughtest therefore to have put my money to the exchangers, and then at my coming I should have received mine own with usury. 28 Take therefore the talent from him, and give it unto him which hath ten talents. 29 For unto every one that hath shall be* given, and he shall have abundance: but from him that hath not shall be taken away even that which he hath. 30 And cast ye the unprofitable servant into outer darkness: there shall be weeping and gnashing of teeth.

Come, ye blessed of my Father, for I was an hungred, and ye gave me meat:
The Lord concludes His Olivet discourse in the same spirit that He has talked about all of the other things: be ready, watching, working, and now, caring for the hungry, the homeless, the naked, the prisoner, and caring for the sick, so when the Lord returns He will say: *Come, ye blessed of my Father, inherit the kingdom prepared for you from the foundation of the world: ....*

Mt 25:31-46   *When the Son of man shall come in his glory, and all the holy angels with him, then shall he sit upon the throne of his glory: 32 And before him shall be gathered all nations: and he shall separate them one from another, as a shepherd divideth his sheep from the goats: 33 And he shall set the sheep on his right hand, but the goats on the left. 34 Then shall the King say unto them on his right hand, Come, ye blessed of my Father, inherit the kingdom prepared for you from the foundation of the world: 35 For I was an hungred, and ye gave me meat: I was thirsty, and ye gave me drink: I was a stranger, and ye took me in: 36 Naked, and ye clothed me: I was sick, and ye visited me: I was in prison, and ye came unto me. 37 Then shall the righteous answer him, saying, Lord, when saw we thee an hungred, and*

80

fed thee? or thirsty, and gave thee drink? 38 When saw we thee a stranger, and took thee in? or naked, and clothed thee? 39 Or when saw we thee sick, or in prison, and came unto thee? 40 And the King shall answer and say unto them, Verily I say unto you, Inasmuch as ye have done it unto one of the least of these my brethren, ye have done it unto me. 41 Then shall he say also unto them on the left hand, Depart from me, ye cursed, into everlasting fire, prepared for the devil and his angels: 42 For I was an hungred, and ye gave me no meat: I was thirsty, and ye gave me no drink: 43 I was a stranger, and ye took me not in: naked, and ye clothed me not: sick, and in prison, and ye visited me not. 44 Then shall they also answer him, saying, Lord, when saw we thee an hungred, or athirst, or a stranger, or naked, or sick, or in prison, and did not minister unto thee? 45 Then shall he answer them, saying, Verily I say unto you, Inasmuch as ye did it not to one of the least of these, ye did it not to me. 46 And these shall go away into everlasting punishment: but the righteous into life eternal.

The end must be very near:

The disciples' original questions were: *Tell us, when shall these things be? and what shall be the sign of thy coming, and of the end of the world?* Jesus then gave his answer in Matthew chapters 24 and 25 and the associated chapters in Mark 13 and Luke 21. To the first question Jesus simply said: *"of that day and hour knoweth no man, no, not the angels of heaven, but my Father only."* He also said once these things start, "*This generation shall not pass, till all these things be fulfilled.*

Jesus addressed the seven churches through the ages giving encouragement and warnings which we should now carefully consider.

4

The Seven Churches of Asia

The Church age:
The time of the Church age is from the time that Jesus said "I will build my church" until the Rapture occurs. During this time the Church of all the ages is in preparation for the coming of the Lord in the Rapture. Every individual in the Church will choose by his/her heart and lifestyle whether he/she goes in the Rapture or stays here for the Tribulation. Soon after the Rapture, the Tribulation begins on earth, with the entrance of the Antichrist. As we wait for the Lord's return let us give sincere consideration to the Lord's messages to the churches.

Mt 16:18   *And I say also unto thee, That thou art Peter, and upon this rock I will build my church; and the gates of hell shall not prevail against it.*

Jesus speaks to the seven churches:
Jesus gave the entire book of Revelation to John in the form of a vision or a visit to heaven in the spirit, showing him all that is to come to pass in the last days. In Rv 4:1-2, John says, "*I was in the spirit.*" Whether John was shown a vision or if he

was actually transported to heaven, is not clear. Before Jesus showed him the many things that will occur, He first gave John very specific messages to the seven churches of Asia and the seven church ages represented by these churches. His concern was that each church and church age and all individuals involved could choose to be ready for the Rapture and all that would follow, both in heaven and on earth.

Rv 4:1-2   *After this I looked, and, behold, a door was opened in heaven: and the first voice which I heard was as it were of a trumpet talking with me; which said, Come up hither, and I will shew thee things which must be hereafter. 2 And immediately I was in the spirit: and, behold, a throne was set in heaven, and one sat on the throne.*

The apostle John addresses the seven churches, saying: grace and peace from God the Father (Him which is and was and is to come), God the Holy Spirit (Seven Spirits), and from God the Son (Jesus Christ), as can be seen in verses 4 and 5. John says of Jesus, that He is the faithful witness, the first begotten of the dead, and the prince of the kings of the earth, who has made us kings and priests unto God and has washed us from our sins in His own blood. One day that same Jesus will come with clouds, seen by all, who will wail because of Him. Jesus himself says, "*I am Alpha and Omega, the beginning and the ending, saith the Lord, which is, and which was, and which is to come, the Almighty.*" It is awesome to think that this entire book was sent by Jesus Himself to the churches and that He is standing outside our hearts knocking to be let in and become a part of our lives, Rv 3:20.

Rv 1:4-8   *John to the seven churches which are in Asia: Grace be unto you, and peace, from him which is, and which was, and which is to come; and from the seven Spirits which are before his throne; 5 And from Jesus Christ, who is the faithful witness, and the first begotten of the dead, and the prince of the kings of the earth. Unto him that loved us, and washed us from our sins in his own blood, 6 And hath made us kings and priests unto God and his Father; to him be glory and dominion for ever and ever. Amen. 7 Behold, he cometh with clouds; and every eye shall see him, and they also which pierced him: and all kindreds of the earth shall wail because of him. Even so, Amen. 8 I am Alpha and Omega, the beginning and the ending, saith the Lord, which is, and which was, and which is to come, the Almighty.*

Jesus tells John to write in a book what he sees and to send it to the seven churches, specifically naming each. The Lord is showing great love for the churches. As we have observed elsewhere, these were seven local churches in Asia, and they each represented seven church ages in church history, and each of us can find ourselves in one or more of these churches. Scholars vary somewhat in their ideas about when the Church ages began and ended, but they generally agree on something like the following: Ephesus, AD 33 to AD 100; Smyrna, AD 100 to AD 312; Pergamos, AD 312 to AD 590; Thyatira, AD 590 to AD 1517;

Sardis, AD 1517 to AD 1750; Philadelphia, AD 1750 to AD 1900; Laodicea, AD 1900 until the Rapture occurs. Even though the above information shows some of the churches belong to past ages, when the Lord returns there will be some elements of each of the churches present.

Rv 1:10-16,20   *I was in the Spirit on the Lord's day, and heard behind me a great voice, as of a trumpet, 11 Saying, I am Alpha and Omega, the first and the last: and, What thou seest, write in a book, and send it unto the seven churches which are in Asia; unto Ephesus, and unto Smyrna, and unto Pergamos, and unto Thyatira, and unto Sardis, and unto Philadelphia, and unto Laodicea. 12 And I turned to see the voice that spake with me. And being turned, I saw seven golden candlesticks; 13 And in the midst of the seven candlesticks one like unto the Son of man, clothed with a garment down to the foot, and girt about the paps with a golden girdle. 14 His head and his hairs were white like wool, as white as snow; and his eyes were as a flame of fire; 15 And his feet like unto fine brass, as if they burned in a furnace; and his voice as the sound of many waters. 16 And he had in his right hand seven stars: and out of his mouth went a sharp twoedged sword: and his countenance was as the sun shineth in his strength. ... 20 The mystery of the seven stars which thou sawest in my right hand, and the seven golden candlesticks. The seven stars are the angels of the seven churches: and the seven candlesticks which thou sawest are the seven churches.*

A great falling Away:

Scripture tells us over and over that there will be a great falling away of the individuals in those churches, in the end time, at some point before the Rapture.

2 Th 2:1-5   *Now we beseech you, brethren, by the coming of our Lord Jesus Christ, and by our gathering together unto him, 2 That ye be not soon shaken in mind, or be troubled, neither by spirit, nor by word, nor by letter as from us, as that the day of Christ is at hand. 3 Let no man deceive you by any means: for that day shall not come, except there come a falling away first, and that man of sin be revealed, the son of perdition; 4 Who opposeth and exalteth himself above all that is called God, or that is worshipped; so that he as God sitteth in the temple of God, shewing himself that he is God. 5 Remember ye not, that, when I was yet with you, I told you these things?*

What the Spirit saith unto the churches:

"He that hath an ear, let him hear what the Spirit saith unto the churches," are words that are spoken to all seven churches. Five of the seven churches were told to "Repent," all but Smyrna and Philadelphia.

Pastor Stephen Armstrong[1], of Verse by Verse Ministry International, gives the meaning of the names of each of the churches, as follows: Ephesus: "desirable"; Smyrna: "myrrh"; Pergamos: "married"; Thyatira: "sacrifice"; Sardis: "escaping"; Philadelphia: "brotherly love"; Laodicea: "people ruling". Other scholars in some cases offer other meanings for the names. Most seem to agree on the meaning of the names of Smyrna, Philadelphia, and Laodicea.

1. Ephesus: The Church of the Apostles
   ### AD 33–100

Jesus commended the Church at Ephesus for their works, labor, and patience. But I have this against you, "thou hast left thy first love. Remember from where you have fallen lest I remove your candlestick from its place," in John's vision, Jesus was walking among the candlesticks (churches) when he said that. Having their candlestick removed would mean they were lost. He then commended them for their rejection of the deeds of the Nicolaitans. According to Strong's Exhaustive Concordance[2] the word Nicolaitans carries the idea of conquest, implying that the Church leadership made efforts to become victorious over the laity, the people. The leadership taught the laity that a relaxed attitude toward the occult and other religions was okay. Like today there are people that say all religions lead to heaven and God, which we know is not true. See John 14:6 where Jesus said, "... no man cometh unto the Father, but by me." Repent, and return to doing your first works. The Lord promised the overcomers among the Ephesians that they would be granted to eat of the tree of life. That would be like it was in the garden of Eden, perfect and sinless and wonderful.

Rv 2:1-7   Unto the angel of the Church of Ephesus write; These things saith he that holdeth the seven stars in his right hand, who walketh in the midst of the seven golden candlesticks; 2 I know thy works, and thy labour, and thy patience, and how thou canst not bear them which are evil: and thou hast tried them which say they are apostles, and are not, and hast found them liars: 3 And hast borne, and hast patience, and for my name's sake hast laboured, and hast not fainted. 4 Nevertheless I have somewhat against thee, because thou hast left thy first love. 5 Remember therefore from whence thou art fallen, and repent, and do the first works; or else I will come unto thee quickly, and will remove thy candlestick out of his place, except thou repent. 6 But this thou hast, that thou hatest the deeds of the Nicolaitans, which I also hate. 7 He that hath an ear, let him hear what the Spirit saith unto the churches; To him that overcometh will I give to eat of the tree of life, which is in the midst of the paradise of God.

Ephesus, " ...you have left your first love." Repent!

2. Smyrna: The persecuted Church
AD 100–312

Jesus told them, outwardly you feel that you are poor and under trial by some in the Jewish population, but actually, you are rich. Among other things, the Lord said to the angel (leader/pastor) of the Church in Smyrna, "ye shall have tribulation ten days." There seem to be many different ideas about what the "ten days of tribulation" means. For the most part, the many ideas can be boiled down to two. One of the two is that the ten-day tribulation is simply a short time. The other idea that is more prevalent is that the ten days is a reference to ten different times of persecution under several different Roman Emperors from about AD 82 to perhaps AD 442. Adam Clarke, Bible commentator, seems to be divided between the two ideas. Matthew Henry seems to go for the idea that the ten days simply means a short period of time, which seems to be the more likely.

Rv 2:8-11 *And unto the angel of the Church in Smyrna write; These things saith the first and the last, which was dead, and is alive; 9 I know thy works, and tribulation, and poverty, (but thou art rich) and I know the blasphemy of them which say they are Jews, and are not, but are the synagogue of Satan. 10 Fear none of those things which thou shalt suffer: behold, the devil shall cast some of you into prison, that ye may be tried; and ye shall have tribulation ten days: be thou faithful unto death, and I will give thee a crown of life. 11 He that hath an ear, let him hear what the Spirit saith unto the churches; He that overcometh shall not be hurt of the second death.*

Smyrna, no rebuke, only praise and encouragement, be faithful and you will receive a crown of life.

3. Pergamos: The pagan church
AD 312–590

In 539 BC when the Persian king, Cyrus the Great conquered Babylon, some of the pagan Babylonian priests escaped and traveled to Pergamos, carrying their idol worshipping practices with them. All of their sun worship and Saturnus sexual cult practices come from as far back as Nimrod when they attempted to build the tower to heaven, Gen 11:1-10. When the Church in Pergamos came into existence all of this evil was still going on. Some in the Church brought these evils into the Church. There were some members who tolerated this activity, but there were some who were pure and faithful to the Lord. As Jesus commended and cautioned those at Pergamos He also recognized two different times that Satan's seat was there in Pergamos, so perhaps their trials and testing was more severe than for others. Pergamos is also the only church among the seven where Jesus threatens the use of the sword of His mouth against those among them who hold the doctrine of Balaam and the doctrine of the Nicolaitans; He calls on them to repent. The doctrine of Balaam and the Nicolaitans is like the evils of Babylon. The sword of His mouth is mentioned several other times and is used to defeat His enemies in war. The overcomers were promised provision and sustenance as well as entrance into the eternal blessings of God, with a new name from God, known only to the one who receives it.

Rv 2:12-17   *And to the angel of the Church in Pergamos write; These things saith he which hath the sharp sword with two edges; 13 I know thy works, and where thou dwellest, even where Satan's seat is: and thou holdest fast my name, and hast not denied my faith, even in those days wherein Antipas was my faithful martyr, who was slain among you, where Satan dwelleth. 14 But I have a few things against thee, because thou hast there them that hold the doctrine of Balaam, who taught Balac to cast a stumblingblock before the children of Israel, to eat things sacrificed unto idols, and to commit fornication. 15 So hast thou also them that hold the doctrine of the Nicolaitans, which thing I hate. 16 Repent; or else I will come unto thee quickly, and will fight against them with the sword of my mouth. 17 He that hath an ear, let him hear what the Spirit saith unto the churches; To him that overcometh will I give to eat of the hidden manna, and will give him a white stone, and in the stone a new name written, which no man knoweth saving he that receiveth it.*

Pergamos, you have those who "... eat things sacrificed to idols, and to commit sexual immorality." Repent!

4. Thyatira: The Church of the dark ages AD 590–1517

In the case of Thyatira, the angel (pastor) was pointedly addressed by none other than "the Son of God", which is a very sobering fact. The pastor was told, "I know your works, love, service, faith, and your patience; and as for your works, the last are more than the first. Nevertheless, I have a few things against you, because you allow that woman Jezebel, who calls herself a prophetess, to teach and seduce my servants to commit sexual immorality and eat things sacrificed to idols." Apparently, there was a dreadful evil going on within the Church at Thyatira which some of the members were involved in. Thyatira's sin was much like that of Pergamos. This greatly disturbed the Lord. He said He had given this Jezebel the opportunity to repent, but she had not done so; He will cast her and her followers into great tribulation and kill her children. The Lord further says, to those of you who have not partaken of this evil, hold fast until I come.

Rv 2:18-29 *And unto the angel of the Church in Thyatira write; These things saith the Son of God, who hath his eyes like unto a flame of fire, and his feet are like fine brass; 19 I know thy works, and charity, and service, and faith, and thy patience, and thy works; and the last to be more than the first. 20 Notwithstanding I have a few things against thee, because thou sufferest that woman Jezebel, which calleth herself a prophetess, to teach and to seduce my servants to commit fornication, and to eat things sacrificed unto idols. 21 And I gave her space to repent of her fornication; and she repented not. 22 Behold, I will cast her into a bed, and them that commit adultery with her into great tribulation, except they repent of their deeds. 23 And I will kill her children with death; and all the churches shall know that I am he which searcheth the reins and hearts: and I will give unto every one of you according to your works. 24 But unto you I say, and unto the rest in Thyatira, as many as have not this doctrine, and which have not known the depths of Satan, as they speak; I will put upon you none other burden. 25 But that which ye have already hold fast till I come. 26 And he that overcometh, and keepeth my works*

*unto the end, to him will I give power over the
nations: 27 And he shall rule them with a rod of
iron; as the vessels of a potter shall they be broken
to shivers: even as I received of my Father. 28 And
I will give him the morning star. 29 He that hath an
ear, let him hear what the Spirit saith unto the
churches.*

Thyatira, those of you who are guilty of
fornication and eating things sacrificed to idols,
Repent: to the others I put no further burden on
you, hold fast until I come.

5. Sardis: The Church of the Reformation AD 1517–1750

The Lord told the Sardis church that they
were dead, which sounds worse than the
accusations of any of the other churches, such as
being lukewarm, or idolatrous, or a fornicator. All
that the Lord demands is repentance; true, sincere
and life-changing repentance for any of these
problems. This accusation of "dead" makes it sound
like many in the Church were not even saved, but
were going through the motions with the rest of the
Church. They were just practicing religion; they
were not true Christians. "Those who had been
faithful and the overcomers are promised they shall
walk with me in white, for they are worthy." They
have a further promise that "I will not blot out his
name out of the book of life, but I will confess his
name before my Father, and before his angels."

Rv 3:1-6 *And unto the angel of the church
in Sardis write; These things saith he that hath the
seven Spirits of God, and the seven stars; I know*

thy works, that thou hast a name that thou livest, and art dead. 2 Be watchful, and strengthen the things which remain, that are ready to die: for I have not found thy works perfect before God. 3 Remember therefore how thou hast received and heard, and hold fast, and repent. If therefore thou shalt not watch, I will come on thee as a thief, and thou shalt not know what hour I will come upon thee. 4 Thou hast a few names even in Sardis which have not defiled their garments; and they shall walk with me in white: for they are worthy. 5 He that overcometh, the same shall be clothed in white raiment; and I will not blot out his name out of the book of life, but I will confess his name before my Father, and before his angels. 6 He that hath an ear, let him hear what the Spirit saith unto the churches.

Sardis, thou art dead. Repent and come alive!

6. Philadelphia: The missionary church AD 1750–1925

The Philadelphian church age was a time of awakening and great missionary effort; aside from Ephesus, there has never been more Christian outreach than with Philadelphia. The Lord offered no rebuke, only encouragement to this church. He tells them plainly that He will keep them from the hour of temptation (the Tribulation) which will come upon all the world to try (test) them that dwell upon the earth.

Rv 3:7-13 *And to the angel of the church in Philadelphia write; These things saith he that is holy, he that is true, he that hath the key of David, he that openeth, and no man shutteth; and shutteth, and no man openeth; 8 I know thy works: behold, I have set before thee an open door, and no man can shut it: for thou hast a little strength, and hast kept my word, and hast not denied my name. 9 Behold, I will make them of the synagogue of Satan, which say they are Jews, and are not, but do lie; behold, I will make them to come and worship before thy feet, and to know that I have loved thee. 10 Because thou hast kept the word of my patience, I also will keep thee from the hour of temptation, which shall come upon all the world, to try them that dwell upon the earth. 11 Behold, I come quickly: hold that fast which thou hast, that no man take thy crown. 12 Him that overcometh will I make a pillar in the temple of my God, and he shall go no more out: and I will write upon him the name of my God, and the name of the city of my God, which is new Jerusalem, which cometh down out of heaven from my God: and I will write upon him my new name. 13 He that hath an ear, let him hear what the Spirit saith unto the churches.*

Philadelphia, I come quickly: hold that fast which thou hast, that no man take thy crown.

7. Laodicea: The lukewarm Church

It seems incredible that the Church could go from being so right, as the Church of Philadelphia was, to become so careless and lukewarm as Laodicea is, especially when we are well aware of what the Philadelphian church age accomplished. In some of the other churches when Jesus mentioned their failures, He acknowledged that some of them were remaining faithful; in the case with Laodicea He does not do that. His accusation is that we are not spiritually hot, nor are we cold, but only lukewarm. That makes it sound like we are at least Christians, but ho-hum Christians. Well, that isn't really all that bad, is it? Why then does he promise to spew us out of His mouth (spit us out)? In April 2020 there are somewhere near 2,300,000,000 (2.3 billion) Christians in the world, 1,200,000,000 (1.2 billion) are Catholics; the others are protestants, Eastern Orthodox or others. There is no doubt that there are many, even millions, of truly born again and on fire Christians in our world today. But when Jesus comes for us, He will decide who is on fire and ready to go in the Rapture and who is only lukewarm and will stay to go through the Tribulation. Here in Laodicea perhaps, as Jesus said to Sardis, "Thou hast a few names which have not defiled their garments; and they shall walk with me in white: for they are worthy." Without repentance and that zeal that He is calling for, there will be many left here to go through the wrath of the Tribulation.

Our problem is that we think, we are "rich, and increased with goods, and have need of nothing;" So, that is our problem, something we think that is not true. Jesus said the real truth is you are "wretched, and miserable, and poor, and blind, and naked:" There is a big difference in what we think about ourselves and what Jesus thinks about us. He is so keenly concerned about our condition that he offers advice for a solution. His advice: buy gold from him and white raiment to cover your nakedness and anoint thine eyes with eye salve so you can see. The gold means to become a truly born-again Christian by trusting in Jesus alone. The white raiment is a reference to living a pure and holy life. And the eye salve anointing is a reference to the baptism of the Holy Spirit. Jesus is even now standing at our heart's door, wanting to come in to sup with us and we with Him. He goes even further and tells us that we can sit with Him in His throne, like he sits with our Father in His throne.

Rv 3:14-22   *And unto the angel of the church of the Laodiceans write; These things saith the Amen, the faithful and true witness, the beginning of the creation of God; 15 I know thy works, that thou art neither cold nor hot: I would thou wert cold or hot. 16 So then because thou art lukewarm, and neither cold nor hot, I will spue thee out of my mouth. 17 Because thou sayest, I am rich, and increased with goods, and have need of nothing; and knowest not that thou art wretched, and miserable, and poor, and blind, and naked: 18 I counsel thee to buy of me gold tried in the fire, that thou mayest be rich; and white raiment, that thou mayest be clothed, and that the shame of thy nakedness do not appear; and anoint thine eyes with eyesalve, that thou mayest see. 19 As many as I love, I rebuke and chasten: be zealous therefore, and repent. 20 Behold, I stand at the door, and knock: if any man hear my voice, and open the door, I will come in to him, and will sup with him, and he with me. 21 To him that overcometh will I grant to sit with me in my throne, even as I also overcame, and am set down with my Father in his throne. 22 He that hath an ear, let him hear what the Spirit saith unto the churches.*

Laodicea: Repent and follow through with the Lord's counsel.

Lk 18:8   *Nevertheless, when the Son of man cometh, shall he find faith on the earth?*

A review of the Chart Timeline will help instill in our minds the order of events that follow the Church age. And now, having considered the messages and encouragement of Jesus to the seven churches and seven church ages, let us go on to take a look at the Rapture and all of the many other things that follow. The Rapture closes the Church age.

Notes:
1. Pastor Stephen Armstrong, Verse by Verse Ministry International. Link: http://www.versebyverseministry.org/bible-answers/determining-the-meaning-of-the-names-of-the-7-churches
2. Strong's Exhaustive Concordance of the Bible (New York: Abingdon Press, 1970).

Chart/Timeline

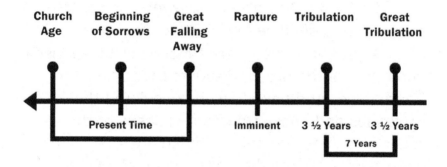

The chart/timeline, as depicted, does not show the timing of all of the events in "the end of the days," but it does show the order in which they occur. As is stated in the chapter above, "The Seven Churches of Asia," the time of the Church age is from the time that Jesus said "I will build my church" until the Rapture occurs. Soon after the Rapture, the Tribulation begins on earth, with the entrance of the Antichrist. The Tribulation is divided into two three-and-one-half year periods, making a total of seven years.

Chart/Timeline

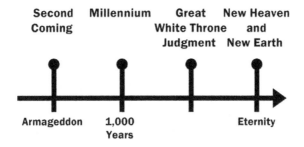

Second Coming | Millennium | Great White Throne Judgment | New Heaven and New Earth

Armageddon | 1,000 Years | Eternity

The Lord's Second Coming occurs, ending the Tribulation with the battle of Armageddon. The Millennium begins then, wherein Jesus reigns as King of Kings for one thousand years. Time is given for the Great White Throne judgment, where all sinners of all time are judged, then separated from God's presence for eternity. The Heaven and earth are made new, and finally the New Jerusalem comes down to earth where Jesus continues to reign, and His faithful ones will reign with Him forever.

5

The Rapture

An astounding event:

The Rapture will be an absolutely breathtaking and wonderful experience for those who have prepared themselves and are accounted as worthy to be taken out of this world and directly into God's holy presence. Nothing like it has ever happened on the scale that will be manifested on that day. Enoch, Elijah, and Jesus were taken to heaven in the same way, but in the Rapture suddenly millions will be taken out of this world, to the clouds and on into heaven. For those who are caught up, it will be an exciting and lovely and awesome experience to meet God face to face. Let us take a look at the Rapture.

There is no such word as "Rapture" found in scripture:

There are many words not found in the Bible, but they are a reality. For example, the word television is not found in the Bible, yet, virtually every home has one. Rv 11:9 speaks of the nations of the world seeing the dead bodies of the two witnesses lying unburied for three days in the city of Jerusalem.

Rv 11:9 *And they of the people and kindreds and tongues and nations shall see their dead bodies three days and an half, and shall not suffer their dead bodies to be put in graves.*

We can easily understand that the whole world can see the dead bodies of the two witnesses in the streets of Jerusalem because of the worldwide availability of television. Going further than that, the word "rapture" is not found in scripture, yet there is an event spoken of in different ways in scripture that is The Rapture.

1 Th 4:16-17   *For the Lord himself shall descend from heaven with a shout, with the voice of the archangel, and with the trump of God: and the dead in Christ shall rise first: 17 Then we which are alive and remain shall be caught up together with them in the clouds, to meet the Lord in the air: and so shall we ever be with the Lord.*

Harpazo[1] (har-pad-zo) is the Greek word for caught up, catch up, pluck, take by force; it carries the idea of a raptor seizing its prey forcefully and carrying it away, thus the idea of the rapture.

What is the Rapture?

Jesus, the Messiah, was born into this world, ministered, was crucified, died, was buried and resurrected on the third day, then 40 days later He ascended to heaven (the KJV says Jesus was taken up). Jesus' ascension might well be considered a rapture.

Ac 1:9   *And when he had spoken these things, while they beheld, he was taken up; and a cloud received him out of their sight.*

Before He went away, Jesus said:

John 14:2-3   *In my Father's house are many mansions: if it were not so, I would have told you. I go to prepare a place for you. 3 And if I go and prepare a place for you, I will come again, and receive you unto myself; that where I am, there ye may be also.*

The Rapture takes place when Jesus "comes again to receive us unto himself". There is a first and second coming of Jesus, spoken of in scripture. The first coming was when He was born into this world as a baby, and eventually went to the cross. The Second Coming will be at the end of the Tribulation when He comes to fight the battle of Armageddon and establish Himself as king over the whole earth for a thousand years. The Rapture and the actual Second Coming are considered as two phases of the Second Coming. In the first coming and the second phase of the second coming of Jesus, He actually comes to the earth and dwells here. In the Rapture, He only comes down to the clouds and calls His prepared and ready people to come up here, then, takes them back into heaven, for the duration of the Tribulation. The Rapture is invisible to the world and the world will not even be aware of its occurrence until they begin to see the evidence of the disappearance of millions, and that those millions are all known as Christians. There will be many millions, who miss the Rapture, and will recognize the disappearance for what it is and begin to turn to Christ in great numbers, then begin to be martyred for Christ during the Tribulation. There will be many millions more of the world who will go into rejoicing, saying "good riddance". From those moments on it will be "hell" on earth, for the next seven years for those who find themselves in that situation. The Rapture is when the Lord comes to claim His waiting bride. Also, there are several places in scripture where the Lord promises to spare her (His bride) from the wrath to come (the Tribulation).

1 Th 1:10   *And to wait for his Son from heaven, whom he raised from the dead, even Jesus, which delivered us from the wrath to come.*

1 Th 5:9-10   *For God hath not appointed us to wrath, but to obtain salvation by our Lord Jesus Christ, 10 Who died for us, that, whether we wake or sleep, we should live together with him.*

Rv 3:10-11   *Because thou hast kept the word of my patience, I also will keep thee from the hour of temptation, which shall come upon all the world, to try them that dwell upon the earth. 11 Behold, I come quickly: hold that fast which thou hast, that no man take thy crown.*

Notice the words "delivered us from the wrath to come", "For God hath not appointed us to wrath", and "keep thee from the hour of temptation, which shall come upon all the world."

These three scripture locations alone, sufficiently show that the Lord is going to deliver His prepared people from His wrath that is coming on the earth in the form of the Tribulation. His prepared people are those that are born again and living in obedience to Him.

The Rapture is all about Christ and the Church:

In these verses Paul is talking about the relationship of husband and wife, and in conclusion he says: I am actually speaking about Christ and the Church. So, in many of the references to the Rapture, we see language speaking of a bridegroom, Christ, coming for His bride, the true church. There is the whole church which includes all involved in the Church in any way, whether they are even saved or not. The true church is made up of those involved who are truly born again and are living fervently in full obedience to the Lord.

Eph 5:22-33 *Wives submit yourselves unto your own husbands, as unto the Lord. 23 For the husband is the head of the wife, even as Christ is the head of the Church: and he is the saviour of the body. 24 Therefore as the Church is subject unto Christ, so let the wives be to their own husbands in every thing. 25 Husbands, love your wives, even as Christ also loved the Church, and gave himself for it; 26 That he might sanctify and cleanse it with the washing of water by the word, 27 That he might present it to himself a glorious church, not having spot, or wrinkle, or any such thing; but that it should be holy and without blemish. 28 So ought men to love their wives as their own bodies. He that loveth his wife loveth himself. 29 For no man ever yet hated his own flesh; but nourisheth and cherisheth it, even as the Lord the church: 30 For we are members of his body, of his flesh, and of his bones. 31 For this cause shall a man leave his father and mother, and shall be joined unto his wife, and they two shall be one flesh. 32 This is a great mystery: but I speak concerning Christ and the church. 33 Nevertheless let every one of you in particular so love his wife even as himself; and the wife see that she reverence her husband.*

Isaac's marriage to Rebekah:

The story of Isaac's marriage to Rebekah is a beautiful picture of Christ and His bride, the Church. In this story Abraham sends his eldest servant, Eliezer, to go find a bride for his son Isaac. Abraham represents God the Father, Isaac represents God the Son, and Eliezer the servant represents God the Holy Spirit. The servant left on his journey with ten camels loaded with all the goods of his master, having sworn an oath that he would not take a wife from the Canaanites, the world, but he would only take a wife from his master's kindred, the true church. He swore also that the woman must be willing to go to Isaac, and that he would never take Isaac back again to where the kindred were living, the world.

As the servant stopped at the water well just outside the city of Nahor, he prayed to Abraham's God, saying:

Gen 24:14-15   *And let it come to pass, that the damsel to whom I shall say, Let down thy pitcher, I pray thee, that I may drink; and she shall say, Drink, and I will give thy camels drink also: let the same be she that thou hast appointed for thy servant Isaac; and thereby shall I know that thou hast shewed kindness unto my master. 15 And it came to pass, before he had done speaking, that, behold, Rebekah came out, who was born to Bethuel, son of Milcah, the wife of Nahor, Abraham's brother, with her pitcher upon her shoulder.*

Before the servant finished his prayer, Rebekah a beautiful young virgin (pure) woman appeared and met all of the servant's requests in his prayer. The servant then gave her three very precious gifts and she invited him to her home, then ran to tell her family of all that happened. Laban, Rebekah's brother, ran out to the well, recognized the servant as a man of God and welcomed him into their home, even washing his feet and preparing a meal. The servant responded by saying, "I will not eat, until I have told mine errand. … I am Abraham's servant." He then made clear to the family all that had transpired in his assignment up to that moment. Then he said:

Gen 24:49-67 *And now if ye will deal kindly and truly with my master, tell me: and if not, tell me; that I may turn to the right hand, or to the left. 50 Then Laban and Bethuel answered and said, The thing proceedeth from the LORD: we cannot speak unto thee bad or good. 51 Behold, Rebekah is before thee, take her, and go, and let her be thy master's son's wife, as the LORD hath spoken. 52 And it came to pass, that, when Abraham's servant heard their words, he worshipped the LORD, bowing himself to the earth. 53 And the servant brought forth jewels of silver, and jewels of gold, and raiment, and gave them to Rebekah: he gave also to her brother and to her* mother precious things. 54 And they did eat and drink, he and the men that were with him, and tarried all night; and they rose up in the morning, and he said, Send me away unto my master. 55 And her brother and her mother said, Let the damsel abide with us a few days, at the least ten; after that she shall go. 56 And he said unto them, Hinder me not, seeing the LORD hath prospered my way; send me away that I may go to my master. 57 And they said, We will call the damsel, and inquire at her mouth. 58 And they called Rebekah, and said unto her, Wilt thou go with this man? And she said, I will go. 59 And they sent away Rebekah their sister, and her nurse, and Abraham's servant, and his men. 60 And they blessed Rebekah, and said unto her, Thou art our sister, be thou the mother of thousands of millions, and let thy seed possess the gate of those which hate them. 61 And Rebekah arose, and her damsels, and they rode upon the camels, and followed the man: and the servant took Rebekah, and went his way. 62 And Isaac came from the way of the well Lahai-roi; for he dwelt in the south country. 63 And Isaac went out to meditate in the field at the eventide: and he lifted up his eyes, and saw, and, behold, the camels were coming. 64 And Rebekah lifted up her eyes, and when she saw Isaac, she lighted off the camel. 65 For she had said unto the servant, What man is this that walketh in the field to meet us? And the servant had said, It is my master: therefore she took a vail, and covered herself. 66 And the servant told Isaac all things that he had done. 67 And Isaac brought her into his mother

Sarah's tent, and took Rebekah, and she became his wife; and he loved her: ....

After explaining in detail, the reason for his trip to the entire family, the servant asked for a definite answer. The father and brother answered and said: this thing is of the Lord, but we cannot answer good or bad, take Rebekah and go and let her be wife to the master's son. So, they celebrated, and the servant gave gifts to the family, and the next morning declared he must be on his way. The family asked that they tarry another ten days, the servant responded with, please don't hinder me, to which the family said: we will ask Rebekah.

Gen 24:58 *Wilt thou go with this man? And she said, I will go.*

So, they left, Rebekah, her nurse, and her damsels, accompanied by the servant and his men.

Rebekah is the bride, her nurse and her damsels are members of the bridal party.

Isaac was out walking and meditating in the field in the evening and saw them coming. Out of respect and modesty Rebekah covered herself with a vail when she saw Isaac. She became his wife and he loved her.

This is a truly great story of Isaac and Rebekah, but representing Jesus and His bride, the true church. The whole family of Rebekah was involved, informed, gifted, and welcomed, but only Rebekah said, "I will go." And only Rebekah, her nurse and her maidens went. In an earlier paragraph, Abraham, Isaac, and the eldest servant were presented as representing God, the Father, the Son, and the Holy Spirit. And here we see Rebekah representing the Church, the Bride of Christ. Rebekah's whole family (the whole church) could have gone as attendants and wedding guests, but they made a choice; they said they could not answer good or bad, ask Rebekah. Rebekah said yes; they said no, we will stay here and not go. Such will be the case with the Church, some will choose to go and others will be happy to stay here, while recognizing that "This is of the Lord." We all must decide and live accordingly.

Please notice that when the servant arrived back home with the bride-to-be, Isaac was out for a walk thinking about the coming bride and anxious to see her, as well, the bride-to-be was anxious to see him. So, it is with Jesus, the bridegroom in heaven and His preparing bride here on earth, both anxious to be with the other, while many in the Church family are not excited enough to get ready to "go."

Great falling away:

One thing that all Christians should be aware of is that the same scripture that teaches us that there will be a Rapture, also teaches us that before that Rapture occurs, there will come about "a great falling away" among many Christians. We are warned again and again that we must stay alert, fervent, and ready for that great moment. But many Christians with good intentions will become drowsy and fall into unreadiness toward the end of days; the Rapture will occur, and many Christians will miss the Rapture and find themselves facing the horrors of the Tribulation.

See what Paul and Jesus had to say about the Church's condition in the end times.

Paul said:

2 Th 2:1-3   *Now we beseech you, brethren, by the coming of our Lord Jesus Christ, and by our gathering together unto him, 2 That ye be not soon shaken in mind, or be troubled, neither by spirit, nor by word, nor by letter as from us, as that the day of Christ is at hand. 3 Let no man deceive you by any means: for that day shall not come, except there come a falling away first, and that man of sin be revealed, the son of perdition; ….*

Suggesting a falling away, Jesus said:

Lk 18:8   *Nevertheless when the Son of man cometh, shall he find faith on the earth?*

They would not come:

Jesus tells a parable of a certain king who made a marriage for his son and sent out invitations to some, but they would not come. Jesus' intentions in telling this parable is to tell us it will be just like that, concerning the Rapture and the marriage of the Lamb that follows. Many are just not interested enough to prepare and go; there are just too many other things that need to be done now, things that just can't wait.

Mt 22:2-6,8-9,14   *The kingdom of heaven is like unto a certain king, which made a marriage for his son, 3 And sent forth his servants to call them that were bidden to the wedding: and they would not come. 4 Again, he sent forth other servants,*

saying, Tell them which are bidden, Behold, I have prepared my dinner: my oxen and my fatlings are killed, and all things are ready: come unto the marriage. 5 But they made light of it, and went their ways, one to his farm, another to his merchandise: 6 And the remnant took his servants, and entreated them spitefully, and slew them. ....
8 Then saith he to his servants, The wedding is ready, but they which were bidden were not worthy. 9 Go ye therefore into the highways, and as many as ye shall find, bid to the marriage. ....
14 For many are called, but few are chosen.

What changes do I need to make:

In Jesus' message to the seven churches in the Revelation, He said,

Rv 2:11 *He that hath an ear, let him hear what the Spirit saith unto the churches; ....*

He said this to all seven of the churches mentioned in Revelation chapters 2 and 3; to five of the seven churches, He said "Repent." We would do well to pay close attention to the idea of repentance. The prophet Daniel had spent most of his life in exile in Babylon because of the sin of the nation of Judah. He had read from Jeremiah's prophecies that they were to spend 70 years in exile because of their sins. Daniel knew that the 70 years was almost over, so he went to his knees in repentance. He did this in preparation for the great event of "going back home to Jerusalem," Judah, somewhat like the great event of going in the Rapture for this present generation. Daniel was a godly man and probably didn't need to repent nearly as much as some Christians today, yet he repented. Much of his prayer of repentance was about his concern for his brothers in the Lord. Maybe today's Christians should take a lesson from Daniel.

Daniel's prayer of repentance:

Dan 9:3-5,17-19   *3 And I set my face unto the Lord God, to seek by prayer and supplication, with fasting, and sackcloth, and ashes: 4 And I prayed unto the LORD my God, and made my confession, and said, O Lord, the great and dreadful God, keeping the covenant and mercy to them that love him, and to them that keep his commandments; 5 We have sinned, and have committed iniquity, and have done wickedly, and have rebelled, even by departing from thy precepts and from thy judgments: …. 17 Now therefore, O our God, hear the prayer of thy servant, and his supplications, and cause thy face to shine upon thy sanctuary that is desolate, for the Lord's sake. 18 O my God, incline thine ear, and hear; open thine eyes, and behold our desolations, and the city which is called by thy name: for we do not present our supplications before thee for our righteousnesses, but for thy great mercies. 19 O Lord, hear; O Lord, forgive; O Lord, hearken and do; defer not, for thine own sake, O my God: ….*

Peter's admonition:

Peter adds to the words of the other prophets by telling us to prepare for "the day of God". We should "be diligent that ye may be found of him in peace, without spot, and blameless."

II Pet 3:10-14   *But the day of the Lord will come as a thief in the night; ... the earth also and the works that are therein shall be burned up. 11 Seeing then that all these things shall be dissolved, what manner of persons ought ye to be in all holy conversation and godliness, 12 Looking for and hasting unto the coming of the day of God, 13 Nevertheless we, according to his promise, look for new heavens and a new earth, wherein dwelleth righteousness. 14 Wherefore, beloved, seeing that ye look for such things, be diligent that ye may be found of him in peace, without spot, and blameless.*

Who is qualified to go in the Rapture? Not everyone is going. Preparations for the Rapture as the Bride:

Many people around the world claim to be Christians, yet, show no concern about their calling or obedience to God. We must understand that obedience to God and staying busy with our calling is vital to our readiness to go in the Rapture.

Mt 7:21-23   *Not everyone who says to Me, Lord, Lord, shall enter the kingdom of heaven, but he who does the will of My Father in heaven. 22 Many will say to Me in that day, Lord, Lord, have we not prophesied in Your name, cast out demons in Your name, and done many wonders in Your name? 23 And then I will declare to them, I never knew you; depart from Me, you who practice lawlessness!*

If any person should find that he/she has missed the Rapture and is in the Tribulation, such a person should immediately call on God in repentance and reach out to God in faith, believing to receive salvation and a right standing with God. Any person finding themselves in the Tribulation, and beginning to truly serve God, will almost certainly not survive, but will go immediately into God's presence upon their martyrdom, which martyrdom will almost certainly happen.

The following scriptures help us to understand that we need to be living seriously and fervently for the Lord if we expect to go in the Rapture. This list can serve as a checklist to see if one is living according to God's word. Take notice of keywords in each verse that shows one's condition such as, if anyone is in Christ, or holiness, or having no spot or wrinkle, or walk in the light. When we sincerely go to God's word for understanding, the Holy Spirit will help us to understand what His word is saying.

We should put on the whole armour of God:

Eph 6:10-18   *Finally, my brethren, be strong in the Lord, and in the power of his might. 11 Put on the whole armour of God, that ye may be able to stand against the wiles of the devil. 12 For we wrestle not against flesh and blood, but against principalities, against powers, against the rulers of the darkness of this world, against spiritual wickedness in high places. 13 Wherefore take unto you the whole armour of God, that ye may be able to withstand in the evil day, and having done all, to stand. 14 Stand therefore, having your loins girt about with truth, and having on the breastplate of righteousness; 15 And your feet shod with the preparation of the gospel of peace; 16 Above all, taking the shield of faith, wherewith ye shall be able to quench all the fiery darts of the wicked. 17 And take the helmet of salvation, and the sword of the Spirit, which is the word of God: 18 Praying always with all prayer and supplication in the Spirit, and watching thereunto with all perseverance and supplication for all saints; ….*

II Ti 4:1-2   I charge thee therefore before God, and the Lord Jesus Christ, who shall judge the quick and the dead at his appearing and his kingdom; 2 Preach the word! Be ready in season and out of season. Convince, rebuke, exhort, with all longsuffering and teaching. …

Tit 2:11-13   For the grace of God that bringeth salvation hath appeared to all men, 12 Teaching us that, denying ungodliness and worldly lusts, we should live soberly, righteously, and godly, in this present world; 13 Looking for that blessed hope, and the glorious appearing of the great God and our Saviour Jesus Christ: …

1 Ti 6:11-14   But thou, O man of God, flee these things; and follow after righteousness, godliness, faith, love, patience, meekness. 12 Fight the good fight of faith, lay hold on eternal life, whereunto thou art also called, and hast professed a good profession before many witnesses. 13 I give thee charge in the sight of God, who quickeneth all things, and before Christ Jesus, who before Pontius

Pilate witnessed a good confession; 14 That thou keep this commandment without spot, unrebukeable, until the appearing of our Lord Jesus Christ: ...

Col 3:1-4   If ye then be risen with Christ, seek those things which are above, where Christ sitteth on the right hand of God. 2 Set your affection on things above, not on things on the earth. 3 For ye are dead, and your life is hid with Christ in God. 4 When Christ, who is our life, shall appear, then shall ye also appear with him in glory.

II Co 7:1   Therefore, having these promises, beloved, let us cleanse ourselves from all filthiness of the flesh and spirit, perfecting holiness in the fear of God.

Add the following scriptures to your reading to get a more complete picture of the lives we should live as we prepare for the coming of the Lord to take us in the rapture.

Mt 24:40-46; Mk 13:32-37; Lk 12:32-37; Jn 3:36; 5:28-29; 15:15-17; 1 Co 1:7-8; 9:24-27; II Co 5:17; Gal 5:24; Eph 5:25-27; Php 3:20-21; 4:5; 1 Thess 5:1-23; Heb 9:28; 12:14; Jas 5:7-8; 1 Pe 1:7; 5:2-4; 2 Pe 1:4-11; I Jn 1:7-10; Jude 21; Rv 2:25; 16:15; 22:7.

Stay busy at your calling:

The Lord told Jeremiah, before you were ever born, I called you. In other words, I brought you into this world for a specific purpose. You have an assignment. I have gifted you for this assignment. Those same words apply to all of us. Some Christians seem to think that is the pastor's job, let him do it. Everyone has a calling, and a gifting for that calling, let us not neglect that calling for it will never be taken away, and we will answer to God for how we responded. That calling varies greatly among us. For some it is full-time ministry here at home or abroad. For some, it may be working weekly in their local church, such as teaching a Sunday school class. For others it may be as simple as living a persistent Godly life before their family, friends, and neighbors. For all, it requires obedience to the Lord. Jeremiah's ministry has reached to many generations all around the world and is still ongoing.

Jer 1:4-7   *Then the word of the LORD came unto me, saying, 5 Before I formed thee in the belly I knew thee; and before thou camest forth out of the womb I sanctified thee, and I ordained thee a prophet unto the nations. 6 Then said I, Ah, Lord GOD! behold, I cannot speak: for I am a child. 7 But the LORD said unto me, Say not, I am a child: for thou shalt go to all that I shall send thee, and whatsoever I command thee thou shalt speak.*

Rom 11:29   *For the gifts and calling of God are without repentance.*

Occupy till I Come:

Jesus made it clear that we should go to work on our calling and stay at it until He comes for us. We should tell the story everywhere we go and if even one soul is won to the Lord, there will come a great reward.

Luke 19:12-13   *He said therefore, A certain nobleman went into a far country to receive for* himself a kingdom, and to return. 13 And he called his ten servants, and delivered them ten pounds, and said unto them, Occupy till I come.

Mark 16:15-16   And he said unto them, Go ye into all the world, and preach the gospel to every creature. 16 He that believeth and is baptized shall be saved; but he that believeth not shall be damned.

Mark 5:17-20   And they began to pray him to depart out of their coasts.18 And when he was come into the ship, he that had been possessed with the devil prayed him that he might be with him. 19 Howbeit Jesus suffered him not, but saith unto him, Go home to thy friends, and tell them how great things the Lord hath done for thee, and hath had compassion on thee. 20 And he departed, and began to publish in Decapolis how great things Jesus had done for him: and all men did marvel.

Luke 10:2   Therefore said he unto them, The harvest truly is great, but the labourers are few: pray ye therefore the Lord of the harvest, that he would send forth labourers into his harvest.

Acts 1: 8   But ye shall receive power, after that the Holy Ghost is come upon you: and ye shall be witnesses unto me both in Jerusalem, and in all Judaea, and in Samaria, and unto the uttermost part of the earth.

John 4:34   Jesus saith unto them, My meat(purpose) is to do the will of him that sent me, and to finish his work.

Let us run the race:

Heb 11:33-40   *Who through faith subdued kingdoms, wrought righteousness, obtained promises, stopped the mouths of lions, 34 Quenched the violence of fire, escaped the edge of the sword, out of weakness were made strong, waxed valiant in fight, turned to flight the armies of the aliens. 35 Women received their dead raised to life again: and others were tortured, not accepting deliverance; that they might obtain a better resurrection: 36 And others had trial of cruel mockings and scourgings, yea, moreover of bonds and imprisonment: 37 They were stoned, they were sawn asunder, were tempted, were slain with the sword: they wandered about in sheepskins and goatskins; being destitute, afflicted, tormented; 38 (Of whom the world was not worthy:) they wandered in deserts, and in mountains, and in dens and caves of the earth. 39 And these all, having obtained a good report through faith, received not the promise: 40 God having provided some better thing for us, that they without us should not be made perfect.*

Heb 12:1   *Wherefore seeing we also are compassed about with so great a cloud of witnesses, let us lay aside every weight, and the sin which doth so easily beset us, and let us run with patience the race that is set before us, ...*

Some Christians pay the supreme price for living for the Lord, while others seem to get off totally free of any cost. We should listen to the writer to the Hebrews and "lay aside every weight, and the sin which doth so easily beset us, and let us run with patience the race that is set before us."

Rv 3:11 *Behold, I come quickly: hold that fast which thou hast, that no man take thy crown.*

There will be a Rapture:

The Lord's last words before His ascension were addressed to the Apostles and others present. He told them the Holy Ghost would empower them to carry the gospel to Jerusalem, and from there to the ends of the earth. Then as He stood before them, He ascended into heaven. As they watched Him ascend, two men (angels) appeared and told them that one day Jesus would come back just like they had seen Him go into heaven. From that moment, the Apostles and all Christians since then have looked for His return. Thus, the timing of the Rapture has been referred to as imminent, or, it could occur at any moment.

Ac 1:8-11 *But ye shall receive power, after that the Holy Ghost is come upon you: and ye shall be witnesses unto me both in Jerusalem, and in all Judaea, and in Samaria, and unto the uttermost part of the earth. 9 And when he had spoken these things, while they beheld, he was taken up; and a cloud received him out of their sight. 10 And while they looked stedfastly toward heaven as he went up, behold, two men stood by them in white apparel; 11 Which also said, Ye men of Galilee, why stand ye gazing up into heaven? this same Jesus, which is taken up from you into heaven, shall so come in like manner as ye have seen him go into heaven.*

The Apostle Paul wrote to the Church at Thessalonica, telling them to take comfort about their deceased loved ones. He says, if we believe that Jesus died and rose again, then the Lord Jesus will bring our loved ones with Him when He comes for us in the Rapture. We which are alive and remain shall be caught up together with our deceased loved ones and ever be with the Lord. The following scripture locations help us to see and understand what actually happens when the Rapture takes place. Paul tells us in the 1 Corinthian letter that we shall not all die, but we shall all be changed; he says this is a mystery, this all occurs at the Rapture.

I Co 15:51-53 *Behold, I tell you a mystery: We shall not all sleep, but we shall all be changed …. 52 in a moment, in the twinkling of an eye, at the last trumpet. For the trumpet will sound, and the dead will be raised incorruptible, and we shall be changed. 53 For this corruptible must put on incorruption, and this mortal must put on immortality.*

1 Th 4:13-17 *But I would not have you to be ignorant, brethren, concerning them which are asleep, that ye sorrow not, even as others which have no hope. 14 For if we believe that Jesus died and rose again, even so them also which sleep in Jesus will God bring with him. 15 For this we say unto you by the word of the Lord, that we which are alive and remain unto the coming of the Lord shall not prevent them which are asleep. 16 For the Lord himself shall descend from heaven with a shout, with the voice of the archangel, and with the*

trump of God: and the dead in Christ shall rise first: 17 Then we which are alive and remain shall be caught up together with them in the clouds, to meet the Lord in the air: and so shall we ever be with the Lord.

We are citizens of heaven and we are waiting for the Lord to come from heaven to take us to be with Him. When He comes, He will transform our body to be like His glorious body, meaning among other things, we cannot die again.

Php 3:20-21   *For our citizenship is in heaven, from which we also eagerly wait for the Savior, the Lord Jesus Christ, 21 who will transform our lowly body that it may be conformed to His glorious body, ….*

1 Jn 3:1-2   *Behold, what manner of love the Father hath bestowed upon us, that we should be called the sons of God: therefore, the world knoweth us not, because it knew him not. 2 Beloved, now are we the sons of God, and it doth not yet appear what we shall be: but we know that, when he shall appear, we shall be like him; for we shall see him as he is.*

These several scripture locations show us beyond dispute that there will be a rapture. If any person takes the word of God seriously, how could there be any doubt about there being a rapture?

The Rapture occurs:

Rv 4:1-2   *After this I looked, and, behold, a door was opened in heaven: and the first voice which I heard was as it were of a trumpet talking with me; which said, Come up hither, and I will shew thee things which must be hereafter. 2 And immediately I was in the spirit: and, behold, a throne was set in heaven, and one sat on the throne.*

Here (Rv 4:1), John is taken into heaven, representing the Rapture as depicted in the Revelation.

His wife has made herself ready:

From the beginning to the end of God's word, He encourages us to fervency in righteous living, and especially in preparation for His coming for us in the Rapture. He wants us to know that it is going to be a very great blessing for us to be in attendance at the marriage supper of the Lamb.

Rev 19:7-9   *Let us be glad and rejoice and give Him glory, for the marriage of the Lamb has come, and His wife has made herself ready." 8 And to her it was granted to be arrayed in fine linen, clean and bright, for the fine linen is the righteous acts of the saints. 9 Then he said to me, "Write: 'Blessed are those who are called to the marriage supper of the Lamb!'" And he said to me, "These are the true sayings of God."*

Even in the Old Testament in the Egyptian Exodus, God gave instruction to the people as to how they should carefully follow Him. As they travelled, the priests carried the ark of the covenant and went before the people. The Lord told them to follow the ark, which represented the presence of God. He told the people that you have never been this way before, so you need to stay back a considerable distance, perhaps 3000 feet, so that you can see which way it is going. In the same way, we should follow the Holy Spirit because we have not gone this way before.

Jos 3:3-4 *When you see the ark of the covenant of the LORD your God, and the priests, the Levites, bearing it, then you shall set out from your place and go after it. 4 Yet there shall be a space between you and it, about two thousand cubits by measure. Do not come near it, that you may know the way by which you must go, for you have not passed this way before.*

God has sent His Holy Spirit to guide us in these New Testament times. We must live our lives so that we are filled with the Holy Spirit, so that He can guide our steps to be sure that we are prepared and ready when Jesus comes for us.

Acts 1:8 *But ye shall receive power, after that the Holy Ghost is come upon you: ….*

Paul reminds us to make full proof of our ministry in preparation for that great day when Jesus comes for us.

II Tim 4:5,7-8 *But watch thou in all things, endure afflictions, do the work of an evangelist, make full proof of thy ministry. …. 7 I have fought a good fight, I have finished my course, I have kept the faith: 8 Henceforth there is laid up for me a crown of righteousness, which the Lord, the righteous judge, shall give me at that day: and not to me only, but unto all them also that love his appearing.*

Eph 1:4 *According as he hath chosen us in him before the foundation of the world, that we should be holy and without blame before him in love: ...*

There will be several rapture events:

• Jesus is the first in the list of the several, and the first to ascend to heaven never to die again.

Ac 1:9 *And when he had spoken these things, while they beheld, he was taken up; and a cloud received him out of their sight.*

• The true church is next in line for being raptured. When the Church (the bride of Christ) is raptured, Jesus will bring the souls of the deceased Christians; their bodies will resurrect from the grave, body and soul rejoined. Then living and prepared Christians will join those freshly resurrected from their graves, and all will ascend together to meet the Lord in the air and go from there on into heaven. At this time all involved will be given glorified bodies which are incapable of death. This group may include all deceased people of God since Abel, who was the first to die, as well as all living Christians, which will be a vast number, probably many millions. Some people teach that The Rapture will involve only New Testament Christians, and Old Testament Saints will be raptured at a later time, but the Lord told Daniel: (Da 12:13) *But go thou thy way till the end be: for thou shalt rest, and stand in thy lot at the end of the days.* From this it seems that Daniel has a definite part in the last days. Quite obviously he will be raptured along with all Old Testament Saints in The Rapture. This rapture event is what we commonly think of as "The Rapture".

Rv 4:1-11   *After this I looked, and, behold, a door was opened in heaven: and the first voice which I heard was as it were of a trumpet talking with me; which said, Come up hither, ...*

1 Th 4:13-18   *But I would not have you to be ignorant, brethren, concerning them which are asleep, that ye sorrow not, even as others which have no hope. 14 For if we believe that Jesus died and rose again, even so them also which sleep in Jesus will God bring with him. 15 For this we say unto you by the word of the Lord, that we which are alive and remain unto the coming of the Lord shall not prevent them which are asleep. 16 For the Lord himself shall descend from heaven with a shout, with the voice of the archangel, and with the trump of God: and the dead in Christ shall rise first: 17 Then we which are alive and remain shall be caught up together with them in the clouds, to meet the Lord in the air: and so shall we ever be with the Lord. 18 Wherefore comfort one another with these words.*

• Later John sees "a great multitude," standing before God's throne, which probably occurs late in the first half of the Tribulation. This group were not seen in John's earlier visions. This includes an enormous number of people who have missed the Rapture of the Church and very soon begin to live for the Lord fervently. Some of these are Christians who have become careless and indifferent and have missed the Rapture, then realize what they have done. They will repent and became fiery and zealous for the Lord during the Tribulation. Others are people who have never accepted the Lord as their Savior. They, soon after the Rapture, will make their hearts right with God, so they all will be ready when this group ascends to heaven.

Rv 7:9,14-17   *After this I beheld, and, lo, a great multitude, which no man could number, of all nations, and kindreds, and people, and tongues, stood before the throne, and before the Lamb, clothed with white robes, and palms in their hands; ... What are these which are arrayed in white robes? and whence came they? 14 And I said unto him, Sir, thou knowest. And he said to me, These are they which came out of great tribulation, and have washed their robes, and made them white in the blood of the Lamb. 15 Therefore are they before the throne of God, and serve him day and night in his temple: and he that sitteth on the throne shall dwell among them. 16 They shall hunger no more, neither thirst any more; neither shall the sun light on them, nor any heat. 17 For the Lamb which is in the midst of the throne shall feed them, and shall lead them unto living fountains of waters: and God shall wipe away all tears from their eyes.*

• The next ascension event, the Two Witnesses, occurs, probably at or very near after the midpoint of the Tribulation when they have been slain, then resurrected and ascended to heaven. Both Enoch and Elijah were raptured in the Old Testament times; neither of them died, but both were taken alive to heaven.

Enoch: Ge 5:24   *And Enoch walked with God: and he was not; for God took him.*

130

Elijah: 2 Ki 2:11 *And it came to pass, as they still went on, and talked, that, behold, there appeared a chariot of fire, and horses of fire, and parted them both asunder; and Elijah went up by a whirlwind into heaven.*

Both of these will possibly return to earth during the Tribulation as the two witnesses. Some say it may be Moses and Elijah rather than Enoch and Elijah. They will live for three-and-a-half years preaching and prophesying; then when they have finished their ministry, they will be killed by the Antichrist. They will lie unburied in the streets of Jerusalem for three-and-one-half days with the whole world viewing their dead bodies (on tv) and rejoicing that these two who had tormented them are now dead. But, after three-and-one-half days they will resurrect and then be taken into heaven.

Rv 11:3-13 *And I will give power unto my two witnesses, and they shall prophesy a thousand two hundred and threescore days, clothed in sackcloth. 4 These are the two olive trees, and the two candlesticks standing before the God of the earth. 5 And if any man will hurt them, fire proceedeth out of their mouth, and devoureth their enemies: and if any man will hurt them, he must in this manner be killed. 6 These have power to shut heaven, that it rain not in the days of their prophecy: and have power over waters to turn them to blood, and to smite the earth with all plagues, as often as they will. 7 And when they shall have finished their testimony, the beast that ascendeth out of the bottomless pit shall make war against them, and shall overcome them, and kill them. 8 And their dead bodies shall lie in the street of the great city, which spiritually is called Sodom and Egypt, where also our Lord was crucified. 9 And they of the people and kindreds and tongues and nations shall see their dead bodies three days and an half, and shall not suffer their dead bodies to be put in graves. 10 And they that dwell upon the earth shall rejoice over them, and make merry, and shall send gifts one to another; because these two prophets tormented them that dwelt on the earth. 11 And after three days and an half the Spirit of life from God entered into them, and they stood upon their feet; and great fear fell upon them which saw them. 12 And they heard a great voice from heaven saying unto them, Come up hither. And they ascended up to heaven in a cloud; and their enemies beheld them. 13 And the same hour was there a great earthquake, and the tenth part of the city fell, and in the earthquake were slain of men seven thousand: and the remnant were affrighted, and gave glory to the God of heaven.*

These two, probably Enoch and Elijah were both raptured long ago, and will be raptured again in the Tribulation, after they have finished their ministry and have been slain and resurrected.

• The next rapture event takes place at some point during the second half of the tribulation when the 144,000 Jewish evangelists are raptured, having finished their ministries, and they now appear in heaven. We first saw this group in Rv 7:3-8.

Rv 14:1-5 *And I looked, and, lo, a Lamb stood on the mount Sion, and with him an hundred forty and four thousand, having his Father's name written in their foreheads. 2 And I heard a voice from heaven, as the voice of many waters, and as the voice of a great thunder: and I heard the voice of harpers harping with their harps: 3 And they sung as it were a new song before the throne, and before the four beasts, and the elders: and no man could learn that song but the hundred and forty and four thousand, which were redeemed from the earth. 4 These are they which were not defiled with women; for they are virgins. These are they which follow the Lamb whithersoever he goeth. These were redeemed from among men, being the firstfruits unto God and to the Lamb. And in their mouth was found no guile: for they are without fault before the throne of God. (Notice they are standing before the throne of God).*

- There seems to be another group which appears in heaven which were not in heaven before. Joseph Chambers[2], says they are "the Jewish remnant" which have rejected the Antichrist, and he has probably slain them. These are found standing on the sea of glass, representing another and different group taken to heaven during the Tribulation.

Rv 15:1-4   *And I saw another sign in heaven, great and marvelous, seven angels having the seven last plagues; for in them is filled up the wrath of God. 2 And I saw as it were a sea of glass mingled with fire: and them that had gotten the victory over the beast, and over his image, and over his mark, and over the number of his name, stand on the sea of glass, having the harps of God. 3 And they sing the song of Moses the servant of*

God, and the song of the Lamb, saying, Great and marvelous are thy works, Lord God Almighty; just and true are thy ways, thou King of saints. 4 Who shall not fear thee, O Lord, and glorify thy name? for thou only art holy: for all nations shall come and worship before thee; for thy judgments are made manifest.

• Chambers[3], also, suggests there is another group that resurrected and raptured, which he calls the "Conclusion of the First Resurrection." Those of the "Conclusion of the First Resurrection" mentioned in Rv 20:4 have obviously been raptured, because, we see that they had been beheaded for "the witness of Jesus" and now they live and reign with Christ a thousand years.

Rv 20:4   *And I saw thrones, and they sat upon them, and judgment was given unto them: and I saw the souls of them that were beheaded for the witness of Jesus, and for the word of God, and which had not worshipped the beast, neither his image, neither had received his mark upon their foreheads, or in their hands; and they lived and reigned with Christ a thousand years.*

• Chambers[4] actually says, "Revelation gives details of seven different resurrections or rapture-type events." He then lists these seven events on pages 186-188 of his book entitled "A Palace for the Antichrist."

These individuals and groups all appear in heaven, there present with both their souls and glorified bodies. Other groups appear there in their souls only, meaning they have died but have not been resurrected, Rv 6:9-11, but will be caught up later.

Pre-tribulation Rapture:

The Rapture is a pre-tribulation event as recorded in the Revelation. There are some who believe that the Rapture occurs in what is called "Midtrib" and others who believe in "Postrib." The midtrib view says the Rapture occurs in the middle of the Tribulation, while the postrib view says the Rapture occurs after the Tribulation. Postrib is sometimes referred to as a U-turn view of the Rapture, because you go up in the Rapture then come right back down in the Second Coming. The pretrib view has a clear and strong scriptural support. The following two scripture selections show the possibility of escaping the Tribulation; notice the words "escape" and "spare" in the two scripture locations.

Lk 21:34-36 *And take heed to yourselves, lest at any time your hearts be overcharged with surfeiting, and drunkenness, and cares of this life, and so that day come upon you unawares. 35 For as a snare shall it come on all them that dwell on the face of the whole earth. 36 Watch ye therefore, and pray always, that ye may be accounted worthy to escape all these things that shall come to pass, and to stand before the Son of man.*

Mal 3:16-18 *Then they that feared the LORD spake often one to another: and the LORD hearkened, and heard it, and a book of remembrance was written before him for them that feared the LORD, and that thought upon his name.*

17 And they shall be mine, saith the LORD of hosts, in that day when I make up my jewels; and I will spare them, as a man spareth his own son that serveth him. 18 Then shall ye return, and discern between the righteous and the wicked, between him that serveth God and him that serveth him not.

Notice that a clear distinction is made in those who are serving God in obedience and those who are not. Those who are born again and living in obedience will go in the rapture.

Here again, in 1 Thessalonians we are told that those who are living in holiness and blamelessness before the Lord while waiting for Him to return will be delivered from the wrath to come, showing that the Rapture occurs before the Tribulation.

1 Th 5:9,23 *For God hath not appointed us to wrath, but to obtain salvation by our Lord Jesus Christ, … 23 And the very God of peace sanctify you wholly; and I pray God your whole spirit and soul and body be preserved blameless unto the coming of our Lord Jesus Christ.*

There will be different orders:

1 Co 15:20-23 *But now is Christ risen from the dead, and become the firstfruits of them that slept. 21 For since by man came death, by man came also the resurrection of the dead. 22 For as in Adam all die, even so in Christ shall all be made alive. 23 But every man in his own order: Christ the firstfruits; afterward they that are Christ's at his coming.*

Joseph Seiss[5] says:

"There are some greatest and some least in the kingdom of heaven. There are some who shall be first and some who shall be last. There are some who get crowns, and there are some who get none. There are some who are assigned dominion over ten cities, some over five, and some who lose all reward, and are saved only "so as by fire." The four Living Ones, and the four-and-twenty Elders, are the representatives of men saved from the earth. But they are in heaven, crowned, glorified, and installed in blessed priesthoods and kinghoods in advance of the vast multitude whose rewards are far inferior."

The Judgment Seat of Christ and the Marriage of the Lamb:

These are two events that will take place in heaven after the Rapture occurs. All who find themselves involved in both of these two events will be greatly blessed. It seems that the Judgment Seat of Christ occurs soon after the Rapture. Then, later, the marriage of the Lamb takes place. The scriptural references to the Judgment seat of Christ help us to understand that this is not a judgment as to whether we are a Christian or not, but it is a judgment regarding the rewards we will receive for the things we have done in our servitude for the Lord.

Ro 14:10   *But why dost thou judge thy brother? or why dost thou set at nought thy brother? for we shall all stand before the judgment seat of Christ.*

2 Co 5:10   *For we must all appear before the judgment seat of Christ; that every one may receive the things done in his body, according to that he hath done, whether it be good or bad.*

After the Judgment Seat of Christ, then comes that great event of the marriage of the Lamb.

Rv 19:7-9   *Let us be glad and rejoice and give Him glory, for the marriage of the Lamb has come, and His wife has made herself ready. 8 And to her it was granted to be arrayed in fine linen, clean and bright, for the fine linen is the righteous acts of the saints. 9 Then he said to me, Write: Blessed are those who are called to the marriage supper of the Lamb! And he said to me, These are the true sayings of God.*

The raptured saints will be with the Lord and return with Him in the Second Coming:

The following scriptures make it clear that the Lord will return with His bride in the Second Coming, which occurs at the end of the Tribulation.

Col 3:4   *When Christ, who is our life, shall appear, then shall ye also appear with him in glory.*

Jude 14-15   *And Enoch also, the seventh from Adam, prophesied of these, saying, Behold, the Lord cometh with ten thousands of his saints, 15 To execute judgment upon all, and to convince all that are ungodly among them of all their ungodly deeds which they have ungodly committed, and of all their hard speeches which ungodly sinners have spoken against him.*

Rv 19:11-14   *And I saw heaven opened, and behold a white horse; and he that sat upon him was called Faithful and True, and in righteousness he doth judge and make war. 12 His eyes were as a flame of fire, and on his head were many crowns; and he had a name written, that no man knew, but he himself. 13 And he was clothed with a vesture dipped in blood: and his name is called The Word of God. 14 And the armies which were in heaven followed him upon white horses, clothed in fine linen, white and clean.*

Zec 14:3-5   *Then shall the LORD go forth, and fight against those nations, as when he fought in the day of battle. 4 And his feet shall stand in that day upon the mount of Olives, which is before Jerusalem on the east, and the mount of Olives shall cleave in the midst thereof toward the east and toward the west, ... 5 ... and the LORD my God shall come, and all the saints with thee.*

Raptured bride is to reign with Christ on the earth as kings and priests:

The saints who go in the Rapture will go immediately to heaven and be greatly blessed in the Judgment Seat of Christ and begin very soon to enjoy the wedding of the Lamb and the great feast that follows. After this the Lord will return to the earth in His Second Coming to destroy His remaining enemies at Armageddon, ending the Tribulation, and we will all accompany Him. As soon as He establishes Himself as king over the whole earth, we will reign with Him as kings and priests for the thousand years of peace.

Rv 5:9-10   *And they sung a new song, saying, Thou art worthy to take the book, and to open the seals thereof: for thou wast slain, and hast redeemed us to God by thy blood out of every kindred, and tongue, and people, and nation; 10 And hast made us unto our God kings and priests: and we shall reign on the earth.*

Rv 22:5 actually says the servants of God shall reign forever and ever.

Rv 22:5   *And there shall be no night there; and they need no candle, neither light of the sun; for the Lord God giveth them light: and they shall reign for ever and ever.*

The Spirit and the Bride say, Come:

One of the concluding words in God's Word is, "Come." Come is the prayer of both the Holy Spirit and the bride. "Please come, Lord Jesus" should be the earnest prayer of every Christian today.

Rv 22:17   *And the Spirit and the bride say, Come. And let him that heareth say, Come. And let him that is athirst come. And whosoever will, let him take the water of life freely.*

Lk 9:62   *And Jesus said unto him, No man, having put his hand to the plough, and looking back, is fit for the kingdom of God.*

Having viewed the Rapture, let us now consider the Antichrist, the main character in the whole world during the seven years of the Tribulation, and a very evil character he is.

Notes:

1. *Harpazo:* Strong's Exhaustive Concordance of the Bible (New York: Abingdon Press, 1970).
2. Joseph R. Chambers, A Palace for the Antichrist (Green Forest, AR: New Leaf Press, 1996), p. 186.
3. Ibid., p. 187.
4. Ibid., p. 186-188.
5. Joseph A. Seiss, The Apocalypse (Grand Rapids, MI: Kregel Publications, 1987), p. 427.

6

The Antichrist

The Spirit of Antichrist is here now:

John the apostle wrote long ago, telling us that the spirit of Antichrist is already in the world. The Covid-19 virus and all of the evil maneuvering associated with it is a good example of the spirit of Antichrist being present in the world today. The whole world has gone mad and is in total chaos. There is corruption and evil on every hand. There are many in our world today not willing to confess that Jesus did indeed come in the flesh. All of this comes under what Jesus was talking about when He spoke of the beginning of sorrows. Yes, John, you were right, the spirit of Antichrist is here now.

1 John 4:3 *And every spirit that confesseth not that Jesus Christ is come in the flesh is not of God: and this is that spirit of antichrist, whereof ye have heard that it should come; and even now already is it in the world.*

The Tribulation opens with an introduction of the Antichrist and an awesome salvo of deadly events within the opening of the first four seals, Rv 6:1-8. Even so, this is as calm as the Tribulation is going to be; it will become demonic and fiendish to an incomprehensible degree by the midpoint of the Tribulation. Enoch, from long ago, spoke of that coming fiend, the Antichrist.

A layman and early church father, Barnabas[1] (AD 100), quotes Enoch when he states: "Enoch says, 'For this end the Lord has cut short the times and the days, that His Beloved may hasten: and He will come to the inheritance.' And the prophet also speaks thus: 'Ten kingdoms shall reign upon the earth, and a little king shall rise up after them, who shall subdue under one, three of the kings.'"

It is remarkable that Enoch, the seventh generation from Adam, was so aware of end time events, while so many who are actually living in the end times know very little about the things that are coming to pass.

The appearance of the Antichrist:

The Tribulation will begin with the Antichrist coming on the scene. In the Antichrist's first appearance, he will be revealed as a very charismatic character, very likeable. He will come up as an eleventh person among the leaders of a ten-nation federation. His first act will be to overcome three of the ten nations and lead the ten through his time in the Tribulation, as is stated in the above quote by Enoch. His next move will be to make a seven-year peace treaty with Israel. At the midpoint of the Tribulation, he will break the treaty and commit the abomination of desolation spoken of by Daniel 11:31. Jesus mentioned what Daniel had said in warning to the Jews, advising them to flee.

Mk 13:14   *But when ye shall see the abomination of desolation, spoken of by Daniel the prophet, standing where it ought not, (let him that readeth understand,) then let them that be in Judaea flee to the mountains: ….*

Antichrist comes from the bottomless pit, continues for a short time; seven years, then goes into perdition.

Rv 17:8-11 *The beast that thou sawest was, and is not; and shall ascend out of the bottomless pit, and go into perdition: and they that dwell on the earth shall wonder, whose names were not written in the book of life from the foundation of the world, when they behold the beast that was, and is not, and yet is. 9 And here is the mind which hath wisdom. The seven heads are seven mountains, on which the woman sitteth. 10 And there are seven kings: five are fallen, and one is, and the other is not yet come; and when he cometh, he must continue a short space. 11 And the beast that was, and is not, even he is the eighth, and is of the seven, and goeth into perdition.*

If these verses can be fully comprehended, then one can more readily understand where and when to look for the Antichrist. He is a person who lived in the past and is now being held in the bottomless pit from which he will ascend when the restrainer releases him from the pit. He is a person who has been a king of one of the seven world empires as is mentioned in Revelation 17. The Antichrist will arise from one of the first seven world empires. The Antichrist is the eighth; the eighth is one of the seven.   Joseph Seiss[2] says the first five empires are: Egyptian, Assyrian, Babylonian, Medo-Persian, Grecian, and scripture says Rome is the sixth (Rv 17:10), with a seventh to come. Actually, the Antichrist person can be narrowed down to a king from one of the first six kingdoms, because, the scripture indicates that in John's time, the person in question has lived and is already held in the bottomless pit. There will come another person among the ten-nation federation kings, in the end time, as the seventh king. Then the Antichrist person arises as the eighth, which is one of the seven.

Antichrist is the great pretender:

The Antichrist will come, pretending to be the Christ, even God. He will be in total opposition to God, but will parade himself as God.

2 Th 2:3-4 *Let no man deceive you by any means: for that day shall not come, except there come a falling away first, and that man of sin be revealed, the son of perdition; 4 Who opposeth and exalteth himself above all that is called God, or that is worshipped; so that he as God sitteth in the temple of God, shewing himself that he is God.*

The Antichrist cannot be revealed until the restrainer is taken out of the way. Some teach that the restrainer is the Church; that is true to some degree, but the ultimate restrainer is the Holy Spirit. When the restrainer is removed, the Rapture occurs, the Antichrist rises to power, and the horrors of the Tribulation begin. When the scripture says the restrainer (the Holy Spirit) is removed; that does not mean that the Holy Spirit actually leaves this world, because He being God is everywhere present; He simply steps aside and lets

146

the Antichrist take his place in the Tribulation. We know that He never leaves this world, because millions, perhaps billions, will be saved during the Tribulation, and no one can be saved without the aid of the Holy Spirit.

2 Th 2:6-7 *And now ye know what withholdeth that he might be revealed in his time. For the mystery of iniquity doth already work: only he who now letteth (holds down) will let (release), until he be taken out of the way.*

Verses 8-12 show us the vile wicked character of Antichrist and how he deceives the many who have not yet made up their minds to serve the Lord. It is made clear, also, that he will ultimately be destroyed by the Lord.

2 Th 2:8-12 *And then shall that Wicked be revealed, whom the Lord shall consume with the spirit of his mouth, and shall destroy with the brightness of his coming: 9 Even him, whose coming is after the working of Satan with all power and signs and lying wonders. 10 And with all deceivableness of unrighteousness in them that perish; because they received not the love of the truth, that they might be saved. 11 And for this cause God shall send them strong delusion, that they should believe a lie: 12 That they all might be damned who believed not the truth, but had pleasure in unrighteousness.*

At or near the mid-point of the Tribulation, the Antichrist receives some sort of deadly wound which will then be healed. As a result, many will be convinced that he is the genuine Messiah.

Rv 13:3 *And I saw one of his heads as it were wounded to death; and his deadly wound was healed: and all the world wondered after the beast.*

Although the name Antichrist is only found four times in the Bible, all four times in the epistles of John; throughout much of scripture, Antichrist is presented with other names and titles, showing us much of his character and actions. Jesus himself said (speaking of the Antichrist):

John 5:43 *I am come in my Father's name, and ye receive me not: if another shall come in his own name, him ye will receive.*

Names of the Antichrist:

There are many scriptural references to the Antichrist, showing us much about his character. Arthur Pink[3] lists many scriptural references to Antichrist; in his book "The Antichrist" Pink says:

"In the book of Job he is referred to as "the Crooked Serpent" (Job 26:13): with this should be compared Isa. 27:1 where, as "the Crooked Serpent", he is connected with the Dragon, though distinguished from him. In the Psalms we find quite a number of references to him; as "the Bloody and Deceitful Man" (5:6); "the Wicked (One)" (9:17); "the Man of the Earth" (10:18); the "Mighty Man" (52:1); "the Adversary" (74:10); "the Head over many countries" (110:6); "the Evil Man" and "the Violent Man" (140:1), etc. Let the student give special attention to Psalms 10, 52, and 55. When we turn to the Prophets there the references to this Monster of Iniquity are so numerous that were, we to cite all of them, even without comment, it would take us quite beyond the bounds of this chapter. Only a few of the more prominent ones can, therefore, be noticed. Isaiah mentions him: first as the "Assyrian", "the Rod" of God's anger (10:5); then as "the Wicked" (11:4); then as "the King of Babylon" (14:11-20 and cf 30:31-33); and also, as the "Spoiler" - Destroyer (16:4). Jeremiah calls him "the Destroyer of the Gentiles" (4:7); the "Enemy", the "Cruel One" and "the Wicked" (30:14 and 23). Ezekiel refers to him as the "Profane Wicked Prince of Israel" (21:25), and again under the figure of the "Prince of Tyre" (28:2-10), and also as "the chief Prince of Meshech and Tubal" (38:2). Daniel gives a full delineation of his character and furnished a complete outline of his career. Hosea speaks of him as "the King of Princes" (8:10), and as the "Merchant" in whose hand are "the balances of deceit" and who "loveth to oppress" (12:7). Joel describes him as the Head of the Northern Army, who shall be overthrown because he "magnified himself to do great things" (2:20). Amos terms him the "Adversary" who shall break Israel's strength and spoil her palaces (3:11). Micah makes mention of him in the fifth chapter of his prophecy (see v. 6). Nahum refers to him under the name of "Belial (Heb.) and tells of his destruction (1:15). Habakkuk speaks of him as "the Proud Man" who "enlarged his desires as hell, and is as death, and cannot be satisfied, but gathereth unto him all nations, and heapeth unto him all peoples" (2:5). Zechariah describes him as "the Idol Shepherd" upon whom is pronounced God's "woe", and upon whom descends His judgment (11:17)."

Arthur Pink has obviously researched the scriptures well, listing all the names of Antichrist in the above paragraph, all from the scriptures.

The Antichrist is also known by other names:

One whose deadly wound was healed, Rv 13:3; Him, whose coming is after the working of Satan, 2 Thess 2:9; That Wicked (one), 2 Thess 2:10; The Lie 2 Thess 2:11. The following scriptural references will give us further understanding of the character of the Antichrist, the man of lawlessness. He will: be boastful, Da 7:20; exalt himself above the God of gods, Da 11:36; have no desire for women, Da 11:37; honor a god of fortresses, Da 11:38; have authority, Da 7:20 and Rv 13:2; seize by intrigue, Da 11:21; be shrewd, deceitful, and powerful, Da 8:25, 11:38, Rv 13:17, Psalm 52:7. Ezekiel 28:4-5; Rv 6:2, 13:4, 17:17. The same Horn made war with the saints and prevailed, Da 7:21-22.

The seven years of Tribulation is the allotted time of the Antichrist's reign:

Although there are various ideas as to the exact time of the beginning of the Tribulation, a strong argument can be made that the confirming of the covenant between the Antichrist and Israel is the beginning of the Tribulation. If the confirming of the covenant is the beginning of the Tribulation, there may be only a short interval of time between the Rapture and the Tribulation.

Da 9:27 *And he shall confirm the covenant with many for one week: and in the midst of the week he shall cause the sacrifice and the oblation to cease, and for the overspreading of abominations he shall make it desolate, even until the consummation, and that determined shall be poured upon the desolate.*

Each of the seven days of the week represents a year in the Tribulation. Perhaps the strongest clue for identifying the Antichrist, is when he makes that seven-year peace agreement with Israel.

The Antichrist rides in on a white horse:

He will come on the scene seeming to have all the answers. He will probably be a very charismatic, appealing world leader, offering peace and prosperity. When the Antichrist first comes on the scene, he will appear as a man of peace, as we see in:

Rv 6:1-2 *And I saw when the Lamb opened one of the seals, and I heard, as it were the noise of thunder, one of the four beasts saying, Come and see. 2 And I saw, and behold a white horse: and he that sat on him had a bow; and a crown was given unto him: and he went forth conquering, and to conquer.*

Daniel speaking perhaps 600 years before John tells us the Antichrist will come in peaceably and obtain the kingdom by flatteries.

Da 11:21-24 *And in his estate shall stand up a vile person, to whom they shall not give the honour of the kingdom: but he shall come in*

*peaceably, and obtain the kingdom by flatteries.
22 And with the arms of a flood shall they be
overflown from before him, and shall be broken;
yea, also the prince of the covenant. 23 And after
the league made with him he shall work
deceitfully: for he shall come up, and shall
become strong with a small people. 24 He shall
enter peaceably even upon the fattest places of
the province; and he shall do that which his
fathers have not done, nor his fathers' fathers; he
shall scatter among them the prey, and spoil, and
riches: yea, and he shall forecast his devices
against the strong holds, even for a time.*

The Antichrist will be a Jew:

The Antichrist will be a Jew, as is indicated by
Ezekiel, when Ezekiel referred to him as the wicked
prince of Israel.

Eze 21:25-27 *And thou, profane wicked
prince of Israel, whose day is come, when iniquity
shall have an end, 26 Thus saith the Lord GOD;
Remove the diadem, and take off the crown: this
shall not be the same: exalt him that is low, and
abase him that is high. 27 I will overturn,
overturn, overturn, it: and it shall be no more, until
he come whose right it is; and I will give it him.*

The Jews have been looking for a Jewish
Messiah for millennia; it seems unreasonable that
they would suddenly give in and accept anything
else. John the apostle lived until near AD 100.
John had a disciple named Polycarp who had a
disciple named Irenaeus (AD 120-202) who had a
disciple named Hippolytus (AD 170-236). Irenaeus

and Hippolytus lived until near or after AD 200, both say that the Antichrist will be a Jew from the tribe of Dan. Irenaeus[4] says, that Jeremiah says that the Antichrist will be a Jew of the tribe of Dan, Irenaeus V XXX 2. *"The snorting of his horses was heard from Dan",* Jer 8:16.

Hippolytus[5] says: "Antichrist will come from the tribe of Dan"; he supports this with reference to: *"Dan shall be a serpent by the way",* Ge 49:17 and Jer 8:16. "Thus did the Scriptures preach before-time of this lion and lion's whelp. And in like manner also we find it written regarding Antichrist. For Moses speaks thus: "Dan is a lion's whelp, and he shall leap from Bashan." But that no one may err by supposing that this is said of the Saviour, let him attend carefully to the matter." "Dan," he says, "is a lion's whelp;" and in naming the tribe of Dan, he declared clearly the tribe from which Antichrist is destined to spring. For as Christ springs from the tribe of Judah, so Antichrist is to spring from the tribe of Dan. And that the case stands thus, we see also from the words of Jacob: "Let Dan be a serpent, lying upon the ground, biting the horse's heel." What, then, is meant by the serpent but Antichrist, that deceiver who is mentioned in Genesis, who deceived Eve and supplanted Adam ...?"

Prophecies showing Antichrist against Israel even though he is a Jew:

The Antichrist is sent, in part, against the hypocritical nation of Israel which has stirred up God's wrath.

Isa 10:5-6 *O Assyrian, the rod of mine anger, and the staff in their hand is mine indignation. 6 I will send him against an hypocritical nation, and against the people of my wrath will I give him a charge, to take the spoil, and to take the prey, and to tread them down like the mire of the streets.*

A question comes to mind: How can the Antichrist be an Assyrian king in past history and a Jew also? The history of the Jews tells us clearly that Babylon carried most Jews into captivity in 586 BC. They were dispersed worldwide again in AD 70. when the Romans destroyed Jerusalem. With such dispersion over all these centuries it is easy to see how the Jewish ethnicity could be spread among other ethnic groups, thereby, producing a Jewish Assyrian king.

Jeremiah 4:5-7 adds another name,"The *Destroyer of the Gentiles*" and the idea that he will be as destructive toward the Gentile nations as he is against Israel.

The Antichrist will be an Assyrian Jew:

The Antichrist will be a Jew, but he will also be an Assyrian, as we shall soon see; worse than these things, he will be a monster from hell.

Isa 10:5 *O Assyrian, the rod of mine anger, and the staff in their hand is mine indignation.*

Isa 14:25 *That I will break the Assyrian in my land, and upon my mountains tread him under foot: then shall his yoke depart from off them, and his burden depart from off their shoulders.*

Isa 30:31 *For through the voice of the LORD shall the Assyrian be beaten down, which smote with a rod.*

Mic 5:5-6 *And this man shall be the peace, when the Assyrian shall come into our land: and when he shall tread in our palaces, then shall we raise against him seven shepherds, and eight principal men. 6 And they shall waste the land of Assyria with the sword, and the land of Nimrod in the entrances thereof: thus shall he deliver us from the Assyrian, when he cometh into our land, and when he treadeth within our borders.*

Since he is clearly an Assyrian, it seems possible that the Antichrist might prove to be a former king of the Assyrian Empire with Jewish blood in his veins.

Will Nimrod prove to be the Antichrist?

Some Bible scholars teach that Nimrod will prove to be the Antichrist. Nimrod was a rebel and the founder of Babylon. Babylon is representative of sinfulness and rebellion against God, and Babylon is ultimately to be destroyed, so it could seem to be fitting that Nimrod will be the Antichrist. The beginning of his (Nimrod's) kingdom is Babylon.

Ge 10:8-11 *And Cush begat Nimrod: he began to be a mighty one in the earth. 9 He was a mighty hunter (rebel) before the LORD: wherefore it is said, Even as Nimrod the mighty hunter before the LORD. 10 And the beginning of his kingdom was Babel, and Erech, and Accad, and Calneh, in the land of Shinar. 11 Out of that land went forth*

*Asshur, and builded Nineveh, and the city
Rehoboth, and Calah, ...*

He being the builder of these cities shows
clearly that he was an Assyrian, and he was a
rebel, but Nimrod is not a Jew, because he lived
before Jews existed. Nimrod is at the least a type
of the Antichrist.

Antichrist is from the Roman Empire:

Many prophecy teachers, today, teach that
the Antichrist is going to arise out of the Revived
Roman Empire, and Daniel 7 states the same.
They then go on to advance the idea that the
European Community is that revived empire,
therefore the Antichrist will arise from somewhere
in Europe. Let us examine the scripture on the
issue. He arises from within a ten-nation
federation: He overcomes three of the ten nations,
then rules over the ten. The fourth beast in
Daniel's vision represents Rome. That fourth beast
had ten horns from which the Antichrist arises at
some point in time in world events, in the last
days.

Da 7:7-8 *After this I saw in the night
visions, and behold a fourth beast, dreadful and
terrible, and strong exceedingly; and it had great
iron teeth: it devoured and brake in pieces, and
stamped the residue with the feet of it: and it was
diverse from all the beasts that were before it; and
it had ten horns. 8 I considered the horns, and,
behold, there came up among them another little
horn, before whom there were three of the first
horns plucked up by the roots: and, behold, in this*

horn were eyes like the eyes of man, and a mouth speaking great things.

According to Hippolytus[6], Antichrist's first strike will be Tyre and Berytus (Beirut), then the three nations of Egypt, Libya, and Ethiopia. Pink[7] suggests that the three nations will be Egypt, Persia, and Greece. This appearance of the Antichrist is from the Roman Empire. So, we see that without question, the Antichrist will arise from somewhere within the Roman Empire. But, in looking further, we see that the Antichrist arises out of the Grecian Empire, as well.

The Antichrist is from the Grecian Empire:

In the paragraph above we saw evidence from Daniel 7 that the Antichrist arises from out of the Roman Empire. In the very next chapter, Daniel 8, we see that he arises from the Grecian Empire.

Da 8:8-12 *Therefore the he goat [Greece] waxed very great: and when he was strong, the great horn was broken; and for it came up four notable ones toward the four winds of heaven. 9 And out of one of them came forth a little horn [the Antichrist], which waxed exceeding great, toward the south, and toward the east, and toward the pleasant land [Israel]. 10 And it waxed great, even to the host of heaven; and it cast down some of the host and of the stars to the ground, and stamped upon them. 11 Yea, he magnified himself even to the prince of the host, and by him the daily sacrifice was taken away, and the place of his sanctuary was cast down. 12 And an host was given him against the daily sacrifice by reason of transgression, and it cast down the truth to the ground; and it practised, and prospered.*

Da 8:21-25 And the rough goat is the king of Grecia: and the great horn that is between his eyes is the first king [Alexander the Great]. 22 Now that being broken, whereas four stood up for it, four kingdoms shall stand up out of the nation, but not in his power. 23 And in the latter time of their kingdom, when the transgressors are come to the full, a king of fierce countenance, and understanding dark sentences, shall stand up. 24 And his power shall be mighty, but not by his own power [Rv 13:2 tells us the dragon, satan, gave him his power]: and he shall destroy wonderfully, and shall prosper, and practise, and shall destroy the mighty and the holy people. 25 And through his policy also he shall cause craft to prosper in his hand; and he shall magnify himself in his heart, and by peace shall destroy many: he shall also stand up against the Prince of princes; but he shall be broken without hand.

The four generals who succeeded Alexander the Great were Gassander (Macedonia/West), Lysimachus (Thrace/North), Seleucia (Syria/East) including Israel, and Ptolemy (Egypt/South) as Daniel 8:9-12 makes clear. Joseph Chambers[8] says: "Isaiah said he would be an Assyrian which places his origination from the Seleucid kingdom, presently Syria, including the eastern area of the old Assyrian kingdom." Daniel very specifically and clearly tells us that the Antichrist will arise from the Grecian Empire as well as from the Roman Empire.

We understand, from Daniel's visions in chapters seven and eight, that the Antichrist will come from some area common to both the Roman and the Grecian Empires. Greece is the only European country that is a part of the Grecian Empire. When Alexander the Great's empire was divided, the Seleucid Empire is the one that went east and south. This Seleucid Empire did not include Greece; it started with Asia Minor (modern-day Turkey) and went east and south all the way to India (including Israel). Modern day countries that are within the bounds of the Roman Empire and the Seleucid Empire are countries such as Lebanon, Turkey, Syria, Iraq, and Iran. There are other countries that could be brought into the mix, but these are the most likely places that fit within the demands of scripture. There presently is no modern-day Assyria. Although in Isaiah 11:1-11 the Lord speaks of Assyria existing during the Millennial Kingdom. However, in southeastern Turkey, northwestern Iran, eastern Syria, and northern Iraq there are pockets of ethnic Assyrian populations. These people have been striving to establish an independent, Assyrian state, since World War I, with promises of just such a state from such as the League of Nations, then from the United Nations. These promises have yet to be fulfilled; who knows what the near future holds. In the northern part of Iraq, there is a large area called the Assyrian Triangle; most of the population is ethnic Assyrian, and Christian rather than

Islamic. Within this "triangle" is the city of Mosul (site of the ancient city of Nineveh). To the south, still within the country of Iraq, lies Al Hillah, the site of ancient Babylon. Both Babylon and Nineveh were built by Nimrod, with whom all of this rebellion against God started after the flood. It is easy to imagine an Assyrian Jew arising from among the Assyrians in northern Iraq, coming into power and by intrigue and deceit, become the President of Iraq, and from there continuing Nimrod's rebellion, fulfilling all that is spoken of the Antichrist in scripture. Such a scenario may very well come about in any one of the countries in the area. So, the Antichrist will very probably appear in one of the following modern-day countries: Syria, Lebanon, Turkey, Iraq, or Iran, or at least in that general area.

If it is as in the paragraphs above (The Antichrist will be a Jew), Hippolytus referring to Moses' words in Dt 33:22, "Dan is a lion's whelp, and he shall leap from Bashan," then, the Antichrist may come from present day Syria.

The fourth beast which had ten horns, spoken of in Daniel seven, produces the ten-nation federation out of which the Antichrist comes. Rather than coming from the European Union, the Antichrist will arise from a federation of nations made up from two groups of nations. One group of five nations could be the European Union, including Italy (Rome) and Greece. The other group will probably be five Arabic countries, possibly including: Turkey, Syria, Iraq, Iran, and possibly Egypt. In consideration of Nebuchadnezzar's

dream, Dan 2, God was showing Nebuchadnezzar what is to be in the last days. In his dream Nebuchadnezzar saw an image with a head of gold, breast and arms of silver, belly and thighs of brass, legs of iron, feet of iron and clay. This image stood for the world empires that had a relationship with Israel. These empires were Babylon the head, Medo-Persia the breast and arms, Greece the belly and thighs, Roman the legs and feet, the toes were the ten-nation federation arising out of the Roman Empire in the last days. The Roman Empire started as a single empire, but in AD 285, divided into two separate empires, as the two legs show us. The two empires were the Eastern Empire governed from Byzantium (today known as Istanbul in Turkey) and the Western Empire governed from Rome. The Western Empire survived until AD 476, while the Byzantine Empire continued until AD 1453. The ten toes of Nebuchadnezzar's dream image help us to understand the ten-nation federation arising out of the Roman Empire in the end times. Daniel 8 helps us to understand that the Antichrist will arise from the Grecian Empire, which seems to point toward the area of the Byzantine Empire. So, it seems as already stated, the Antichrist will most likely arise from somewhere in the middle east (Asia rather than Europe).

Further considerations of the Antichrist:

During the first three-and-one-half years of the Tribulation: The Antichrist appears, as a man of peace, and he secures and solidifies his position with Israel and the rest of the whole world; he develops his position with the False Prophet, the two witnesses, the great whore, and Babylon.

The midpoint of the Tribulation seems to be somewhere between the end of Revelation 8 and the end of chapter 11 and involving the "three woes"; all that follows in the last half of the tribulation is straight out of hell. All that God brings about is horrific, yet, righteous judgment.

Revelation 6 shows us the opening of the Tribulation with an introduction of the Antichrist. In this first appearance of the Antichrist, he comes in and with intrigue and deception, establishes himself firmly as the world ruler for the remainder of the seven-year Tribulation. Notice also, the judgments of God begin immediately. Under the opening of the first seal, the first appearance of the Antichrist occurs. When the second seal is opened, with all else that occurs, either terrible murder and mass slaughter or war will break out which may be the war of Gog and Magog, as is mentioned in Eze 38 and 39. All of this is followed by worldwide famine under the third seal. Finally, under the fourth seal, one fourth of the world's population dies; nearly 2 billion people will die. All of this probably occurs in the first few months of the Tribulation. Then things get really bad.

Rv 6:1-8 *And I saw when the Lamb opened one of the seals, and I heard, as it were the noise of thunder, one of the four beasts saying, Come and see. 2 And I saw, and behold a white horse: and he that sat on him had a bow; and a crown was given unto him: and he went forth conquering, and to conquer. 3 And when he had opened the* second seal, I heard the second beast say, Come and see. 4 And there went out another horse that was red: and power was given to him that sat thereon to take peace from the earth, and that they should kill one another: and there was given unto him a great sword. 5 And when he had opened the third seal, I heard the third beast say, Come and see. And I beheld, and lo a black horse; and he that sat on him had a pair of balances in his hand. 6 And I heard a voice in the midst of the four beasts say, A measure of wheat for a penny, and three measures of barley for a penny; and see thou hurt not the oil and the wine. 7 And when he had opened the fourth seal, I heard the voice of the fourth beast say, Come and see. 8 And I looked, and behold a pale horse: and his name that sat on him was Death, and Hell followed with him. And power was given unto them over the fourth part of the earth, to kill with sword, and with hunger, and with death, and with the beasts of the earth.

Antichrist and the two witnesses:

In the middle of all that is going on God sends the two witnesses, perhaps Enoch and Elijah, or some say it might be Moses and Elijah. Hippolytus[9] says that the two witnesses are: Enoch and Elijah.

It is prophesied that Elijah is to come to restore all things, so he seems to be almost certainly one of the two witnesses.

Mal 4:5-6   Behold, I will send you Elijah the prophet before the coming of the great and dreadful day of the LORD: 6 And he shall turn the *heart of the fathers to the children, and the heart of the children to their fathers, lest I come and smite the earth with a curse.*

Mt 17:10-11   *And his disciples asked him, saying, Why then say the scribes that Elias must first come? 11 And Jesus answered and said unto them, Elias truly shall first come, and restore all things.*

The writer to the Hebrews says "it is appointed unto men once to die".

Heb 9:27   *And as it is appointed unto men once to die, but after this the judgment: ….*

Both Enoch and Elijah were translated to heaven alive and did not die, so it seems that they would be good candidates to fill the position of these witnesses.

Rv 11:3   *And I will give power unto my two witnesses, and they shall prophesy a thousand two hundred and threescore days, clothed in sackcloth.*

The words "two witnesses" give us a strong hint as to why they are sent. God has sent these two to give their testimony for three-and-one-half years, preaching and prophesying and telling the whole world that the Antichrist and the False Prophet are indeed false and should be rejected. Hopefully, many who find themselves in this terrible situation will listen to them and accept the Lord Jesus and reject this godless Antichrist.

Rv 11:4   *These are the two olive trees, and the two candlesticks standing before the God of the earth.*

We see a reference to these same two in the book of Zechariah.

Zec 4:11-14 *Then answered I, and said unto him, What are these two olive trees upon the right side of the candlestick and upon the left side thereof? 12 And I answered again, and said unto him, What be these two olive branches which through the two golden pipes empty the golden oil out of themselves? 13 And he answered me and said, Knowest thou not what these be? And I said, No, my lord. 14 Then said he, These are the two anointed ones, that stand by the LORD of the whole earth.*

These two come directly from heaven with a definite anointing and a specific assignment. They have tremendous power and cannot be harmed until they have finished their ministry, after which the Antichrist kills them and refuses them burial. The whole world has seen their ministry and their slaughter. There is little doubt that many will accept the Lord because of their witness, but there will be many more who will rejoice over their deaths. After three-and-one-half days they will resurrect and be raptured, adding greatly to their witness, perhaps adding even more converts.

Rv 11:5-13 *And if any man will hurt them, fire proceedeth out of their mouth, and devoureth their enemies: and if any man will hurt them, he must in this manner be killed. 6 These have power to shut heaven, that it rain not in the days of their prophecy: and have power over waters to turn them to blood, and to smite the earth with all plagues, as often as they will. 7 And when they shall have finished their testimony, the beast that ascendeth out of the bottomless pit shall make war against them, and shall overcome them, and kill them. 8 And their dead bodies shall lie in the street of the great city [Jerusalem], which spiritually is called Sodom and Egypt, where also our Lord was crucified. 9 And they of the people and kindreds and tongues and nations shall see their dead bodies three days and an half, and shall not suffer their dead bodies to be put in graves. 10 And they that dwell upon the earth shall rejoice over them, and make merry, and shall send gifts one to another; because these two prophets tormented them that dwelt on the earth. 11 And after three days and an half the Spirit of life from God entered into them, and they stood upon their feet; and great fear fell upon them which saw them. 12 And they heard a great voice from heaven saying unto them, Come up hither. And they ascended up to heaven in a cloud; and their enemies beheld them. 13 And the same hour was there a great earthquake, and the tenth part of the city fell, and in the earthquake were slain of men seven thousand: and the remnant were affrighted, and gave glory to the God of heaven.*

The Woman, the Child, and the Dragon:

In Revelation 12, the Antichrist is not mentioned, but a terrific story is told. In the story, a woman (the nation of Israel) is about to give birth to a child (the child is Jesus), when she is confronted by a great red dragon (Satan), who intends to devour the child as soon as it is born. All of this is a look back in history when Jesus was born in Bethlehem. The child was caught up to God and His throne (at Jesus' ascension). The rest of this story takes place near the midpoint of the Tribulation. The dragon has seven heads with crowns and ten horns. The heads/crowns are seven empires from which the Antichrist comes. The ten horns are the ten-nation federation in which the Antichrist appears as an eleventh person among the kings of that federation. There is a war in heaven, and the dragon (Satan) is cast out of heaven, and with the angels who followed him, he is cast to the earth, and will never gain access to heaven again. A great voice announces woe to the inhabitants of the earth because Satan has come down having great anger, because he knows he has but a short time remaining. Remember in Job's time Satan had access to heaven to attend meetings that God called for His angels, but not anymore. The dragon (Satan) persecutes the woman (through the Antichrist), and she flees to the wilderness where she is to be cared for three-and-one-half years until the Antichrist's time is finished. Remember how the Lord fed Israel for forty years in the wilderness when they left Egypt. In pursuing the woman, the dragon sends a flood after her (perhaps the flood is the armies of the Antichrist) but the earth opens up and swallows the flood and the woman is able to escape to the wilderness. The dragon then pursues (by means of the efforts of the Antichrist) the remnant of the woman's seed (Christians and Jews in the Tribulation). Read all of Revelation 12 to see the full story. This is an amazing story with tremendous repercussions for the inhabitants of earth. Through all of earth's history, Satan has been allowed access to heaven; now, suddenly he is limited to earth with but little time left, and he takes it out on all the inhabitants of the earth and especially God's people (manifesting himself through the Antichrist). This will make a big difference in the last half of the Tribulation. The Tribulation will now become the great Tribulation.

Rv 12:12 *Therefore rejoice, ye heavens, and ye that dwell in them. Woe to the inhabiters of the earth and of the sea! for the devil is come down unto you, having great wrath, because he knoweth that he hath but a short time.*

Throughout the story in Rv 12, it is the great red dragon that is being talked about, two times he is referred to as the serpent. Through the remaining time in the great Tribulation he will manifest himself through the actions and deeds of the Antichrist.

Antichrist at the midpoint of the Tribulation:

The 13th chapter of Revelation presents a fearsome appearance of the Antichrist and his False Prophet; the Antichrist is referred to as the beast from the sea. This appearance is at the midpoint of the Tribulation when he has become fully possessed of and impowered by the devil and is turned into a hellish monster with most of the world still in awe of and worshipping him. In verses 1-9 the Antichrist receives the power necessary for his worldly conquest. However, he seems to suffer a fatal wound but is miraculously resurrected;

astonishing the world and convincing them he is the true messiah.

Rv 13:1-9 *And I stood upon the sand of the sea, and saw a beast rise up out of the sea, having seven heads and ten horns, and upon his horns ten crowns, and upon his heads the name of blasphemy. 2 And the beast which I saw was like unto a leopard, and his feet were as the feet of a bear, and his mouth as the mouth of a lion: and the dragon gave him his power, and his seat, and great authority. 3 And I saw one of his heads as it were wounded to death; and his deadly wound was healed: and all the world wondered after the beast. 4 And they worshipped the dragon which gave power unto the beast: and they worshipped the beast, saying, Who is like unto the beast? who is able to make war with him? 5 And there was given unto him a mouth speaking great things and blasphemies; and power was given unto him to continue forty and two months. 6 And he opened his mouth in blasphemy against God, to blaspheme his name, and his tabernacle, and them that dwell in heaven. 7 And it was given unto him to make war with the saints, and to overcome them: and power was given him over all kindreds, and tongues, and nations. 8 And all that dwell upon the earth shall worship him, whose names are not written in the book of life of the Lamb slain from the foundation of the world. 9 If any man have an ear, let him hear.*

Abomination of Desolation:

Jesus spoke of the abomination of desolation, an awful event committed by the Antichrist, which had been prophesied by the prophet Daniel more than 500 years earlier. Jesus tells those in Judea at that time to flee to the mountains, showing that it is an awful event, also, that the killing of Christians from then on will be much worse.

Mt 24:15-16 *When ye therefore shall see the abomination of desolation, spoken of by Daniel the prophet, stand in the holy place, (whoso readeth, let him understand 16 Then let them which be in Judaea flee into the mountains: ...*

The abomination of desolation is when the Antichrist goes into the newly built temple, takes away the daily sacrifice and announces that he is God, and demands worship of himself as God, along with some other god. The mark of the beast will be put into place near that time. All who refuse to take the mark and refuse to worship the Antichrist as God will be killed.

Da 11:31-39 *And arms shall stand on his part, and they shall pollute the sanctuary of strength, and shall take away the daily sacrifice, and they shall place the abomination that maketh desolate. 32 And such as do wickedly against the covenant shall he corrupt by flatteries: but the people that do know their God shall be strong, and do exploits. 33 And they that understand among the people shall instruct many: yet they shall fall by the sword, and by flame, by captivity, and by spoil, many days. 34 Now when they shall fall, they shall be holpen with a little help: but many shall cleave to them with flatteries. 35 And some of them of understanding shall fall, to try them, and to purge, and to make them white, even to the time of the end: because it is yet for a time appointed. 36 And the king shall do according to his will; and he shall exalt himself, and magnify himself above every god, and shall speak marvellous things against the God of gods, and shall prosper till the indignation be accomplished: for that that is determined shall be done. 37 Neither shall he regard the God of his fathers, nor the desire of women, nor regard any god: for he shall magnify himself above all. 38 But in his estate shall he honour the God of forces: and a god whom his fathers knew not shall he honour with gold, and silver, and with precious stones, and pleasant things. 39 Thus shall he do in the most strongholds with a strange god, whom he shall acknowledge and increase with glory: and he shall cause them to rule over many, and shall divide the land for gain.*

The False Prophet:

The False Prophet accompanies the Antichrist, promoting the Antichrist's program, threatening all with death who do not worship the Antichrist, performing miracles to prove the Antichrist is God. All that the False Prophet does is done to deceive the whole world. This False Prophet is referred to as the beast out of the earth.

Rv 13:11-18 *And I beheld another beast coming up out of the earth; and he had two horns like a lamb, and he spake as a dragon. 12 And he exerciseth all the power of the first beast before him, and causeth the earth and them which dwell therein to worship the first beast, whose deadly wound was healed. 13 And he doeth great wonders, so that he maketh fire come down from heaven on the earth in the sight of men, 14 And deceiveth them that dwell on the earth by the means of those miracles which he had power to do in the sight of the beast; saying to them that dwell on the earth, that they should make an image to the beast, which had the wound by a sword, and did live. 15 And he had power to give life unto the image of the beast, that the image of the beast should both speak, and cause that as many as would not worship the image of the beast should be killed. 16 And he causeth all, both small and great, rich and poor, free and bond, to receive a mark in their right hand, or in their foreheads: 17 And that no man might buy or sell, save he that had the mark, or the name of the beast, or the number of his name. 18 Here is wisdom. Let him that hath understanding count the number of the beast: for it is the number of a man; and his number is Six hundred threescore and six.*

The Second Beast now arises, this one from the earth, and he possesses the same power as the First Beast. The mark of the beast is instituted by the False Prophet, making it mandatory for all to receive the mark or be killed. As proof of his authority, he performs amazing signs, even calling down fire from the sky: further, he gives "life" to an image of the First Beast, made by the people of the earth. Anyone who doesn't worship this ungodly image is immediately put to death. Famous or unknown, wealthy or poor, imprisoned or free, any who wish to engage in commerce during the Antichrist's reign must come under the authority of the Second Beast via the image. It will be virtually impossible to earn wages, buy food, sell or trade anything for food without the First Beast's mark or the number of his name on the forehead or right hand. Scripture states the number of his name plainly (666), and it will be plain to the wise.

The Antichrist and the False Prophet both are referred to as beasts, with the Antichrist being the first beast and the False Prophet being the second beast. *Therion* is the Greek word for beast, meaning a dangerous animal or a venomous wild beast. Yet for some reason the Lord has chosen to label them as beasts. These two are not animals, but, human beings, empowered by the Devil. The first beast, the Antichrist, is a human being who has lived in the past probably as a king over one of the empires such as Assyria, having been held in the bottomless pit, until he is released to take part in the Tribulation. Not so much is known about the second beast as to where he comes from. He is referred to as the Second Beast as well as the False Prophet three times in the Revelation. Make no mistake, both of these two beings are devilish and fiendish beyond comprehension. They both will become responsible for the death of billions of Christians as well as others during the seven-year Tribulation, so, it is proper that they are labeled as beasts.

The destruction of Mystery Babylon, all false religion:

There is a distinct relationship between Mystery Babylon and the Antichrist. The 17th chapter of the Revelation tells of a woman sitting upon a scarlet colored beast. The woman is referred to as the great whore, by whom the inhabitants of the earth have been made drunk with the wine of her fornication. The blasphemous beast (the Antichrist) she is riding upon has seven heads and ten horns, showing a relationship with past world empires and the ten-nation confederation that is coming in the end times. In Rv 17:5 the woman is called Mystery Babylon the Great, The Mother of Harlots and Abominations of the Earth. The scripture, also, tells us she is guilty of the blood of the saints and martyrs of Jesus. This woman is the false religions of all of history riding on the back of the Antichrist during the time of the Tribulation, the coming together of two horrible evils. John seems to have been stunned by what he saw in this woman. Through much of the Tribulation the ten-nation confederation will support the great whore along with the Antichrist; toward the end of the Tribulation the ten-nation confederation along with the Antichrist will turn from her and destroy her, so that the Antichrist alone can be worshipped as god.

Rv 17:7-8,12-18   *And the angel said unto me, Wherefore didst thou marvel? I will tell thee the mystery of the woman, and of the beast that carrieth her, which hath the seven heads and ten* horns. 8 *The beast that thou sawest was, and is not; and shall ascend out of the bottomless pit, and go into perdition: and they that dwell on the earth shall wonder, whose names were not written in the book of life from the foundation of the world, when they behold the beast that was, and is not, and yet is. ... 12 And the ten horns which thou sawest are ten kings, which have received no kingdom as yet; but receive power as kings one hour with the beast. 13 These have one mind, and shall give their power and strength unto the beast. 14 These shall make war with the Lamb, and the Lamb shall overcome them: for he is Lord of lords, and King of kings: and they that are with him are called, and chosen, and faithful. 15 And he saith unto me, The waters which thou sawest, where the whore sitteth, are peoples, and multitudes, and nations, and tongues. 16 And the ten horns which thou sawest upon the beast, these shall hate the whore, and shall make her desolate and naked, and shall eat her flesh, and burn her with fire. 17 For God hath put in their hearts to fulfil his will, and to agree, and give their kingdom unto the beast, until the words of God shall be fulfilled. 18 And the woman which thou sawest is that great city, which reigneth over the kings of the earth.*

In the above paragraph and scripture, we see the destruction of Mystery Babylon, which is all false religions of all history. The first of false religions, after the flood, began under Nimrod in the city of Babylon.

Babylon the Great, evil commercialism of the world destroyed:

Much that is said of Mystery Babylon can be said of Babylon the Great with the understanding that Mystery Babylon is all false religion while Babylon the Great is all of the evil commerce in the world. The Antichrist does have a part in the destruction of false religion because he wants the worship of the world for himself. He probably has no part in the destruction of the world's commercialism or of the actual city of Babylon, that can be attributed to the Lord. The destruction of these will happen at or very near the same time as the Antichrist and his False Prophet are destroyed. The Lord says, "*Come out of her, my people, that ye be not partakers of her sins, and that ye receive not of her plagues.*" We should receive the Lord's words of caution both physically and spiritually. Get out of Babylon.

Rv 18:1-13 *And after these things I saw another angel come down from heaven, having great power; and the earth was lightened with his glory. 2 And he cried mightily with a strong voice, saying, Babylon the great is fallen, is fallen, and is become the habitation of devils, and the hold of every foul spirit, and a cage of every unclean and hateful bird. 3 For all nations have drunk of the wine of the wrath of her fornication, and the kings of the earth have committed fornication with her, and the merchants of the earth are waxed rich through the abundance of her delicacies. 4 And I heard another voice from heaven, saying, Come out of her, my people, that ye be not partakers of her sins, and that ye receive not of her plagues. 5 For her sins have reached unto heaven, and God hath remembered her iniquities. 6 Reward her even as she rewarded you, and double unto her double according to her works: in the cup which she hath filled fill to her double. 7 How much she hath glorified herself, and lived deliciously, so much torment and sorrow give her: for she saith in her heart, I sit a queen, and am no widow, and shall see no sorrow. 8 Therefore shall her plagues come in one day, death, and mourning, and famine; and she shall be utterly burned with fire: for strong is the Lord God who judgeth her. 9 And the kings of the earth, who have committed fornication and lived deliciously with her, shall bewail her, and lament for her, when they shall see the smoke of her burning, 10 Standing afar off for the fear of her torment, saying, Alas, alas, that great city Babylon, that mighty city! for in one hour is thy judgment come. 11 And the merchants of the earth shall weep and mourn over her; for no man buyeth their merchandise any more: 12 The merchandise of gold, and silver, and precious stones, and of pearls, and fine linen, and purple, and silk, and scarlet, and all thyine wood, and all manner vessels of ivory, and all manner vessels of most precious wood, and of brass, and iron, and marble, 13 And cinnamon, and odours, and ointments, and frankincense, and wine, and oil, and fine flour, and wheat, and beasts, and sheep, and horses, and chariots, and slaves, and souls of men.*

Antichrist's demise:

Daniel 8 says that in the latter time when sin has come to the full, a king of fierce countenance (the Antichrist) will come into power, and that power will be mighty, but it is not his own power (his power comes from the devil). He will use that power to destroy the mighty and holy people. He will actually stand up against the Prince of Princes (Jesus), but he will be defeated. Jesus will simply speak the words and the Antichrist will be defeated and cast into the lake of fire burning with brimstone.

Dan 8:23-25   *And in the latter time of their kingdom, when the transgressors are come to the full, a king of fierce countenance, and understanding dark sentences, shall stand up. 24 And his power shall be mighty, but not by his own power: and he shall destroy wonderfully, and shall prosper, and practice, and shall destroy the mighty and the holy people. 25 And through his policy also he shall cause craft to prosper in his hand; and he shall magnify himself in his heart, and by peace shall destroy many: he shall also stand up against the Prince of princes; but he shall be broken without hand.*

The 16th chapter of Revelation reveals a blasphemous, satanic trinity, made up of the Dragon (Satan), the Beast out of the sea (Antichrist), and the Beast out of the earth (the False Prophet). Demonic spirits come out of the mouths of these three and go forth to gather the kings of the earth to the battle of the great day of God Almighty to the place called Armageddon.

Rv 16:13-16   *And I saw three unclean spirits like frogs come out of the mouth of the dragon, and out of the mouth of the beast, and out of the mouth of the false prophet. 14 For they are the spirits of devils, working miracles, which go forth unto the kings of the earth and of the whole world, to gather them to the battle of that great day of God Almighty. 15 Behold, I come as a thief. Blessed is he that watcheth, and keepeth his garments, lest he walk naked, and they see his shame. 16 And he gathered them together into a place called in the Hebrew tongue Armageddon.*

Notice, in the middle of this passage of scripture concerning the armies gathering for Armageddon, in verse 15, Jesus is encouraging any who will to remain faithful; any who are yet unsaved at this point should call on the Lord for salvation.

The Lord Jesus himself will stop the Antichrist at Armageddon. Eventually the Antichrist, the False Prophet, and even Satan will be stopped! Their day is coming. At the end of the seven years of Tribulation, Jesus returns to earth to put an end to this tyrant and his hellish actions and establish Himself as King of Kings over the earth.

Revelation 19 shows us the return of Jesus and the destruction of Antichrist:

Rv 19:11-16,19-20   *And I saw heaven opened, and behold a white horse; and he that sat upon him was called Faithful and True, and in righteousness he doth judge and make war. 12 His eyes were as a flame of fire, and on his head were many crowns; and he had a name written, that no man knew, but he himself. 13 And he was clothed with a vesture dipped in blood: and his name is called The Word of God. 14 And the armies which were in heaven followed him upon white horses, clothed in fine linen, white and clean. 15 And out of his mouth goeth a sharp sword, that with it he should smite the nations: and he shall rule them with a rod of iron: and he treadeth the winepress of the fierceness and wrath of Almighty God. 16 And he hath on his vesture and on his thigh a name written, KING OF KINGS, AND LORD OF LORDS. ... 19 And I saw the beast, and the kings of the earth, and their armies, gathered together to make war against him that sat on the horse, and against his army. 20 And the beast was taken, and with him the false prophet that wrought miracles before him, with which he deceived them that had received the mark of the beast, and them that worshipped his image. These both were cast alive into a lake of fire burning with brimstone.*

The Antichrist will be broken (captured) in the mountains of Israel, Jerusalem, as is shown by:

Isa 14:25   *That I will break the Assyrian in my land, and upon my mountains tread him under foot: then shall his yoke depart from off them, and his burden depart from off their shoulders.*

Da 11:44-45   *But tidings out of the east and out of the north shall trouble him: therefore he shall go forth with great fury to destroy, and utterly to make away many. 45 And he shall plant the tabernacles of his palace between the seas in the glorious holy mountain; yet he shall come to his end, and none shall help him.*

Eze 21:25-27 *And thou, profane wicked prince of Israel, whose day is come, when iniquity shall have an end, 26 Thus saith the Lord GOD; Remove the diadem, and take off the crown: this shall not be the same: exalt him that is low, and abase him that is high. 27 I will overturn, overturn, overturn, it: and it shall be no more, until he come whose right it is; and I will give it him.*

This Ezekiel passage also shows that the Antichrist is indeed a Jew; he is called the "profane wicked prince of Israel," and he has an end. That end comes suddenly with the return of our Lord Jesus.

Satan's doom:

Along with what happens to the Antichrist, the devil himself is bound in chains and cast into the bottomless pit for the 1000 years of the Millennial reign of Christ.

Rv 20:1-3 *And I saw an angel come down from heaven, having the key of the bottomless pit and a great chain in his hand. 2 And he laid hold on the dragon, that old serpent, which is the Devil, and Satan, and bound him a thousand years, 3 And cast him into the bottomless pit, and shut him up, and set a seal upon him, that he should deceive the nations no more, till the thousand years should be fulfilled: and after that he must be loosed a little season.* [Satan will be

181

imprisoned for the 1000 years then released for a short while to deceive the nations once again.]

Rv 20:7-10 *And when the thousand years are expired, Satan shall be loosed out of his prison, 8 And shall go out to deceive the nations which are in the four quarters of the earth, Gog and Magog, to gather them together to battle: the number of whom is as the sand of the sea. 9 And they went up on the breadth of the earth, and compassed the camp of the saints about, and the beloved city: and fire came down from God out of heaven, and devoured them. 10 And the devil that deceived them was cast into the lake of fire and brimstone, where the beast and the false prophet are, and shall be tormented day and night for ever and ever.*

Satan has been the driving force, driving the Antichrist in all that the Antichrist has done, so it is fitting that they both come to a horrible ending. Daniel 7 paints an encouraging picture of the Tribulation and the Antichrist both coming to an end. Daniel had a dream which he did not understand, so, he asked for help to know the meaning, which was given.

Da 7:19,23-27 *Then I would know the truth of the fourth beast, ... 23 Thus he said, The fourth beast shall be the fourth kingdom upon earth, which shall be diverse from all kingdoms, and shall devour the whole earth, and shall tread it down, and break it in pieces. 24 And the ten horns out of this kingdom are ten kings that shall arise: and another shall rise after them; and he shall be diverse from the first, and he shall subdue three*

182

kings. 25 And he shall speak great words against the most High, and shall wear out the saints of the most High, and think to change times and laws: and they shall be given into his hand until a time and times and the dividing of time. 26 But the judgment shall sit, and they shall take away his dominion, to consume and to destroy it unto the end. 27 And the kingdom and dominion, and the greatness of the kingdom under the whole heaven, shall be given to the people of the saints of the most High, whose kingdom is an everlasting kingdom, and all dominions shall serve and obey him.

So, we see the Tribulation, the most horrible time in all of history, led by the two most evil of all beings, Satan and the Antichrist, come to an end. The Millennium, led by Jesus, with the saints of God, working with Jesus, as kings and priests forever, is now in place.

Since the Lord has provided a way to escape the wrath to come, including the evil of the Antichrist and his False Prophet, we must watch and pray always that we may escape.

Lk 21:36 *Watch ye therefore, and pray always, that ye may be accounted worthy to escape all these things that shall come to pass, and to stand before the Son of man.*

Every person present in the world during these awful times will suffer greatly at the hands of the Antichrist and others especially during the last half of the Tribulation. We will look now at the Tribulation.

Notes:

1. Barnabas, The Epistle of Barnabas, 4:3-4. Link: http://www.earlychristianwritings.com/text/barnabas-lightfoot.html

2. Joseph A. Seiss, The Apocalypse (Grand Rapids, MI: Kregel Publications, 1987), p. 393.

3. Arthur Pink, The Antichrist, Chapter One. Link: http://www.biblebelievers.com/Pink/antichrist03.htm

4. Irenaeus of Lyons, V XXX 2. Link: http://www.earlychristianwritings.com/text/irenaeus-book5.html

5. Hippolytus of Rome, Treatise on Christ and Antichrist, 14. Link: http://www.earlychristianwritings.com/text/hippolytus-christ.html

6. Hippolytus of Rome, Treatise on Christ and Antichrist, 52. Link: http://www.earlychristianwritings.com/text/hippolytus-christ.html

7. Arthur Pink, The Antichrist, Chapter Six. Link: http://www.biblebelievers.com/Pink/antichrist03.htm

8. Joseph R. Chambers, A Palace for the Antichrist (Green Forest, AR: New Leaf Press, 1996), p. 138-139.

9. Hippolytus of Rome, Treatise on Christ and Antichrist, 43. Link: http://www.earlychristianwritings.com/text/hippolytus-christ.html

7

Tribulation/Great Tribulation

A time of judgment:

Many people consider the Tribulation a time when the Antichrist comes and takes over the world and demands to be worshipped as god, in the process causing unimaginable chaos and death. This is true but only part of the truth. The full truth is that the Tribulation is a time when God chooses to judge the nations including Israel. The words "the wrath of God" are found ten times in the King James Version of the Bible, five of these references are speaking directly about the Tribulation. This fact tells us much of what the Tribulation is all about. Much that happens in the Tribulation is brought about by the direct action of God. In the process He allows Satan to use the Antichrist and his False Prophet to bring on added death and destruction to this judgment of the world. God's judgments come in three sevens: seven seals, seven trumpets, and seven vials including horrendous earthquakes and many other calamities. And God's judgments are fulfilled in righteousness.

The above paragraph is a very brief introduction to the opening of the Tribulation period, including a few comments on the appearance of the Antichrist and his False Prophet. Much more study is needed to understand the full scope of the Tribulation; begin by reading the entire book of the Revelation and Daniel and other scripture such as Zechariah and Joel.

The Tribulation ends with the appearance of the Lord in what is called the Second Coming of Jesus. Jesus will destroy all the armies of the earth that are gathered around the nation of Israel to destroy Israel and actually then attempt to war with and overthrow God Himself. At that time blood will flow to the depth of the horse's bridles in what is called the battle of Armageddon.

1 Th 5:2-10 *For yourselves know perfectly that the day of the Lord so cometh as a thief in the night. 3 For when they shall say, Peace and safety; then sudden destruction cometh upon them, as travail upon a woman with child; and they shall not escape. 4 But ye, brethren, are not in darkness, that that day should overtake you as a thief. 5 Ye are all the children of light, and the children of the day: we are not of the night, nor of darkness. 6 Therefore let us not sleep, as do others; but let us watch and be sober. 7 For they that sleep sleep in the night; and they that be drunken are drunken in the night. 8 But let us, who are of the day, be sober, putting on the breastplate of faith and love; and for an helmet, the hope of salvation. 9 For God hath not appointed us to wrath, but to obtain salvation by our Lord Jesus Christ, 10 Who died for*

us, that, whether we wake or sleep, we should live together with him.

In looking at the Tribulation and how awful it will be, we should take careful note in 1 Th 5:9 that the Lord tells us that "God hath not appointed us to wrath." In fact, we see that He tells us that if we live in obedience to Him, "I also will keep thee from the hour of temptation," the Tribulation.

Rv 3:10-11   *Because thou hast kept the word of my patience, I also will keep thee from the hour of temptation, which shall come upon all the world, to try them that dwell upon the earth.   11 Behold, I come quickly: hold that fast which thou hast, that no man take thy crown.*

Jesus actually goes even further to tell us that He is knocking at our heart's door wanting to sup with us and that if we overcome, He will have us to sit with Him in His throne. Sitting with Jesus in His throne during the Tribulation, would be far better than remaining here through the terrors of the Tribulation. All He requires of us is to choose Him as our Savior, then live an overcoming and obedient life. Let us take heed.

Rv 3:20-21   *Behold, I stand at the door, and knock: if any man hear my voice, and open the door, I will come in to him, and will sup with him, and he with me.   21 To him that overcometh will I grant to sit with me in my throne, even as I also overcame, and am set down with my Father in his throne.*

The Day of the Lord:

The Tribulation is a period of seven years and is referred to by several different names including "the day of the Lord". The day of the Lord appears 26 times in the Old and New Testaments. The Tribulation is perhaps often associated with the Antichrist and the mark of the beast; these two do indeed play a significant part. The outstanding part of the day of the Lord is God Himself bringing judgment on the nations including Israel. In talking about "the day of the Lord," words like destruction, cruel, vengeance, alarm, terrible, darkness, bitter, and dreadful all tell us what the character of God's wrath and the Tribulation will be like. The following scriptural quotes concerning the day of the Lord will help everyone to have a good understanding of what the Tribulation is all about. In these scripture locations, we see God's anger at: sin and sinning, those individuals and nations that have been abusive toward Israel, and all that are sinful heathen even whole heathen nations.

Isa 2:12   *For the day of the LORD of hosts shall be upon every one that is proud and lofty, and upon every one that is lifted up; and he shall be brought low: ….*

Isa 13:6,9   *Howl ye; for the day of the LORD is at hand; it shall come as a destruction from the Almighty. … 9 Behold, the day of the LORD cometh, cruel both with wrath and fierce anger, to lay the land desolate: and he shall destroy the sinners thereof out of it.*

Isa 34:8   *For it is the day of the LORD 's vengeance, and the year of recompences for the controversy of Zion.*

Jer 46:10   *For this is the day of the Lord GOD of hosts, a day of vengeance, that he may avenge him of his adversaries: and the sword shall devour, and it shall be satiate and made drunk with their blood: for the Lord GOD of hosts hath a sacrifice in the north country by the river Euphrates.*

Lam 2:22   *Thou hast called as in a solemn day my terrors round about, so that in the day of the LORD 's anger none escaped nor remained: those that I have swaddled and brought up hath mine enemy consumed.*

Eze 13:5   *Ye have not gone up into the gaps, neither made up the hedge for the house of Israel to stand in the battle in the day of the LORD.*

Eze 30:3   *For the day is near, even the day of the LORD is near, a cloudy day; it shall be the time of the heathen.*

The day of the Lord is mentioned three different times in the book of Joel. The entire book seems to be given to addressing different things that will be happening during the Tribulation, especially the restoration of Israel.

Joel 1:15   *Alas for the day! for the day of the LORD is at hand, and as a destruction from the Almighty shall it come.*

Joel 2:1,11   *Blow ye the trumpet in Zion, and sound an alarm in my holy mountain: let all the inhabitants of the land tremble: for the day of the LORD cometh, for it is nigh at hand; ... 11 And* the LORD shall utter his voice before his army: for his camp is very great: for he is strong that executeth his word: for the day of the LORD is great and very terrible; and who can abide it?

Joel 3:11-14   Assemble yourselves, and come, all ye heathen, and gather yourselves together round about: thither cause thy mighty ones to come down, O LORD. 12 Let the heathen be wakened, and come up to the valley of Jehoshaphat: for there will I sit to judge all the heathen round about. 13 Put ye in the sickle, for the harvest is ripe: come, get you down; for the press is full, the fats overflow; for their wickedness is great. 14 Multitudes, multitudes in the valley of decision: for the day of the LORD is near in the valley of decision.

Am 5:18,20   Woe unto you that desire the day of the LORD! to what end is it for you? the day of the LORD is darkness, and not light. ... 20 Shall not the day of the LORD be darkness, and not light? even very dark, and no brightness in it?

Ob 1:15   For the day of the LORD is near upon all the heathen: as thou hast done, it shall be done unto thee: thy reward shall return upon thine own head.

Zep 1:7-8,14,18   Hold thy peace at the presence of the Lord GOD: for the day of the LORD is at hand: for the LORD hath prepared a sacrifice, he hath bid his guests. 8 And it shall come to pass in the day of the LORD 's sacrifice, that I will punish the princes, and the king's children, and all such as are clothed with strange apparel. ... 14 The great day of the LORD is near, it is near, and

hasteth greatly, even the voice of the day of the LORD: the mighty man shall cry there bitterly. …
18 Neither their silver nor their gold shall be able to deliver them in the day of the LORD 's wrath; but the whole land shall be devoured by the fire of his jealousy: for he shall make even a speedy riddance of all them that dwell in the land.

Zep 2:2-3 *Before the decree bring forth, before the day pass as the chaff, before the fierce anger of the LORD come upon you, before the day of the LORD 's anger come upon you. 3 Seek ye the LORD, all ye meek of the earth, which have wrought his judgment; seek righteousness, seek meekness: it may be ye shall be hid in the day of the LORD's anger.*

Zephaniah helps us to understand that the Lord's anger is manifest in judgment during the Tribulation, and also, that we may be hid during that time. The word hid is referring to escaping in the Rapture. It may be that the Lord will indeed hide some who find themselves in the Tribulation, although, many Christians will die as martyrs during this time.

Zec 14:1 *Behold, the day of the LORD cometh, and thy spoil shall be divided in the midst of thee.*

Notice Malachi's use of the word "dreadful". The whole time of seven years of God's righteous wrath poured out is indeed going to be dreadful for all who remain sinners, both individuals and nations.

Mal 4:5   *Behold, I will send you Elijah the prophet before the coming of the great and dreadful day of the LORD: ...*

1 Th 5:2   *For yourselves know perfectly that the day of the Lord so cometh as a thief in the night.*

The apostle Peter makes it sound as if the day of the Lord includes the time of Tribulation and extends beyond the seven-year Tribulation. The burning of the earth with a fervent heat occurs more than a thousand years after the Tribulation.

2 Pe 3:10   *But the day of the Lord will come as a thief in the night; in the which the heavens shall pass away with a great noise, and the elements shall melt with fervent heat, the earth also and the works that are therein shall be burned up.*

The Tribulation begins soon after the Rapture:

From the viewpoint of the Revelation, the Rapture takes place in Rv 4:1.

Rv 4:1   *After this I looked, and, behold, a door was opened in heaven: and the first voice which I heard was as it were of a trumpet talking with me; which said, Come up hither, and I will shew thee things which must be hereafter.*

In his vision, after he ascends to heaven, John depicts scenes that he sees both in heaven and on earth through the rest of the Revelation. Many of the events occurring on earth are the direct result of God's wrath bringing the destruction of the ungodly. Other events are God allowing

Satan through the Antichrist to bring about the destruction of sinners, as well as the martyrdom of saints. None of the scenes that occur on earth can occur until allowed by God in heaven.

Scenes in heaven:

John was raptured within his vision, as a type of the Rapture; when the vision was over, John was back on the island of Patmos. The first scene John sees after his rapture and arrival in heaven is a throne scene in heaven: 24 elders and the 4 living ones.

Rv 4:1-2,4,6   *After this I looked, and, behold, a door was opened in heaven: ... 2 And immediately I was in the spirit: and, behold, a throne was set in heaven, ... 4 And round about the throne were four and twenty seats: and upon the seats I saw four and twenty elders sitting, clothed in white raiment; and they had on their heads crowns of gold. ... 6 And before the throne there was a sea of glass like unto crystal: and in the midst of the throne, and round about the throne, were four beasts full of eyes before and behind.*

These 24 elders and 4 beasts (living ones) are all redeemed human beings and are representative groups of the redeemed. These beasts are not beasts as animals. Several versions of the Bible use the words "living ones" rather than beasts.

The Shulamite:

In answer to the question, "What will ye see in the Shulamite?" and the answer, "As it were the company of two armies", Dan Muse[1] says, in his book, "The Song of Songs": "That is, two perfect ranks, or files. This statement coincides with that of scripture which indicates that two companies, or ranks, will be caught up in the Rapture. In the fourth chapter of Revelation these two perfect armies are called "the Living ones" and "the Elders," who testify to having been redeemed by the blood of the Lamb, out of every kindred, and tongue, and people, and nation. They kept rank. They constitute two armies, or ranks, of the redeemed."

SS 6:13   *Return, return, O Shulamite; return, return, that we may look upon thee. What will ye see in the Shulamite? As it were the company of two armies.*

The seven sealed book:

John then sees the seven sealed book in the hand of God (the title deed to the redeemed inheritance) and only the slain Lamb, our kinsman redeemer, Jesus, who could open it.

Rv 5:1-7   *And I saw in the right hand of him that sat on the throne a book written within and on the backside, sealed with seven seals. 2 And I saw a strong angel proclaiming with a loud voice, Who is worthy to open the book, and to loose the seals thereof? 3 And no man in heaven, nor in earth, neither under the earth, was able to open the book, neither to look thereon. 4 And I wept much, because no man was found worthy to open and to read the book, neither to look thereon. 5 And one of the elders saith unto me, Weep not: behold, the Lion of the tribe of Juda, the Root of David, hath prevailed to open the book, and to loose the seven seals thereof. 6 And I beheld, and, lo, in the midst of the throne and of the four beasts, and in the midst of the elders, stood a Lamb as it had been slain, having seven horns and seven eyes, which are the seven Spirits of God sent forth into all the earth. 7 And he came and took the book out of the right hand of him that sat upon the throne.*

Opening of the seals:

The white horse rider is the "Antichrist" pretending to be the true Christ; compare with Rv 19:11-16, where Jesus Christ rides forth in His Second Coming, saints riding with Him.

• **First Seal:** Rv 6:2 *And I saw, and behold a white horse: and he that sat on him had a bow; and a crown was given unto him: and he went forth conquering, and to conquer.*

The red horse rider takes Peace from the earth; that they should kill one another; red is the symbol of blood; the sword is the symbol of war. Refer to Mt 24:6-7. It is possible that the war of Gog/Magog, mentioned in Ezekiel 38 and 39, could occur under this seal at or near this time.

• **Second Seal:** Rv 6:4 *And there went out another horse that was red: and power was given to him that sat thereon to take peace from the earth, and that they should kill one another: and there was given unto him a great sword.*

The black horse rider signifies "famine." Famine follows war. This famine will be so severe that a person working can earn enough in one day of labor to buy enough food to feed one person. So, a man with a wife and three children, will be able to feed one of the five. What will the other four in the family do? Well, so, the wife works too. Good! Now, two can eat. What about the other three? As we will see later, neither of them can work unless they take the mark of the beast.

• **Third Seal:** Rv 6:5-6 *And when he had opened the third seal, I heard the third beast say, Come and see. And I beheld, and lo a black horse; and he that sat on him had a pair of balances in his hand. 6 And I heard a voice in the midst of the four beasts say, A measure of wheat for a penny, and three measures of barley for a penny; and see thou hurt not the oil and the wine.*

The pale (livid) horse rider is "Death" and "Hell" followed with him; the fourth part of men killed with sword, hunger, death, (probably some great pestilence;) and beasts of the earth. In July 2019 earth's population was about 7,583,315,000, in the year since then, the earth's population has increased by almost 200,000,000. Earth's present population, as of July 2020, is 7,780,000,000. One fourth of that number is 1,925,000,000 slain, or 753,424 per day for 7 years, or 31,392 per hour. All of this dying comes under the fourth seal. All of this action under the fourth seal may not take seven years; it could happen in a few weeks or months. According to the World Health Organization, about 56 million people die worldwide per year in past years, so death then will far exceed the present death rate. Earth's population is growing daily, so with the passage of time these figures will increase.

• **Fourth Seal:** Rv 6:7-8   *And when he had opened the fourth seal, I heard the voice of the fourth beast say, Come and see. 8 And I looked, and behold a pale horse: and his name that sat on him was Death, and Hell followed with him. And power was given unto them over the fourth part of the earth, to kill with sword, and with hunger, and with death, and with the beasts of the earth.*

The souls under the altar:

Souls under the altar, "slain for the word of God and for their testimony." This is a picture of persecution and martyrdom, through fire and blood. The persecution is against the Jews but will also include Gentile Christians from many other nations. These are those who have died as martyrs on earth and their souls are now in heaven; they will be raptured later.

• **Fifth Seal:** Rv 6:9   *And when he had opened the fifth seal, I saw under the altar the souls of them that were slain for the word of God, and for the testimony which they held: ….*

Men of the earth are awed and terrified by these actions of God's judgments, but seemingly no repentance among most, even though seemingly all on earth recognize what is going on as the righteous judgmental actions of an angry God.

• **Sixth Seal:** Rv 6:12-17   *And I beheld when he had opened the sixth seal, and, lo, there was a*

*great earthquake; and the sun became black as
sackcloth of hair, and the moon became as blood;
13 And the stars of heaven fell unto the earth,
even as a fig tree casteth her untimely figs, when
she is shaken of a mighty wind. 14 And the heaven
departed as a scroll when it is rolled together; and
every mountain and island were moved out of their
places. 15 And the kings of the earth, and the great
men, and the rich men, and the chief captains, and
the mighty men, and every bondman, and every
free man, hid themselves in the dens and in the
rocks of the mountains; 16 And said to the
mountains and rocks, Fall on us, and hide us from
the face of him that sitteth on the throne, and from
the wrath of the Lamb: 17 For the great day of his
wrath is come; and who shall be able to stand?*

**144,000 from twelve tribes sealed, first
of Israel to be saved:**

These 144,000 are the first fruits among the
Jews that will evangelize the rest of the Jews
throughout the world. From the days of the
Apostles there have been some Jews in each
generation who have received Jesus as the
Messiah, but for the most part they have not done
so in large numbers. This group of Jews, 144,000,
are the first in large numbers during the
Tribulation; they will minister to the other Jews.
Before the Tribulation is over many of the Jews in
the world will accept Jesus as the Messiah, once
again becoming the people of God. In the process,
the Gentile people of the world will hear the story

of redemption, and will perhaps have another opportunity of making a choice for God.

Rv 7:2-4   *And I saw another angel ascending from the east, having the seal of the living God: and he cried with a loud voice to the four angels, to whom it was given to hurt the earth and the sea, 3 Saying, Hurt not the earth, neither the sea, nor the trees, till we have sealed the servants of our God in their foreheads. 4 And I heard the number of them which were sealed: and there were sealed an hundred and forty and four thousand of all the tribes of the children of Israel.*

Rapture of a great multitude:

There is also a great multitude, in chapter 7, which no man could number out of all nations, kindreds, peoples, and tongues, who appear before God's throne. This enormous multitude is made up of people who have never known the Lord, as well as a lot of people who were Christians but missed the rapture for various reasons of unreadiness. Many of them are careless and indifferent Christians, others are people who were not born-again Christians when the rapture occurred, but have since accepted the Lord as their Savior and are taken when this rapture event occurs, probably during the first half of the Tribulation.

Rv 7:9,13-15   *After this I beheld, and, lo, a great multitude, which no man could number, of all nations, and kindreds, and people, and tongues, stood before the throne, and before the Lamb, clothed with white robes, and palms in their hands; ... 13 And one of the elders answered, saying unto* me, *What are these which are arrayed in white robes? and whence came they? 14 And I said unto him, Sir, thou knowest. And he said to me, These are they which came out of great tribulation, and have washed their robes, and made them white in the blood of the Lamb. 15 Therefore are they before the throne of God, and serve him day and night in his temple: and he that sitteth on the throne shall dwell among them.*

• **Seventh Seal:** Rv 8:1-2 *And when he had opened the seventh seal, there was silence in heaven about the space of half an hour. 2 And I saw the seven angels which stood before God; and to them were given seven trumpets.*

Seven angels are given seven trumpets to sound under the opening of this seventh seal. Under the opening of the first six seals there has already been unimaginable death and destruction. Now under the opening of this seventh seal, the door is opened for the sounding of the seven trumpets, and what occurs under these trumpets is so awesome that all of heaven stands in silence and wonder for half an hour at what is about to happen on earth.

Sounding of the trumpets:

Seven trumpet judgments come under the seventh seal, of which the first four apparently come in quick succession. Under the first trumpet a violent hailstorm occurs with added fire and blood, which destroys one third of all trees on earth and all of the grass.

- **First Trumpet:** Rv 8:7 *The first angel sounded, and there followed hail and fire mingled with blood, and they were cast upon the earth: and the third part of trees was burnt up, and all green grass was burnt up.*

    With the second trumpet apparently a very large mountain, maybe a meteor, strikes the sea which has effects in one thirds: 1/3 of the sea became blood, 1/3 of the sea creatures died, 1/3 of all ships destroyed.

- **Second Trumpet:** Rv 8:8-9 *And the second angel sounded, and as it were a great mountain burning with fire was cast into the sea: and the third part of the sea became blood; 9 And the third part of the creatures which were in the sea, and had life, died; and the third part of the ships were destroyed.*

    When the third trumpet sounds a great star, named Wormwood, maybe another meteor, falls from the sky, even though the word bitter is used, it seems to poison fresh water supplies, killing many people.

- **Third Trumpet:** Rv 8:10-11 *And the third angel sounded, and there fell a great star from heaven, burning as it were a lamp, and it fell upon the third part of the rivers, and upon the fountains of waters; 11 And the name of the star is called Wormwood: and the third part of the waters became wormwood; and many men died of the waters, because they were made bitter.*

    As the fourth trumpet sounds 1/3 of the sun, moon, and stars are smitten affecting both the day and night with darkness.

• **Fourth Trumpet:** Rv 8:12 *And the fourth angle sounded, and the third part of the sun was smitten, and the third part of the moon, and the third part of the stars; so as the third part of them was darkened, and the day shone not for a third part of it, and the night likewise.*

Notice, an angel intervenes, flying through the midst of heaven (in the airspace above the earth), sounding a warning to the inhabitants of the earth of the terrible events coming soon to pass, again a warning and accompanying opportunity to call on God in repentance. The angel flying through the heavens announcing the three woes is very probably at the midpoint of the Tribulation. In Rv 12, we are told that Satan is cast down to the earth with great anger, chapter 13 tells us that the Antichrist demands worship as God; he is fully empowered by Satan as a monster from hell. Much that occurs after chapter 8 involves millions of demons directly from hell.

Rv 8:13 *And I beheld, and heard an angel flying through the midst of heaven, saying with a loud voice, Woe, woe, woe, to the inhabiters of the earth by reason of the other voices of the trumpet of the three angels, which are yet to sound!*

Jesus said: Mt 24:21-22 *For then shall be great tribulation, such as was not since the beginning of the world to this time, no, nor ever shall be. 22 And except those days should be shortened, there should no flesh be saved: but for the elect's sake those days shall be shortened.*

If any person finds themselves present in the world at this time, he/she should accept Jesus

202

Christ as his/her Savior and prepare for martyrdom. The Tribulation from this point on will be horrifying beyond imagination.

First Woe:

With the sounding of the fifth trumpet, the first woe takes place. From out of the bottomless pit there comes forth smoke, and from out of the smoke there comes forth locusts. As of July 2020, there is a plague of desert locusts across East Africa, affecting seven countries, inflicting great harm and problems to the people of those countries. This sounds bad, and it is, but the plague under the fifth trumpet will be far worse, for it will be worldwide and the locusts will be demonic straight out of hell. They will inflict horrendous pain on people who have rejected God and have not the seal of God in their foreheads. Those stricken by these demonic creatures will wish to die because of all the pain, but they cannot die. The description given of these creatures sounds hideous and nothing like a common locust. The king of the bottomless pit mentioned here is some very great demonic angel, maybe Satan himself, or some other great demonic being, and you know what to expect from him.

• **Fifth Trumpet:** Rv 9:1-12 *Then the fifth angel sounded: And I saw a star fallen from heaven to the earth. To him was given the key to the bottomless pit. 2 And he opened the bottomless pit, and smoke arose out of the pit like the smoke of a great furnace. So the sun and the air were darkened because of the smoke of the pit. 3 Then* out of the smoke locusts came upon the earth. And to them was given power, as the scorpions of the earth have power. 4 They were commanded not to harm the grass of the earth, or any green thing, or any tree, but only those men who do not have the seal of God on their foreheads. 5 And they were not given authority to kill them, but to torment them for five months. Their torment was like the torment of a scorpion when it strikes a man. 6 In those days men will seek death and will not find it; they will desire to die, and death will flee from them. 7 The shape of the locusts was like horses prepared for battle. On their heads were crowns of something like gold, and their faces were like the faces of men. 8 They had hair like women's hair, and their teeth were like lions' teeth. 9 And they had breastplates like breastplates of iron, and the sound of their wings was like the sound of chariots with many horses running into battle. 10 They had tails like scorpions, and there were stings in their tails. Their power was to hurt men five months. 11 And they had as king over them the angel of the bottomless pit, whose name in Hebrew is Abaddon, but in Greek he has the name Apollyon. 12 One woe is past. Behold, still two more woes are coming after these things.

All that occurs under the coming second and third woes is demonic, straight out of hell, and more horrible and terrifying than can be imagined, the stuff of true nightmares.

Second Woe:

The description of these demonic creatures is frightening. 200,000,000 demonic horse creatures which will slay a third part of men in an hour, a day, a month, and a year. Under the fourth seal, we noted that one fourth of the world's population would die, leaving a world population of 5,775,000,000. One third of the remaining number is 1,923,075,000 or 4,918,350 per day. All of these die in an hour, a day, a month, and a year. After the action of the horse creatures under the sixth trumpet, the world population will be down to 3,851,000,000. All of this slaughter as a result of the fourth seal and the sixth trumpet only, has taken away one half of the world's population. There will be millions of others dying from all of the other things going on, such as war and those being martyred by the Antichrist.

• **Sixth Trumpet:** Rv 9:13-21 *Then the sixth angel sounded: And I heard a voice from the four horns of the golden altar which is before God, 14 saying to the sixth angel who had the trumpet, "Release the four angels who are bound at the great river Euphrates." 15 So the four angels, who had been prepared for the hour and day and month and year, were released to kill a third of mankind. 16 Now the number of the army of the horsemen was two hundred million; I heard the number of them. 17 And thus I saw the horses in the vision: those who sat on them had breastplates of fiery red, hyacinth blue, and sulfur yellow; and the heads of the horses were like the heads of lions; and out of their mouths came fire, smoke, and* *brimstone. 18 By these three plagues a third of mankind was killed — by the fire and the smoke and the brimstone which came out of their mouths. 19 For their power is in their mouth and in their tails; for their tails are like serpents, having heads; and with them they do harm. 20 But the rest of mankind, who were not killed by these plagues, did not repent of the works of their hands, that they should not worship demons, and idols of gold, silver, brass, stone, and wood, which can neither see nor hear nor walk. 21 And they did not repent of their murders or their sorceries or their sexual immorality or their thefts.*

Parenthesis between sixth and seventh trumpets:

When John ate (read) the book there were things there that sounded good (sweet), but then as he absorbed the whole reading, there were horrifying (bitter) events coming for the Jews and other nations during the last three-and-one-half years of the Tribulation. In his book, "The Book of Revelation", Clarence Larkin[2] talks about "the little book"; he says that "the little book" is bitter because it is addressing terrible events that will happen to the Jews during the Great Tribulation.

The little book: Rv 10:1-2,8-10   *And I saw another mighty angel come down from heaven, clothed with a cloud: and a rainbow was upon his head, and his face was as it were the sun, and his feet as pillars of fire: 2 And he had in his hand a little book open: and he set his right foot upon the sea, and his left foot on the earth, ... 8*

And the voice which I heard from heaven spake unto me again, and said, Go and take the little book which is open in the hand of the angel which standeth upon the sea and upon the earth. 9 And I went unto the angel, and said unto him, Give me the little book. And he said unto me, Take it, and eat it up; and it shall make thy belly bitter, but it shall be in thy mouth sweet as honey. 10 And I took the little book out of the angel's hand, and ate it up; and it was in my mouth sweet as honey: and as soon as I had eaten it, my belly was bitter.

Measure the Temple but not the court:

In the first two verses of Revelation 11, John is told to measure the temple but not the court for it is given to the Gentiles and they are going to trample it and the holy city for forty-two months. Among other things, this means that the Jews are going to suffer terribly as well as much destruction in the city of Jerusalem during the last 42 months of the Tribulation.

Rv 11:1-2   *And there was given me a reed like unto a rod: and the angel stood, saying, Rise, and measure the temple of God, and the altar, and them that worship therein. 2 But the court which is without the temple leave out, and measure it not; for it is given unto the Gentiles: and the holy city shall they tread under foot forty and two months.*

Two witnesses appear, probably Enoch and Elijah:

The Two Witnesses play a major role in the Tribulation. Go to the Antichrist chapter to see observations about the Two Witnesses. The Two Witnesses play a major role in all that is going on.

Rv 11:3-4 *And I will give power unto my two witnesses, and they shall prophesy a thousand two hundred and threescore days, clothed in sackcloth. 4 These are the two olive trees, and the two candlesticks standing before the God of the earth.*

Third Woe:

Rv 11:14 *The second woe is past; and, behold, the third woe cometh quickly.*

The third woe seems to include everything through Revelation chapter 19, especially the seven vials in Rv 16:1-17, and the Lord's return to fight Armageddon, ending the Tribulation.

At the sounding of the 7th trumpet, it seems that a significant turning point has been reached. In the verses above, notice the proclamation of the angels, the Lord is taking possession of the kingdoms of this world, and His wrath is come, and the time of judgment and reward is come. Also, remarkably the Ark of his testament is seen in the temple in heaven. This solves a great question in that the Ark disappeared around the time that the Jews were carried into exile by the Babylonians, near 600 BC. Some think that Jeremiah may have hidden the Ark in the mountains. At this point it shows up in heaven.

• **Seventh Trumpet:** Rv 11:15-19 *And the seventh angel sounded; and there were great voices in heaven, saying, The kingdoms of this world are become the kingdoms of our Lord, and of* his Christ; and he shall reign for ever and ever. 16 And the four and twenty elders, which sat before God on their seats, fell upon their faces, and worshipped God, 17 Saying, We give thee thanks, O Lord God Almighty, which art, and wast, and art to come; because thou hast taken to thee thy great power, and hast reigned. 18 And the nations were angry, and thy wrath is come, and the time of the dead, that they should be judged, and that thou shouldest give reward unto thy servants the prophets, and to the saints, and them that fear thy name, small and great; and shouldest destroy them which destroy the earth. 19 And the temple of God was opened in heaven, and there was seen in his temple the ark of his testament: and there were lightnings, and voices, and thunderings, and an earthquake, and great hail.

Satan is thrown down to the earth:

Revelation 12 takes a look back at Satan's efforts to stop the birth and ministry of the Lord Jesus. When Satan sees that Jesus is out of reach, having ascended to heaven, he turns his attention to destroy the woman, Israel. She then flees to the wilderness, where she is fed for three-and-one-half years. Christian Jews are persecuted, and God hides them in the wilderness during this time; they are hidden virtually under the Antichrist's nose, and he can't find them. Notice that Satan is described as having seven heads and ten horns, and seven crowns upon his heads; this description is applied to the Antichrist at least eight other times later. This makes it clear that this whole plan originates with Satan; he has been working on these plans for centuries in the past and hopes to bring them to fruition in the Tribulation. Take notice of the warning given in verse 12 to the inhabitants of the earth because the devil has been cast down from heaven to earth, he is very angry and is gone forth to make war with those who have the testimony of Jesus Christ. Satan is going to do a lot of terrible things through the Antichrist during the remaining three-and-one-half years of the Great Tribulation.

Rv 12:1-3,4-9,12,17   *And there appeared a great wonder in heaven; a woman ... 2 And she being with child cried, travailing in birth, and pained to be delivered. 3 And there appeared another wonder in heaven; and behold a great red dragon, having seven heads and ten horns, and seven crowns upon his heads. ... 4 ... the dragon stood before the woman which was ready to be delivered, for to devour her child as soon as it was born. 5 And she brought forth a man child, who was to rule all nations with a rod of iron: and her child was caught up unto God, and to his throne. 6 And the woman fled into the wilderness, where she hath a place prepared of God, that they should feed her there a thousand two hundred and threescore days. 7 And there was war in heaven: Michael and his angels fought against the dragon; and the dragon fought and his angels, 8 And prevailed not; neither was their place found any more in heaven. 9 And the great dragon was cast out, that old serpent, called the Devil, and Satan, which deceiveth the whole world: he was cast out into the earth, and his angels were cast out with him. ... 12*

Therefore rejoice, ye heavens, and ye that dwell in them. Woe to the inhabiters of the earth and of the sea! for the devil is come down unto you, having great wrath, because he knoweth that he hath but a short time. ... 17 And the dragon was wroth with the woman, and went to make war with the remnant of her seed, which keep the commandments of God, and have the testimony of Jesus Christ.

Antichrist at the midpoint of the Tribulation:

During the Tribulation as shown in the Revelation, the Antichrist made his first appearance in Rv 6:2 under the opening of the first seal. He rode in on a white horse conquering and to conquer under the guise of being the promised Messiah. Under his presentation in the thirteenth chapter, blasphemy is associated with his name and character four different times; it is clear that he is everything evil, and not the Messiah at all. This first beast arises out of the sea; the sea represents Gentile nations. He comes fully empowered by the devil, with the evil of past empires (the leopard, bear, and lion; these represent Greece, Medo-Persia, and Babylon) still a part of his character, plans, and intentions for his work in the Tribulation. The world is in awe of him and worship both Satan and the Antichrist as god; the Antichrist's response is to blaspheme God, God's name, God's tabernacle, and all who dwell in heaven. He then goes on to war against the saints on earth and overcome them. The Lord concludes His comments about the Antichrist by warning us, "If any man have an ear, Let him hear." So, let us all pay close attention.

Rv 13:1-9   *And I stood upon the sand of the sea, and saw a beast rise up out of the sea, having seven heads and ten horns, and upon his horns ten crowns, and upon his heads the name of blasphemy. 2 And the beast which I saw was like unto a leopard, and his feet were as the feet of a bear, and his mouth as the mouth of a lion: and the dragon gave him his power, and his seat, and great authority. 3 And I saw one of his heads as it were wounded to death; and his deadly wound was healed: and all the world wondered after the beast. 4 And they worshipped the dragon which gave power unto the beast: and they worshipped the beast, saying, Who is like unto the beast? who is able to make war with him? 5 And there was given unto him a mouth speaking great things and blasphemies; and power was given unto him to continue forty and two months. 6 And he opened his mouth in blasphemy against God, to blaspheme his name, and his tabernacle, and them that dwell in heaven. 7 And it was given unto him to make war with the saints, and to overcome them: and power was given him over all kindreds, and tongues, and nations. 8 And all that dwell upon the earth shall worship him, whose names are not written in the book of life of the Lamb slain from the foundation of the world. 9 If any man have an ear, let him hear.*

Daniel prophesied of the coming Antichrist nearly 700 years before John wrote about the same subject, the appearance of Antichrist during the awful time of the Tribulation. Daniel's prophesy adds to our knowledge of the things the Antichrist does during the Tribulation. In Daniel 7, it tells us that Antichrist has a relationship with the Ancient Roman Empire through the ten kingdoms that will arise out of that Roman Empire. In chapter 8 he tells us that the Antichrist himself will arise directly out of the Grecian Empire. In both of these presentations the Antichrist appears in the Tribulation, fully empowered by Satan ready to do all of the vile and evil work that Satan has concocted, including the destruction of "the mighty and the holy people."

Da 7:7-8   *After this I saw in the night visions, and behold a fourth beast, dreadful and terrible, and strong exceedingly; and it had great iron teeth: it devoured and brake in pieces, and stamped the residue with the feet of it: and it was diverse from all the beasts that were before it; and it had ten horns. 8 I considered the horns, and, behold, there came up among them another little horn, before whom there were three of the first horns plucked up by the roots: and, behold, in this horn were eyes like the eyes of man, and a mouth speaking great things.*

Da 8:21-24   *And the rough goat is the king of Grecia: and the great horn that is between his eyes is the first king. 22 Now that being broken, whereas four stood up for it, four kingdoms shall stand up out of the nation, but not in his power. 23 And in the latter time of their kingdom, when the transgressors are come to the full, a king of fierce countenance, and understanding dark sentences, shall stand up. 24 And his power shall be mighty, but not by his own power: and he shall destroy wonderfully, and shall prosper, and practise, and shall destroy the mighty and the holy people.*

The Abomination of Desolation:

In the Antichrist's first appearance, he will be revealed as a very charismatic character, very likeable. He will come up as an eleventh person among the leaders of a ten-nation federation. His first act will be to overcome three of the ten nations and lead the ten through his time in the Tribulation. His next move will be to make a seven-year peace treaty with Israel. Seeing these two things occur in an individual shortly after the Rapture has occurred will be strong clues that this is the Antichrist. At the midpoint of the Tribulation he will break the treaty and commit the abomination of desolation spoken of by Daniel.

Da 11:31   *And arms shall stand on his part, and they shall pollute the sanctuary of strength, and shall take away the daily sacrifice, and they shall place the abomination that maketh desolate.*

Jesus made reference to the abomination of desolation and cautioned anyone who is in Judea and sees this event take place to immediately flee to the mountains without taking the time to go get extra clothing, for there is a terrible time of suffering about to take place.

Mt 24:15-18,21   *When ye therefore shall see the abomination of desolation , spoken of by Daniel the prophet, stand in the holy place, (whoso*

214

readeth, let him understand:) 16 Then let them which be in Judaea flee into the mountains: 17 Let him which is on the housetop not come down to take any thing out of his house: 18 Neither let him which is in the field return back to take his clothes. ... 21 For then shall be great tribulation, such as was not since the beginning of the world to this time, no, nor ever shall be.

The False Prophet comes on the scene:

This second beast arises out of the earth, perhaps from the underworld, as is true with the Antichrist, as Joseph Seiss[3] suggests in his book, The Apocalypse. Much less information is given us about the second beast.   He is later called the False Prophet and he comes with two horns as a lamb. Notice in the same sentence scripture says he speaks as a dragon. He like the first beast is a farce, a pretender. He is not the Lamb of God he pretends to be, but he is of the dragon, Satan. From Satan, he receives the same power as the first beast. He is able to do great wonders deceiving those on the earth. He instigates the creation of an image of the Antichrist, then gives life to the image and demands of all worship of the beast as well as the image of the beast or be killed. This False Prophet demands that everyone receive the mark of the beast in their right hand or forehead, if they hope to buy or sell. That mark is 666, perhaps in the form of a tattoo or a computer chip, or some other type of mark. Even though this False Prophet demands ungodly worship of the Antichrist, God sends an angel, Rv 14:9-12, to tell the whole world that any person who does so will "be tormented in fire and brimstone." Please understand, "NO ONE SHOULD EVER TAKE THE MARK OF THE BEAST."

Rv 13:11-18   *And I beheld another beast coming up out of the earth; and he had two horns like a lamb, and he spake as a dragon. 12 And he exerciseth all the power of the first beast before him, and causeth the earth and them which dwell therein to worship the first beast, whose deadly wound was healed. 13 And he doeth great wonders, so that he maketh fire come down from heaven on the earth in the sight of men, 14 And deceiveth them that dwell on the earth by the means of those miracles which he had power to do in the sight of the beast; ... 16 And he causeth all, both small and great, rich and poor, free and bond, to receive a mark in their right hand, or in their foreheads: 17 And that no man might buy or sell, save he that had the mark, or the name of the beast, or the number of his name. 18 Here is wisdom. Let him that hath understanding count the number of the beast: for it is the number of a man; and his number is Six hundred threescore and six.*

144,000 Jewish evangelists taken to heaven:

As the events in the Tribulation occur one after another, and we at this point have passed into the horrors of the last half of the Tribulation, we are shown another scene in heaven. The 144,000 Jewish evangelists have been raptured and now stand before the throne of God.

Rv 14:1,5   *And I looked, and, lo, a Lamb stood on the mount Sion, and with him an hundred forty and four thousand, having his Father's name written in their foreheads. ... 5 And in their mouth was found no guile: for they are without fault before the throne of God.*

The Gospel is preached to all the world:

Following that scene in heaven, Rv 14:6, an angel flies through the midst of heaven, preaching the everlasting gospel, for the hour of his judgment is come. During the centuries since Jesus ascended to the Father, having told us to go into the world and preach the gospel; the gospel has been preached many times over to most if not all of the world. Now at this point the Rapture has occurred and the Tribulation is well on its way, even approaching the finish; first there were the 144,000 Jewish evangelists, then the two witnesses, and now this angel "flies through the midst of heaven, preaching the everlasting gospel." The world has heard the gospel, the world knows the gospel; the world will know again. The world is without excuse. The world will repent or experience the righteous judgment of God.

Babylon is fallen:

Babylon's evils date all the way back to the days of Nimrod, great-grandson to Noah. Nimrod was evil, and Babylon from those early days is evil. Babylon is mentioned dozens of times in the Old Testament with several references to its complete destruction. Babylon has been destroyed, but never to the extent prophesied of in scripture. There are six references to Babylon's destruction in the Revelation. This destruction is to happen during the Tribulation, and it will be complete and total. Time is running out. The reference in Rv 14:8 tells that the reason for this destruction is "because she made all nations drink of the wrath of her fornication." This makes it very obvious as to how sin and evil can influence others. The sin of Babylon from long ago reaches even, as an example, to the modern nations of the world today.

Rv 14:8   *And there followed another angel, saying, Babylon is fallen, is fallen, that great city, because she made all nations drink of the wine of the wrath of her fornication.*

Do not worship the Beast nor receive his mark:

Again, and again, the Lord is faithful to make it clear to all the world that worship of the Antichrist will lead to eternal tragedy. It appears that the whole world will hear the loud voice of this angel as he flies over the world to warn all not to worship the beast. This knowledge will warn the world and help to sustain any Christians present at the time of these events. So, again, never worship the beast, the Antichrist, nor receive the mark of the beast.

Rv 14:9-12   *And the third angel followed them, saying with a loud voice, If any man worship the beast and his image, and receive his mark in his forehead, or in his hand, 10 The same shall drink of the wine of the wrath of God, which is poured out without mixture into the cup of his indignation; and he shall be tormented with fire and brimstone in the presence of the holy angels, and in the presence of the Lamb: 11 And the smoke of their torment ascendeth up for ever and ever: and they have no rest day nor night, who worship the beast and his image, and whosoever receiveth the mark of his name. 12 Here is the patience of the saints: here are they that keep the commandments of God, and the faith of Jesus.*

A fore view of Armageddon:

The scripture gives a fore view of the Lord's Second Coming and Armageddon. In Rv 14:8, the destruction of Babylon is declared, and verses 14 and 16 mention the Second Coming and Armageddon. These things are beginning to come together; they all happen either simultaneously or in quick succession at the very end of the Tribulation, as is shown in Rv 19.

Rv 14:8,14-20   *And there followed another angel, saying, Babylon is fallen, is fallen, that great city, because she made all nations drink of the wine of the wrath of her fornication. ... . 14 And I looked, and behold a white cloud, and upon the cloud one sat like unto the Son of man, having on his head a golden crown, and in his hand a sharp sickle. 15 And another angel came out of the temple, crying with a loud voice to him that sat on the cloud, Thrust in thy sickle, and reap: for the time is come for thee to reap; for the harvest of the earth is ripe. 16 And he that sat on the cloud thrust in his sickle on the earth; and the earth was reaped. 17*

And another angel came out of the temple which is in heaven, he also having a sharp sickle. 18 And another angel came out from the altar, which had power over fire; and cried with a loud cry to him that had the sharp sickle, saying, Thrust in thy sharp sickle, and gather the clusters of the vine of the earth; for her grapes are fully ripe. 19 And the angel thrust in his sickle into the earth, and gathered the vine of the earth, and cast it into the great winepress of the wrath of God. 20 And the winepress was trodden without the city, and blood came out of the winepress, even unto the horse bridles, by the space of a thousand and six hundred furlongs. [about 185/200 miles]

The seven vials of God's wrath:

No man can enter the temple in heaven until the results of the seven vials is fulfilled. The righteous judgments of God are obviously very serious when events in heaven are placed on pause until God's judgments take place.

Rv 15:5-8 *And after that I looked, and, behold, the temple of the tabernacle of the testimony in heaven was opened: 6 And the seven angels came out of the temple, having the seven plagues, clothed in pure and white linen, and having their breasts girded with golden girdles. 7 And one of the four beasts gave unto the seven angels seven golden vials full of the wrath of God, who liveth for ever and ever. 8 And the temple was filled with smoke from the glory of God, and from his power; and no man was able to enter into the temple, till the seven plagues of the seven angels were fulfilled.*

As the pouring out of the vials begins with the first vial, a terrible plague strikes those who have received the mark of the beast or those who have worshipped his image. Under vial number two, the sea is smitten, this time the sea becomes like the blood of a dead man. As the third vial is poured out, fresh water sources become blood. The fourth vial is poured out on the sun and men are scorched with heat. With the fifth vial, darkness fills the kingdom of the Antichrist. The sixth vial is poured out on the river Euphrates to prepare the way of the kings of the east. Demons come from the mouth of the Devil, the Antichrist, and the False Prophet. These demons go to the kings all over the earth and gather them to Armageddon. As the seventh vial is poured out, God declares it is finished; the greatest earthquake that ever has been strikes, the cities of the nations fall, an unheard-of hailstorm strikes.

- **First Vial:** Rv 16:2 *And the first went, and poured out his vial upon the earth; and there fell a noisome and grievous sore upon the men which had the mark of the beast, and upon them which worshipped his image.*
- **Second Vial:** Rv 16:3 *And the second angel poured out his vial upon the sea; and it became as the blood of a dead man: and every living soul died in the sea.*
- **Third Vial:** Rv 16:4-7 *And the third angel poured out his vial upon the rivers and fountains of waters; and they became blood. 5 And I heard the*

angel of the waters say, Thou art righteous, O Lord, which art, and wast, and shalt be, because thou hast judged thus. 6 For they have shed the blood of saints and prophets, and thou hast given them blood to drink; for they are worthy. 7 And I heard another out of the altar say, Even so, Lord God Almighty, true and righteous are thy judgments.

- **Fourth Vial:**   Rv 16:8-9   And the fourth angel poured out his vial upon the sun; and power was given unto him to scorch men with fire. 9 And men were scorched with great heat, and blasphemed the name of God, which hath power over these plagues: and they repented not to give him glory.

- **Fifth Vial:**   Rv 16:10-11   And the fifth angel poured out his vial upon the seat of the beast; and his kingdom was full of darkness; and they gnawed their tongues for pain, 11 And blasphemed the God of heaven because of their pains and their sores, and repented not of their deeds.

- **Sixth Vial:**   Rv 16:12-16   And the sixth angel poured out his vial upon the great river Euphrates; and the water thereof was dried up, that the way of the kings of the east might be prepared. 13 And I saw three unclean spirits like frogs come out of the mouth of the dragon, and out of the mouth of the beast, and out of the mouth of the false prophet. 14 For they are the spirits of devils, working miracles, which go forth unto the kings of the earth and of the whole world, to gather them to the battle of that great day of God Almighty. 15 Behold, I come as a thief. Blessed is he that watcheth, and keepeth his garments, lest he walk *naked, and they see his shame. 16 And he gathered them together into a place called in the Hebrew tongue Armageddon.*

• **Seventh Vial:** Rv 16:17-21 *And the seventh angel poured out his vial into the air; and there came a great voice out of the temple of heaven, from the throne, saying, It is done. 18 And there were voices, and thunders, and lightnings; and there was a great earthquake, such as was not since men were upon the earth, so mighty an earthquake, and so great. 19 And the great city was divided into three parts, and the cities of the nations fell: and great Babylon came in remembrance before God, to give unto her the cup of the wine of the fierceness of his wrath. 20 And every island fled away, and the mountains were not found. 21 And there fell upon men a great hail out of heaven, every stone about the weight of a talent: and men blasphemed God because of the plague of the hail; for the plague thereof was exceeding great.*

This is another fore view of Armageddon. A talent is about 75 pounds. Imagine what 75-pound hailstones will do to everything involved, especially human beings.

Mystery Babylon:

Chapter 17 shows the destruction of Mystery Babylon, the false religions of all history in their relationship with all of the evils of Babylon, going all the way back to Babylon's origins. The woman depicted in this chapter is what God calls a whore, the city of Babylon, false religion. This vile person is destroyed by the very Antichrist and ten horns (kings) that had carried her through most of the Tribulation.

Rv 17:1,4-6,12,16,18 *And there came one of the seven angels which had the seven vials, and talked with me, saying unto me, Come hither; I will shew unto thee the judgment of the great whore that sitteth upon many waters: …. 4 And the woman was arrayed in purple and scarlet colour, and decked with gold and precious stones and pearls, having a golden cup in her hand full of abominations and filthiness of her fornication: 5 And upon her forehead was a name written, MYSTERY, BABYLON THE GREAT, THE MOTHER OF HARLOTS AND ABOMINATIONS OF THE EARTH. 6 And I saw the woman drunken with the blood of the saints, and with the blood of the martyrs of Jesus: …. 12 And the ten horns which thou sawest are ten kings, which have received no kingdom as yet; but receive power as kings one hour with the beast. … 16 And the ten horns which thou sawest upon the beast, these shall hate the whore, and shall make her desolate and naked, and shall eat her flesh, and burn her with fire. … 18 And the woman which thou sawest is that great city, which reigneth over the kings of the earth.*

Babylon the Great:

Chapter 18 reveals to us that through her history the evil spirit of Babylon has had a close association with the commerce of the whole world. It is stated three times that "in one hour" the judgments of God will bring evil Babylon and all that is associated with her to an end. There is no doubt that Babylon has been vile and evil throughout history; and there is no doubt that her destruction will be complete for eternity. This destruction will apply to an actual city called Babylon as well as the world of commerce and all of the other sins Babylon is guilty of. Notice that at Babylon's destruction, heaven rejoices while the kings of the earth *"bewail her, and lament for her, when they shall see the smoke of her burning."* The destruction of Babylon takes place at the same time as Armageddon. This is shown to us in the scripture location above, as well as Rv 16:7-21, where it is talking about events in Armageddon, and in the middle of those descriptions it says *"great Babylon came in remembrance before God."*

Rv 18:1-2,8-10,21,23-24   *And after these things I saw another angel come down from heaven, having great power; and the earth was lightened with his glory. 2 And he cried mightily with a strong voice, saying, Babylon the great is fallen, is fallen, and is become the habitation of devils, and the hold of every foul spirit, and a cage of every unclean and hateful bird. …. 8 Therefore shall her plagues come in one day, death, and mourning, and famine; and she shall be utterly burned with fire: for strong is the Lord God who judgeth her. 9 And the kings of the earth, who have committed fornication and lived deliciously with her, shall bewail her, and lament for her, when they shall see the smoke of her burning, 10 Standing afar off for the fear of her torment, saying, Alas, alas, that great city Babylon, that*

*mighty city! for in one hour is thy judgment come.
... 21 And a mighty angel took up a stone like a
great millstone, and cast it into the sea, saying,
Thus with violence shall that great city Babylon be
thrown down, and shall be found no more at all. ...
23 ... for by thy sorceries were all nations
deceived. 24 And in her was found the blood of
prophets, and of saints, and of all that were slain
upon the earth.*

Armageddon:

The name Armageddon is only found one
time in the Bible. Yet, it is a very important event
that brings forth the end of the Tribulation and the
destruction of the Antichrist, the False Prophet, and
the armies of the nations of the world who are
gathered to fight against the armies of God. Even
though the name is only mentioned once, there are
numerous Old and New Testament prophecies of
this great event.

The battle of Armageddon brings an end to
the Tribulation; it is brought about by the righteous
judgment of an angry God, who is angry at all of
the nations of the world who have all acted in
sinfulness and rebellion against a loving and
righteous God. All of the following scripture
locations concerning Armageddon paint a picture of
the horrible deaths of hundreds of millions, or more
likely billions, of the evil and desperately wicked
who have survived all of the events in the previous
years of the Tribulation. This great battle stretches
from Mount Megiddo in the north of Israel, down to
Jerusalem and on to the valley of Jehoshaphat,

then to Bozrah which is in present day Jordan; a distance of about 200 miles, north to south, where blood flows to the depth of the horse's bridle. That is a nearly unbelievable amount of blood, but that is what the word of God tells us, and that is what will be.

Rv 16:16 *And he gathered them together into a place called in the Hebrew tongue Armageddon.*

This presentation of Armageddon in Rv 16 is a fore view of Armageddon. The actual battle occurs down in Rv 19:20 following the Second Coming. Notice the several scripture locations below which help us to understand the many things that occur in this battle.

Zec 12:1-9 is a part of the Tribulation and the battle of Armageddon. The Lord's anger is stirred against all of the other nations of the world who have come against Israel and Judah in particular. The Lord promises to destroy all of these other nations even though it includes every other nation on earth. In the battle of Armageddon all of the other nations of the world will be gathered against Israel to destroy Israel, and to actually fight against God Himself.

Zec 12:2-3,6,8-9 *Behold, I will make Jerusalem a cup of trembling unto all the people round about, when they shall be in the siege both against Judah and against Jerusalem. 3 And in that day will I make Jerusalem a burdensome stone for all people: all that burden themselves with it shall be cut in pieces, though all the people of the earth be gathered together against it. ... 6 In that day will*

I make the governors of Judah like an hearth of fire among the wood, and like a torch of fire in a sheaf; and they shall devour all the people round about, on the right hand and on the left: and Jerusalem shall be inhabited again in her own place, even in Jerusalem. ... 8 In that day shall the LORD defend the inhabitants of Jerusalem; and he that is feeble among them at that day shall be as David; and the house of David shall be as God, as the angel of the LORD before them. 9 And it shall come to pass in that day, that I will seek to destroy all the nations that come against Jerusalem.

Zec 14:1-3   Behold, the day of the LORD cometh, and thy spoil shall be divided in the midst of thee. 2 For I will gather all nations against Jerusalem to battle; and the city shall be taken, and the houses rifled, and the women ravished; and half of the city shall go forth into captivity, and the residue of the people shall not be cut off from the city. 3 Then shall the LORD go forth, and fight against those nations, as when he fought in the day of battle.

Joel 3:1-2,12,14   For, behold, in those days, and in that time, when I shall bring again the captivity of Judah and Jerusalem, 2 I will also gather all nations, and will bring them down into the valley of Jehoshaphat, and will plead with them there for my people and for my heritage Israel, whom they have scattered among the nations, and parted my land. ... 12 Let the heathen be wakened, and come up to the valley of Jehoshaphat: for there will I sit to judge all the heathen round about. ... 14 Multitudes, multitudes in the valley of *decision: for the day of the LORD is near in the valley of decision.*

Isa 34:1-2,5,6,8   Come near, ye nations, to hear; and hearken, ye people: let the earth hear, and all that is therein; the world, and all things that come forth of it. 2 For the indignation of the LORD is upon all nations, and his fury upon all their armies: he hath utterly destroyed them, he hath delivered them to the slaughter. ... 5 For my sword shall be bathed in heaven: behold, it shall come down upon Idumea, ... 6 ... for the LORD hath a sacrifice in Bozrah, and a great slaughter in the land of Idumea. ... 8 For it is the day of the LORD's vengeance, and the year of recompences for the controversy of Zion.

Isaiah prophesied 700 years before Christ; he was among the early Old Testament prophets who spoke of God becoming angry with the nations and promising to take vengeance for the cause of Israel. Many nations in these end times are very much against Israel and the Jews all over the world. The 63rd chapter of Isaiah seems to be a continuation and a support of the 34th chapter, with a bloody trampling of the nations in the area of Bozrah in Edom, present day Jordan.

Isa 63:1-4   Who is this that cometh from Edom, (Jesus) with dyed garments from Bozrah? this that is glorious in his apparel, travelling in the greatness of his strength? I that speak in righteousness, mighty to save. 2 Wherefore art thou red in thine apparel, and thy garments like him that treadeth in the winefat? 3 I have trodden the winepress alone; and of the people there was none with me: for I will tread them in mine anger, and trample them in my fury; and their blood shall be sprinkled upon my garments, and I will stain all my raiment. 4 For the day of vengeance is in mine heart, and the year of my redeemed is come.

The four places named in the above scripture locations beginning with Armageddon will be one great battle involving all of these and perhaps many other locations. Jesus will not be running here and there trying in desperation to stay up with all of the challenges thrown at Him. He fights this battle with the sword of His mouth. When He descends from heaven, He will pass in the air over the whole area and speak the words of judgment, and the masses gathered there against Him will be slaughtered. All of the saints who went in the Rapture will be there with the Lord, but Jesus in His anger takes care of this job alone, just as He took care of our redemption on the cross, all alone.

Marriage Supper of the Lamb:
After much praise glorifying God, the voice of a great multitude announces, "the marriage of the Lamb has come". This is a tremendous and awesome event which occurs in heaven with those that are there at that time; Christ and His Bride and Guests. This event may be of short or long endurance, that is not made clear. The very next verses tell us that Jesus is mounted on a white horse in preparation to come to earth, in what is called the Second Coming, to judge and make war in righteousness with earth's godless and unrepentant inhabitants at Armageddon, including

the Antichrist, the False Prophet, and even Satan himself.

Rv 19:7-9   *Let us be glad and rejoice, and give honour to him: for the marriage of the Lamb is come, and his wife hath made herself ready. 8 And to her was granted that she should be arrayed in fine linen, clean and white: for the fine linen is the righteousness of saints. 9 And he saith unto me, Write, Blessed are they which are called unto the marriage supper of the Lamb. And he saith unto me, These are the true sayings of God.*

The Second Coming:

In scripture, this is when the Second Coming and the actual Battle of Armageddon takes place. A description of Jesus is given as he arrives to destroy the evil forces at Armageddon. Rv 19 gives us a final picture of the actual event of Armageddon when the Lord Jesus treads the winepress, destroying all of the remaining godless ones at the end of the Tribulation. The fowls (birds) are called to come to the great supper of God. The Antichrist and the kings of the earth with their armies are gathered to make war against Jesus Christ. The Antichrist and the False Prophet are taken and cast alive into the lake of fire (hell). All of their armies are slain with the *"sword of him that sat upon the horse, which sword proceeded out of his mouth: and all the fowls were filled with their flesh."*

Rv 19:11-16,19-21   *And I saw heaven opened, and behold a white horse; and he that sat upon him was called Faithful and True, and in righteousness he doth judge and make war. 12 His eyes were as a flame of fire, and on his head were many crowns; and he had a name written, that no man knew, but he himself. 13 And he was clothed with a vesture dipped in blood: and his name is called The Word of God. 14 And the armies which were in heaven followed him upon white horses, clothed in fine linen, white and clean. 15 And out of his mouth goeth a sharp sword, that with it he should smite the nations: and he shall rule them with a rod of iron: and he treadeth the winepress of the fierceness and wrath of Almighty God. 16 And he hath on his vesture and on his thigh a name written, KING OF KINGS, AND LORD OF LORDS. ... 19 And I saw the beast, and the kings of the earth, and their armies, gathered together to make war against him that sat on the horse, and against his army. 20 And the beast was taken, and with him the false prophet that wrought miracles before him, with which he deceived them that had received the mark of the beast, and them that worshipped his image. These both were cast alive into a lake of fire burning with brimstone. 21 And the remnant were slain with the sword of him that sat upon the horse, which sword proceeded out of his mouth: and all the fowls were filled with their flesh.*

The Devil is bound in the bottomless pit for a thousand years:

With that, the seven years of the Tribulation is finished. It seems very fitting that the final event in this awful time of trouble, called the Tribulation, is God taking this evil being, the Devil, who has troubled billions of human beings over the last 6000 years and chaining and confining him to the bottomless pit where he can trouble no one for the next 1000 years of the Millennial Kingdom. After Armageddon and the confining of Satan, Christ Jesus will then establish Himself as King of Kings and Lord of Lords over all the nations on earth in what is called the Millennial Reign or the 1000 years of peace. After the Millennial Kingdom, Satan will be loosed for a short time for one last effort to deceive the untried ones.

Rv 20:1-3   *And I saw an angel come down from heaven, having the key of the bottomless pit and a great chain in his hand. 2 And he laid hold on the dragon, that old serpent, which is the Devil, and Satan, and bound him a thousand years, 3 And cast him into the bottomless pit, and shut him up, and set a seal upon him, that he should deceive the nations no more, till the thousand years should be fulfilled: and after that he must be loosed a little season.*

As we think of all that is yet coming, let us give heed to Zephaniah's wise words of advice.

Zep 2:2-3   *Before the decree bring forth, before the day pass as the chaff, before the fierce anger of the LORD come upon you, before the day of the LORD 's anger come upon you. 3 Seek ye the LORD, all ye meek of the earth, which have wrought his judgment; seek righteousness, seek meekness: it may be ye shall be hid in the day of the LORD's anger.*

Rv 16:15 *Behold, I come as a thief. Blessed is he that watcheth, and keepeth his garments, lest he walk naked, and they see his shame.*

We should now go and take a look at what is going to happen with Israel during the Tribulation.

Notes:

1. Dan T. Muse, The Song of Songs (Franklin Springs, GA: Pentecostal Holiness Publishing House, 1947), p. 199.
2. Clarence Larkin, The Book of Revelation (Philadelphia, PA: Erwin W. Moyer, Printers) p. 82.
3. Joseph A. Seiss, The Apocalypse, (Grand Rapids, MI: Kregel Publications, 1987), p. 334.

8

Israel in the Tribulation

The time of Jacob's trouble:

Israel has suffered a lot in history past, even to being scattered over the face of the earth among the world's other nations, hated by many and enduring the holocaust under Hitler; and it is going to get much worse during the Tribulation. All of this because Israel, God's special and chosen nation has turned away from Him in unbelief. It is amazing that a prophecy that addresses the end times would also look back hundreds of years and tell what caused all of this to come about. Ezekiel 38 and 39 tell of the battle of Gog/Magog. The battle of Gog/Magog is well known by many and was prophesied by Ezekiel sometime around 600 BC. In Ezekiel's concluding remarks about Gog/Magog he tells exactly why Jacob (Israel) was to have so much trouble.

Eze 39:22-29 *So the house of Israel shall know that I am the LORD their God from that day and forward. 23 And the heathen shall know that the house of Israel went into captivity for their iniquity: because they trespassed against me, therefore hid I my face from them, and gave them into the hand of their enemies: so fell they all by* the sword. 24 According to their uncleanness and according to their transgressions have I done unto them, and hid my face from them. 25 Therefore thus saith the Lord GOD; Now will I bring again the captivity of Jacob, and have mercy upon the whole house of Israel, and will be jealous for my holy name; 26 After that they have borne their shame, and all their trespasses whereby they have trespassed against me, when they dwelt safely in their land, and none made them afraid. 27 When I have brought them again from the people, and gathered them out of their enemies' lands, and am sanctified in them in the sight of many nations; 28 Then shall they know that I am the LORD their God, which cause them to be led into captivity among the heathen: but I have gathered them unto their own land, and have left none of them any more there. 29 Neither will I hide my face any more from them: for I have poured out my spirit upon the house of Israel, saith the Lord GOD.*

The time of Jacob's trouble is yet in the future, in the time of the Tribulation. Israel has known lots of trouble, but the time that Jeremiah spoke of as "the time of Jacob's trouble is worse than all the others. It is a time of fear and trembling, so much so that men's faces will turn pale. The prophecy says there is no other day like it."

Jer 30:4-9   And these are the words that the LORD spake concerning Israel and concerning Judah. 5 For thus saith the LORD; We have heard a voice of trembling, of fear, and not of peace. 6 Ask ye now, and see whether a man doth travail with child? wherefore do I see every man with his hands on his loins, as a woman in travail, and all faces are turned into paleness? 7 Alas! for that day is great, so that none is like it: it is even the time of Jacob's trouble; but he shall be saved out of it. 8 For it shall come to pass in that day, saith the LORD of hosts, that I will break his yoke from off thy neck, and will burst thy bonds, and strangers shall no more serve themselves of him: 9 But they shall serve the LORD their God, and David their king, whom I will raise up unto them.

God warns Israel:

Israel was removed out of their own land and scattered over many nations in the world for many centuries because of her sins against God. Actually, God's repeated warnings to Israel go all the way back to Moses' time, sometime near 1475 BC.

Dt 4:25-31 *When thou shalt beget children, and children's children, and ye shall have remained long in the land, and shall corrupt yourselves, and make a graven image, or the likeness of any thing, and shall do evil in the sight of the LORD thy God, to provoke him to anger: 26 I call heaven and earth to witness against you this day, that ye shall soon utterly perish from off the land whereunto ye go over Jordan to possess it; ye shall not prolong your days upon it, but shall utterly be destroyed. 27 And the LORD shall scatter you among the nations, and ye shall be left few in number among the heathen, whither the LORD shall lead you. 28 And there ye shall serve gods, the work of men's hands, wood and stone, which neither see, nor hear, nor eat, nor smell. 29 But if from thence thou shalt seek the LORD thy God, thou shalt find him, if thou seek him with all thy heart and with all thy soul. 30 When thou art in tribulation, and all these things are come upon thee, even in the latter days, if thou turn to the LORD thy God, and shalt be obedient unto his voice; 31 (For the LORD thy God is a merciful God;) he will not forsake thee, neither destroy thee, nor forget the covenant of thy fathers which he sware unto them.* [Also, Deut 28:64]

Israel taken into captivity by Assyria 722 BC:

At the death of Solomon there arose a dispute, between Jeroboam and Rehoboam, which brought on a division between the two nations. Under Saul, David, and Solomon they were known as Israel. After the division, they were known as Judah, made up of two southern tribes, and Israel, made up of the ten northern tribes. Jeroboam immediately led Israel into sinning against God, building two golden calves to worship rather than worship God, and thus they continued for about two hundred and fifty years until the Assyrians came and carried them away into captivity. After many warnings from the Lord, it seems that for all those many years Israel just grew further and further from the Lord rather than listening to him. Then came the Assyrians to carry them away.

2 Ki 17:5-18 *Then the king of Assyria came up throughout all the land, and went up to Samaria, and besieged it three years. 6 In the ninth year of Hoshea the king of Assyria took*

Samaria, and carried Israel away into Assyria, and placed them in Halah and in Habor by the river of Gozan, and in the cities of the Medes. 7 For so it was, that the children of Israel had sinned against the LORD their God, which had brought them up out of the land of Egypt, from under the hand of Pharaoh king of Egypt, and had feared other gods, 8 And walked in the statutes of the heathen, whom the LORD cast out from before the children of Israel, and of the kings of Israel, which they had made. 9 And the children of Israel did secretly those things that were not right against the LORD their God, and they built them high places in all their cities, from the tower of the watchmen to the fenced city. 10 And they set them up images and groves in every high hill, and under every green tree: 11 And there they burnt incense in all the high places, as did the heathen whom the LORD carried away before them; and wrought wicked things to provoke the LORD to anger: 12 For they served idols, whereof the LORD had said unto them, Ye shall not do this thing. 13 Yet the LORD testified against Israel, and against Judah, by all the prophets, and by all the seers, saying, Turn ye from your evil ways, and keep my commandments and my statutes, according to all the law which I commanded your fathers, and which I sent to you by my servants the prophets. 14 Notwithstanding they would not hear, but hardened their necks, like to the neck of their fathers, that did not believe in the LORD their God. 15 And they rejected his statutes, and his covenant that he made with their fathers, and his testimonies which he testified against them; and they followed vanity, and became vain, and went after the heathen that were round about them, concerning whom the LORD had charged them, that they should not do like them. 16 And they left all the commandments of the LORD their God, and made them molten images, even two calves, and made a grove, and worshipped all the host of heaven, and served Baal. 17 And they caused their sons and their daughters to pass through the fire, and used divination and enchantments, and sold themselves to do evil in the sight of the LORD, to provoke him to anger. 18 Therefore the LORD was very angry with Israel, and removed them out of his sight: there was none left but the tribe of Judah only.

Judah taken into exile by Babylon
605 BC to 586 BC:

136 years later, Judah was taken into exile to Babylon, beginning 605 BC to 586 BC, for sinning against God, and refusing to listen to the prophets which God sent to them.

2 Ch 36:15-21 And the LORD God of their fathers sent to them by his messengers, rising up betimes, and sending; because he had compassion on his people, and on his dwelling place: 16 But they mocked the messengers of God, and despised his words, and misused his prophets, until the wrath of the LORD arose against his people, till there was no remedy. 17 Therefore he brought upon them the king of the Chaldees, who slew their young men with the sword in the house of their sanctuary, and had no compassion upon young

man or maiden, old man, or him that stooped for age: he gave them all into his hand. 18 And all the vessels of the house of God, great and small, and the treasures of the house of the LORD, and the treasures of the king, and of his princes; all these he brought to Babylon. 19 And they burnt the house of God, and brake down the wall of Jerusalem, and burnt all the palaces thereof with fire, and destroyed all the goodly vessels thereof. 20 And them that had escaped from the sword carried he away to Babylon; where they were servants to him and his sons until the reign of the kingdom of Persia: 21 To fulfil the word of the LORD by the mouth of Jeremiah, until the land had enjoyed her sabbaths: for as long as she lay desolate she kept sabbath, to fulfil threescore and ten years.

Return home to Judah from Babylon:

At the end of 70 years of exile in Babylon, Cyrus the Persian had come into power over the Jewish exiles. By an edict from Cyrus, the Jews were allowed to return to Jerusalem and their home country, Judah. Even though any and all could go, only about 50,000 chose to return to rebuild Jerusalem and the Temple and settle in the land. When Jesus came to earth, 500-plus years later, there were Jews in the land ruled over by the Romans. 40 years after Jesus ascended back to heaven, the Romans destroyed Jerusalem including the temple; most of the Jews had rejected Jesus as the Messiah.

Jerusalem and the Temple destroyed by the Romans AD 70 because of continuing sin against and rejection of God:

Mt 24:2   *And Jesus said unto them, See ye not all these things? verily I say unto you, There shall not be left here one stone upon another, that shall not be thrown down.*

Lk 21:24   *And they shall fall by the edge of the sword, and shall be led away captive into all nations: and Jerusalem shall be trodden down of the Gentiles, until the times of the Gentiles be fulfilled.*

This actually took place under Titus in the year AD 70. Josephus[1] tells of the tremendous loss of life when Titus came and destroyed Jerusalem, the siege at Masada took place finishing off the last standouts and ending the War of the Jews. There was never a Judea or an Israel again until 1948, when the nation of Israel was established again, in a day.

The people who were carried away from Israel by the Assyrians have since been scattered over the earth, but they will find their way back to Israel; many already have in the last generation or two. While they were scattered the land lay desolate and controlled by other Gentile nations with a promise of restoration.

Eze 36:34-35   *And the desolate land shall be tilled, whereas it lay desolate in the sight of all that passed by. 35 And they shall say, This land that was desolate is become like the garden of Eden; and the waste and desolate and ruined cities are become fenced, and are inhabited.*

Israel returns to the land, Hebrew language restored:

The Lord showed Ezekiel a valley full of dry bones and told Ezekiel to prophesy over the bones and they shall live. This is a prophecy telling that one day the deceased nation of Israel would come to life again.

Eze 37:11-14,21-22   *Then he said unto me, Son of man, these bones are the whole house of Israel: behold, they say, Our bones are dried, and our hope is lost: we are cut off for our parts. 12 Therefore prophesy and say unto them, Thus saith the Lord GOD; Behold, O my people, I will open your graves, and cause you to come up out of your graves, and bring you into the land of Israel. 13 And ye shall know that I am the LORD, when I have opened your graves, O my people, and brought you up out of your graves, 14 And shall put my spirit in you, and ye shall live, and I shall place you in your own land: then shall ye know that I the LORD have spoken it, and performed it, saith the LORD. ... 21 And say unto them, Thus saith the Lord GOD; Behold, I will take the children of Israel from among the heathen, whither they be gone, and will gather them on every side, and bring them into their own land: 22 And I will make them one nation in the land upon the mountains of Israel; and one king shall be king to them all: and they shall be no more two nations, neither shall they be divided into two kingdoms any more at all: ....*

Israel restored 1948:

After centuries of absence as a nation, on May 14, 1948, Israel arose and declared her independence as a nation, as Egypt, Iraq, Jordan, Syria, and others in the Arab League, stood in opposition against Israel. Isaiah spoke of this event many centuries before it happened. A lot of things came together over decades, but when the time came, it all happened in a day.

Isa 66:8-10 *Who hath heard such a thing? who hath seen such things? Shall the earth be made to bring forth in one day? or shall a nation be born at once? for as soon as Zion travailed, she brought forth her children. 9 Shall I bring to the birth, and not cause to bring forth? saith the LORD: shall I cause to bring forth, and shut the womb? saith thy God. 10 Rejoice ye with Jerusalem, and be glad with her, all ye that love her: rejoice for joy with her, all ye that mourn for her: ….*

Israel's spiritual blindness will one day be removed:

Paul tells us a very amazing thing, that because the Jews rejected Jesus as the Messiah, "blindness in part has happened to Israel." A relative few will accept Jesus as the Messiah, but for the most part they will continue to reject Jesus until that blindness is lifted at some time in the Tribulation.

Ro 11:25-27 *For I would not, brethren, that ye should be ignorant of this mystery, lest ye should be wise in your own conceits; that blindness in part is happened to Israel, until the fulness of*

244

the Gentiles be come in. 26 And so all Israel shall be saved: as it is written, There shall come out of Sion the Deliverer, and shall turn away ungodliness from Jacob: 27 For this is my covenant unto them, when I shall take away their sins.

Six-day War, Jerusalem restored:

In the 72-plus years since, there have been many ups and downs, but Israel still stands today (as of May 2020). In June of 1967, again Israel was threatened by the nations of Egypt, Jordan, and Syria, yet in six days Israel was victorious and had gained control over the city of Jerusalem in the process, which had been under the control of Jordan. It wasn't until December of 2017 that Jerusalem was recognized as the capital of Israel by the USA. And at this point, May of 2020, Israel is surrounded by plenty of enemies today, yet standing strong.

We are in the season of the end times:

At this point we await the Rapture, then, the beginning of the Tribulation, a terrible time for Israel and the rest of the world. We must keep Jesus' words in mind, warning us of wars, pestilences, like Corona virus, famines, earthquakes, and other calamities happening before His coming. Jesus told us no one knows the day or hour when He will come for us, but He told us you can know the season is near. We are in the season now.

Mk 13:28-32   *Now learn a parable of the fig tree; When her branch is yet tender, and putteth forth leaves, ye know that summer is near: 29 So ye in like manner, when ye shall see these things come to pass, know that it is nigh, even at the doors. 30 Verily I say unto you, that this generation shall not pass, till all these things be done. 31 Heaven and earth shall pass away: but my words shall not pass away. 32 But of that day and that hour knoweth no man, no, not the angels which are in heaven, neither the Son, but the Father.*

Events that will happen involving Israel during the Tribulation:

The next thing to happen will be the Rapture, then the Antichrist will come on the scene amid a ten-nation federation, who will overpower three of the ten, then sign a seven-year covenant with the Jews. At the midpoint of the seven years, the Antichrist will break his covenant and commit the Abomination of Desolation in the newly built temple. The Jewish people will realize that the Antichrist is not the Messiah and will turn from him; hell on earth will begin for them for the remaining three-and-one-half years of "the time of Jacob's trouble."

Da 9:27   *And he shall confirm the covenant with many for one week: and in the midst of the week he shall cause the sacrifice and the oblation to cease, and for the overspreading of abominations he shall make it desolate, even until the consummation, and that determined shall be poured upon the desolate.*

No one who will be on earth during that time, is ready for what will be happening during those awful years. There are a relatively few Jews who have accepted Jesus as the Messiah and will go in the Rapture when He comes, but for the most part, the Jewish people the world over will go through the Tribulation, and they for sure are not ready for what will happen to them at that time.

The 144,000 appear and minister to the world:

As rebellious as the Jewish people have been, early during the Tribulation, there will be 144,000 Jewish evangelists that appear, 12,000 from each of the twelve tribes. How this comes about is not explained, they just show up. Results from their ministry are spectacular and is the beginning of the Jews as a whole turning to Christ.

Rv 7:2-8 *And I saw another angel ascending from the east, having the seal of the living God: and he cried with a loud voice to the four angels, to whom it was given to hurt the earth and the sea, 3 Saying, Hurt not the earth, neither the sea, nor the trees, till we have sealed the servants of our God in their foreheads. 4 And I heard the number of them which were sealed: and there were sealed an hundred and forty and four thousand of all the tribes of the children of Israel. 5 Of the tribe of Juda were sealed twelve thousand. Of the tribe of Reuben were sealed twelve thousand. Of the tribe of Gad were sealed twelve thousand. 6 Of the tribe of Aser were sealed twelve thousand. Of the tribe of Nepthali were sealed*

*twelve thousand. Of the tribe of Manasses were
sealed twelve thousand. 7 Of the tribe of Simeon
were sealed twelve thousand. Of the tribe of Levi
were sealed twelve thousand. Of the tribe of
Issachar were sealed twelve thousand. 8 Of the
tribe of Zabulon were sealed twelve thousand. Of
the tribe of Joseph were sealed twelve thousand. Of
the tribe of Benjamin were sealed twelve thousand.*

A great multitude raptured from out of great Tribulation:

The verses immediately following tell of
countless numbers that are saved from all nations.
We are not told that these are saved as a result of
the ministry of the 144,000, but we are probably
safe in assuming that the 144,000 play a part in
winning this multitude to Christ.

Rv 7:9-17   *After this I beheld, and, lo, a
great multitude, which no man could number, of all
nations, and kindreds, and people, and tongues,
stood before the throne, and before the Lamb,
clothed with white robes, and palms in their hands;
10 And cried with a loud voice, saying, Salvation to
our God which sitteth upon the throne, and unto
the Lamb. 11 And all the angels stood round about
the throne, and about the elders and the four
beasts, and fell before the throne on their faces,
and worshipped God, 12 Saying, Amen: Blessing,
and glory, and wisdom, and thanksgiving, and
honour, and power, and might, be unto our God for
ever and ever. Amen. 13 And one of the elders
answered, saying unto me, What are these which
are arrayed in white robes? and whence came*

they? 14 And I said unto him, Sir, thou knowest. And he said to me, These are they which came out of great tribulation, and have washed their robes, and made them white in the blood of the Lamb. 15 Therefore are they before the throne of God, and serve him day and night in his temple: and he that sitteth on the throne shall dwell among them. 16 They shall hunger no more, neither thirst any more; neither shall the sun light on them, nor any heat. 17 For the Lamb which is in the midst of the throne shall feed them, and shall lead them unto living fountains of waters: and God shall wipe away all tears from their eyes.

The Gog/Magog war takes place at some point during or previous to the Tribulation:

Already, there are a number of nations that are gathered in Syria regarding the Syrian Civil War. This puts them in place for the Gog/Magog invasion into Israel, that will very likely take place before or early on in the Tribulation. Magog (Russia) and many other nations with her will invade the nation of Israel in the hopes of gaining great riches. See "Gog/Magog War" in the chapter entitled "War in the Tribulation."

Eze 38:1-12 *And the word of the LORD came unto me, saying, 2 Son of man, set thy face against Gog, the land of Magog, the chief prince of Meshech and Tubal, and prophesy against him, 3 And say, Thus saith the Lord GOD; Behold I am against thee, O Gog, the chief prince of Meshech and Tubal: ... 5 Persia, Ethiopia, and Libya with them; all of them with shield and helmet: 6 Gomer,* and all his bands; the house of Togarmah of the north quarters, and all his bands: and many people with thee. ... 8 After many days thou shalt be visited: in the latter years thou shalt come into the land that is brought back from the sword, and is gathered out of many people, against the mountains of Israel, which have been always waste: but it is brought forth out of the nations, and they shall dwell safely all of them. 9 Thou shalt ascend and come like a storm, thou shalt be like a cloud to cover the land, thou, and all thy bands, and many people with thee. 10 Thus saith the Lord GOD; It shall also come to pass, that at the same time shall things come into thy mind, and thou shalt think an evil thought: 11 And thou shalt say, I will go up to the land of unwalled villages; I will go to them that are at rest, that dwell safely, all of them dwelling without walls, and having neither bars nor gates, 12 To take a spoil, and to take a prey; to turn thine hand upon the desolate places that are now inhabited, and upon the people that are gathered out of the nations, which have gotten cattle and goods, that dwell in the midst of the land. ...

Eze 38:18-23   And it shall come to pass at the same time when Gog shall come against the land of Israel, saith the Lord GOD, that my fury shall come up in my face. 19 For in my jealousy and in the fire of my wrath have I spoken, Surely in that day there shall be a great shaking in the land of Israel; 20 So that the fishes of the sea, and the fowls of the heaven, and the beasts of the field, and all creeping things that creep upon the earth,

and all the men that are upon the face of the earth, shall shake at my presence, and the mountains shall be thrown down, and the steep places shall fall, and every wall shall fall to the ground. 21 And I will call for a sword against him throughout all my mountains, saith the Lord GOD: every man's sword shall be against his brother. 22 And I will plead against him with pestilence and with blood; and I will rain upon him, and upon his bands, and upon the many people that are with him, an overflowing rain, and great hailstones, fire, and brimstone. 23 Thus will I magnify myself, and sanctify myself; and I will be known in the eyes of many nations, and they shall know that I am the LORD. ...

Eze 39:2,9,11-12,22-23   And I will turn thee back, and leave but the sixth part of thee, and will cause thee to come up from the north parts, and will bring thee upon the mountains of Israel: ... 9 And they that dwell in the cities of Israel shall go forth, and shall set on fire and burn the weapons, both the shields and the bucklers, the bows and the arrows, and the handstaves, and the spears, and they shall burn them with fire seven years: ... 11 And it shall come to pass in that day, that I will give unto Gog a place there of graves in Israel, the valley of the passengers on the east of the sea: and it shall stop the noses of the passengers: and there shall they bury Gog and all his multitude: and they shall call it The valley of Hamon-gog. 12 And seven months shall the house of Israel be burying of them, that they may cleanse the land. ... 22 So the house of Israel shall know that I am the LORD their God from that day and forward. 23 And the heathen shall know that the house of Israel went into captivity for their iniquity: because they trespassed against me, therefore hid I my face from them, and gave them into the hand of their enemies: so fell they all by the sword.

Israel's future riches:

There are a number of scripture locations, including the ones above in Eze 38 and 39, that support the idea that when Israel comes back into the land as an independent nation, she will become very wealthy. After 70 years as a nation again, Israel ranks as the 32nd wealthiest nation (which is not the top, but she is at least doing fairly well). There are those, including Joel Rosenberg, who believe that verses like the one listed below are suggesting the possibility that Israel may one day strike oil, and become extremely wealthy.

Jacob prophesied over Joseph:

Ge 49:25   *Even by the God of thy father, who shall help thee; and by the Almighty, who shall bless thee with blessings of heaven above, blessings of the deep that lieth under, blessings of the breasts, and of the womb: ...*

Moses prophesied over the 12 tribes:

Dt 32:13   *He made him ride on the high places of the earth, that he might eat the increase of the fields; and he made him to suck honey out of the rock, and oil out of the flinty rock; ...*

Dt 33:13,19,24   *And of Joseph he said, Blessed of the LORD be his land, for the precious*

things of heaven, for the dew, and for the deep
that coucheth beneath, …. 19 They shall call the
people unto the mountain; there they shall offer
sacrifices of righteousness: for they shall suck of
the abundance of the seas, and of treasures hid in
the sand. …. 24 And of Asher he said, Let Asher be
blessed with children; let him be acceptable to his
brethren, and let him dip his foot in oil.

Isa 45:3   And I will give thee the treasures
of darkness, and hidden riches of secret places,
that thou mayest know that I, the LORD, which call
thee by thy name, am the God of Israel.

Damascus destroyed:

The oldest inhabited city in the world,
Damascus, is to be destroyed. If this destruction is
the work of Israel or an ally of Israel, such action
may be an encouragement to the nations involved
in the Gog/Magog War to go and take revenge on
Israel.

Isa 17:1,14   The burden of Damascus.
Behold, Damascus is taken away from being a city,
and it shall be a ruinous heap. … 14 And behold at
eveningtide trouble; and before the morning he is
not. This is the portion of them that spoil us, and
the lot of them that rob us.

The Little Book:

John sees a person with a little book standing
with one foot on the earth and the other on the
sea. Seven thunders uttered their voice. John was
told to take the little book and eat it. He was told it
would be sweet in his mouth and bitter in his belly.

When he ate it, it was sweet to his taste and became bitter in his belly.

Rv 10:1-4,8-10   *And I saw another mighty angel come down from heaven, clothed with a cloud: and a rainbow was upon his head, and his face was as it were the sun, and his feet as pillars of fire: 2 And he had in his hand a little book open: and he set his right foot upon the sea, and his left foot on the earth, 3 And cried with a loud voice, as when a lion roareth: and when he had cried, seven thunders uttered their voices. 4 And when the seven thunders had uttered their voices, I was about to write: and I heard a voice from heaven saying unto me, Seal up those things which the seven thunders uttered, and write them not. ... 8 And the voice which I heard from heaven spake unto me again, and said, Go and take the little book which is open in the hand of the angel which standeth upon the sea and upon the earth. 9 And I went unto the angel, and said unto him, Give me the little book. And he said unto me, Take it, and eat it up; and it shall make thy belly bitter, but it shall be in thy mouth sweet as honey. 10 And I took the little book out of the angel's hand, and ate it up; and it was in my mouth sweet as honey: and as soon as I had eaten it, my belly was bitter.*

Joseph Seiss[2], in his book, "The Apocalypse," says the little book is the same as the seven sealed book, back in Rv 5. John is told he "must prophesy again before many peoples, and nations, and tongues, and kings." Seiss says in this "little book" are many wonderful things spoken of that are sweet to think on and to look forward to, but in the process of them coming to pass, and in ministering to the world of them, there are many hardships and much bitterness. In this situation, there is an involvement with the little book and what the seven thunders uttered. For Israel there will be bitterness involved in the little book and in what the thunders said. John, for some reason, was told to not write what the seven thunders said.

The two witnesses:

Moses and Elijah, or maybe it is Enoch and Elijah, that will appear as the two witnesses. Among other things, the two witnesses, like the 144,000, come to preach the gospel and warn the world about the Antichrist. The two are not defenseless and cannot be harmed until they have finished their ministry. When they have finished their ministry, they will be slain by the Antichrist, lie in the streets of Jerusalem unburied, and after three days resurrect and ascend back into heaven.

Rv 11:3-12 *And I will give power unto my two witnesses, and they shall prophesy a thousand two hundred and threescore days, clothed in sackcloth. 4 These are the two olive trees, and the two candlesticks standing before the God of the earth. 5 And if any man will hurt them, fire proceedeth out of their mouth, and devoureth their enemies: and if any man will hurt them, he must in this manner be killed. 6 These have power to shut heaven, that it rain not in the days of their prophecy: and have power over waters to turn them to blood, and to smite the earth with all plagues, as often as they will. 7 And when they shall have finished their testimony, the beast that ascendeth out of the bottomless pit shall make war against them, and shall overcome them, and kill them. 8 And their dead bodies shall lie in the street of the great city, which spiritually is called Sodom and Egypt, where also our Lord was crucified. 9 And they of the people and kindreds and tongues and nations shall see their dead bodies three days and an half, and shall not suffer their dead bodies to be put in graves. 10 And they that dwell upon the earth shall rejoice over them, and make merry, and shall send gifts one to another; because these two prophets tormented them that dwelt on the earth. 11 And after three days and an half the Spirit of life from God entered into them, and they stood upon their feet; and great fear fell upon them which saw them. 12 And they heard a great voice from heaven saying unto them, Come up hither. And they ascended up to heaven in a cloud; and their enemies beheld them.*

Satan makes war with Christians and Jews:

Satan has always waged war with all people, and especially God's people. In Rv 12, Satan is thrown out of heaven and is cast down to the earth and is very angry and determined to persecute God's people, especially the Jews and Christians. At the midpoint of the Tribulation when the Antichrist commits the Abomination of Desolation and begins to really persecute the people, God tells His people to flee to the mountains where he has prepared a place to protect them for the remainder of the Tribulation.

Rv 12:13-17 *And when the dragon saw that he was cast unto the earth, he persecuted the woman which brought forth the man child. 14 And to the woman were given two wings of a great eagle, that she might fly into the wilderness, into her place, where she is nourished for a time, and times, and half a time, from the face of the serpent. 15 And the serpent cast out of his mouth water as a flood after the woman, that he might cause her to be carried away of the flood. 16 And the earth helped the woman, and the earth opened her mouth, and swallowed up the flood which the dragon cast out of his mouth. 17 And the dragon was wroth with the woman, and went to make war with the remnant of her seed, which keep the commandments of God, and have the testimony of Jesus Christ.*

Israel in Great Tribulation:

At this point it is becoming clear, that even though the Antichrist's involvement includes the whole world, much of what he is doing centers right around Jerusalem and the land of Israel and surrounding area. Toward the end of the Tribulation period, the Antichrist will actually locate his headquarters in the city of Jerusalem.

Antichrist's palace is located in Jerusalem:

Da 11:45 *And he shall plant the tabernacles of his palace between the seas in the glorious holy mountain; yet he shall come to his end, and none shall help him.*

Jerusalem surrounded by armies:

Somewhere near that same time, Jerusalem will once again be surrounded by armies and be hit terribly hard, near to destruction. Two thirds of the population of Jerusalem will die. The third that survives will be tried as by fire. We first see in Zec 12, the Lord promising to stand strong for Jerusalem and Israel, because finally Israel begins turning to the Lord, recognizing Jesus as the Messiah. Then in Zec 13 and 14, Jerusalem is surrounded and nearly destroyed, but then the Lord intervenes and destroys those enemy nations.

Zec 12:1-11 *The burden of the word of the LORD for Israel, saith the LORD, which stretcheth forth the heavens, and layeth the foundation of the earth, and formeth the spirit of man within him. 2 Behold, I will make Jerusalem a cup of trembling unto all the people round about, when they shall be in the siege both against Judah and against Jerusalem. 3 And in that day will I make Jerusalem a burdensome stone for all people: all that burden themselves with it shall be cut in pieces, though all the people of the earth be gathered together against it. 4 In that day, saith the LORD, I will smite every horse with astonishment, and his rider with madness: and I will open mine eyes upon the house of Judah, and will smite every horse of the people with blindness. 5 And the governors of Judah shall say in their heart, The inhabitants of Jerusalem shall be my strength in the LORD of* hosts their God. 6 In that day will I make the governors of Judah like an hearth of fire among the wood, and like a torch of fire in a sheaf; and they shall devour all the people round about, on the right hand and on the left: and Jerusalem shall be inhabited again in her own place, even in Jerusalem. 7 The LORD also shall save the tents of Judah first, that the glory of the house of David and the glory of the inhabitants of Jerusalem do not magnify themselves against Judah. 8 In that day shall the LORD defend the inhabitants of Jerusalem; and he that is feeble among them at that day shall be as David; and the house of David shall be as God, as the angel of the LORD before them. 9 And it shall come to pass in that day, that I will seek to destroy all the nations that come against Jerusalem. 10 And I will pour upon the house of David, and upon the inhabitants of Jerusalem, the spirit of grace and of supplications: and they shall look upon me whom they have pierced, and they shall mourn for him, as one mourneth for his only son, and shall be in bitterness for him, as one that is in bitterness for his firstborn. 11 In that day shall there be a great mourning in Jerusalem, as the mourning of Hadadrimmon in the valley of Megiddon.

Zec 13:1-2,8-9   In that day there shall be a fountain opened to the house of David and to the inhabitants of Jerusalem for sin and for uncleanness. 2 And it shall come to pass in that day, … 8 And it shall come to pass, that in all the land, saith the LORD, two parts therein shall be cut off and die; but the third shall be left therein. 9

And I will bring the third part through the fire, and will refine them as silver is refined, and will try them as gold is tried: they shall call on my name, and I will hear them: I will say, It is my people: and they shall say, The LORD is my God.

Zec 14:1-3 Behold, the day of the LORD cometh, and thy spoil shall be divided in the midst of thee. 2 For I will gather all nations against Jerusalem to battle; and the city shall be taken, and the houses rifled, and the women ravished; and half of the city shall go forth into captivity, and the residue of the people shall not be cut off from the city. 3 Then shall the LORD go forth, and fight against those nations, as when he fought in the day of battle.

Jesus' Second Coming and Armageddon:

In God's timing the Tribulation is closed with the Second Coming of Jesus. He appears on a white horse in great majesty, accompanied by the armies in heaven (all who went in the Rapture). Out of His mouth goeth a sharp sword, with which He smites the nations, He but speaks and destroys His enemies and ours. Blood flows to the horse's bridle for 200 miles. He comes to rule the world as King of Kings. The Antichrist and the False Prophet are taken and cast alive into the lake of fire forever.

Rv 19:11-16,19-21 And I saw heaven opened, and behold a white horse; and he that sat upon him was called Faithful and True, and in righteousness he doth judge and make war. 12 His eyes were as a flame of fire, and on his head were many crowns; and he had a name written, that no man knew, but he himself. 13 And he was clothed with a vesture dipped in blood: and his name is called The Word of God. 14 And the armies which were in heaven followed him upon white horses, clothed in fine linen, white and clean. 15 And out of his mouth goeth a sharp sword, that with it he should smite the nations: and he shall rule them with a rod of iron: and he treadeth the winepress of the fierceness and wrath of Almighty God. 16 And he hath on his vesture and on his thigh a name written, KING OF KINGS, AND LORD OF LORDS. ... 19 And I saw the beast, and the kings of the earth, and their armies, gathered together to make war against him that sat on the horse, and against his army. 20 And the beast was taken, and with him the false prophet that wrought miracles before him, with which he deceived them that had received the mark of the beast, and them that worshipped his image. These both were cast alive into a lake of fire burning with brimstone. 21 And the remnant were slain with the sword of him that sat upon the horse, which sword proceeded out of his mouth: and all the fowls were filled with their flesh.

Satan in chains for a thousand years:

Satan is taken by one angel, at the word of Jesus, bound with a great chain and cast into the bottomless pit for 1000 years as we enjoy the peace of the Millennial kingdom. After the Millennium, Satan will be released briefly one last time; he deceives millions, then he is thrown into the lake of fire forever.

Rv 20:1-3   *And I saw an angel come down from heaven, having the key of the bottomless pit and a great chain in his hand. 2 And he laid hold on the dragon, that old serpent, which is the Devil, and Satan, and bound him a thousand years, 3 And cast him into the bottomless pit, and shut him up, and set a seal upon him, that he should deceive the nations no more, till the thousand years should be fulfilled: and after that he must be loosed a little season.*

The Millennial Reign of Jesus:

During His Millennial reign, Jesus will rule the world from Jerusalem. There will be a great returning of Jews to Israel from the other nations of the world where they have been scattered.

Isa 2:2-3   *And it shall come to pass in the last days, that the mountain of the LORD's house shall be established in the top of the mountains, and shall be exalted above the hills; and all nations shall flow unto it. 3 And many people shall go and say, Come ye, and let us go up to the mountain of the LORD, to the house of the God of Jacob; and he will teach us of his ways, and we will walk in his paths: for out of Zion shall go forth the law, and the word of the LORD from Jerusalem.*

During this time, people will live long lives and be very prosperous. All will be peaceful, so much so that this time is referred to as the thousand years of peace, even the animals will be at peace with each other.

Isa 65:20-25   *There shall be no more thence an infant of days, nor an old man that hath not filled his days: for the child shall die an hundred years old; but the sinner being an hundred years old shall be accursed. 21 And they shall build houses, and inhabit them; and they shall plant vineyards, and eat the fruit of them. 22 They shall not build, and another inhabit; they shall not plant, and another eat: for as the days of a tree are the days of my people, and mine elect shall long enjoy the work of their hands. 23 They shall not labour in vain, nor bring forth for trouble; for they are the seed of the blessed of the LORD, and their offspring with them. 24 And it shall come to pass, that before they call, I will answer; and while they are yet speaking, I will hear. 25 The wolf and the lamb shall feed together, and the lion shall eat straw like the bullock: and dust shall be the serpent's meat. They shall not hurt nor destroy in all my holy mountain, saith the LORD.*

The earth will be ruled over by the KING OF KINGS, and LORD OF LORDS for a thousand years. God told Daniel:

Da 12:13 *But go thou thy way till the end be: for thou shalt rest, and stand in thy lot at the end of the days.*

Rv 20:6 *Blessed and holy is he that hath part in the first resurrection: on such the second death hath no power, but they shall be priests of God and of Christ, and shall reign with him a thousand years.*

Israel and all of the nations will learn plenty about war during the Tribulation, so let us go and learn for ourselves about "War in the Tribulation."

Notes:

1. The Complete Works of Flavius Josephus, War of the Jews, Book VII, Chapter 8, Section 7. Link: http://www.ultimatebiblereferencelibrary.com/Complete_Works_of_Josephus.pdf

2. Joseph A. Seiss, The Apocalypse (Grand Rapids, MI: Kregel Publications, 1987), p. 227.

9

War in the Tribulation

War:

During the Tribulation, there will be many things happening thick and fast, some separate and different from each other and some simultaneous, but plenty going on. There will be war among the many other things, almost nonstop. Some of these war events can be located as to near the time when they actually occur, and for others it cannot be known when they will occur. The following are war events during the end time.

War of Psalm 83:

The war of Psalms 83 is one of those wars in question. Some say it is not a war but simply a prayer. It seems that it is a war and that it may well have taken place in Israel in 1967 in the Six Day War, because all of the enemy nations to Israel listed in Psalm 83 were present and defeated at that time. If it is still future and has not taken place yet, it is not known when it will occur. Some are guessing that it will occur before the Tribulation or shortly after it begins. This war could be a precursor to the Gog/Magog War, because victory for Israel will get at least a brief time of peace urging Gog/Magog to come down to take a spoil; scripture says Israel will be at peace when

Gog/Magog occurs. The first eight verses of Psalm 83 tell of the surrounding countries that will come against Israel in war; all of these are adjoining countries to Israel. The verses after verse eight are a prayer for victory.

Ps 83:1-8   *Keep not thou silence, O God: hold not thy peace, and be not still, O God. 2 For, lo, thine enemies make a tumult: and they that hate thee have lifted up the head. 3 They have taken crafty counsel against thy people, and consulted against thy hidden ones. 4 They have said, Come, and let us cut them off from being a nation; that the name of Israel may be no more in remembrance. 5 For they have consulted together with one consent: they are confederate against thee: 6 The tabernacles of Edom, and the Ishmaelites; of Moab, and the Hagarenes; 7 Gebal, and Ammon, and Amalek; the Philistines with the inhabitants of Tyre; 8 Assur also is joined with them: they have holpen the children of Lot. Selah.*

Damascus is to become a ruinous heap:

Among the many other conflicts during the Tribulation, Isa 17, Jer 49:22-27, and Am 1:3-5 all tell us that Damascus will be destroyed during the end of days. Damascus is thought to be the oldest inhabited city in the world, yet because she has chosen to "spoil, and rob," Israel, she is to be destroyed. This conflict may or may not be a war on its own. It may be a part of one of the other wars.

Isa 17:1,14   *The burden of Damascus. Behold, Damascus is taken away from being a city, and it shall be a ruinous heap. … 14 And behold at evening tide trouble; and before the morning he is not. This is the portion of them that spoil us, and the lot of them that rob us.*

Jer 49:22-27   Behold, he shall come up and fly as the eagle, and spread his wings over Bozrah: and at that day shall the heart of the mighty men of Edom be as the heart of a woman in her pangs. 23 Concerning Damascus. Hamath is confounded, and Arpad: for they have heard evil tidings: they are fainthearted; there is sorrow on the sea; it cannot be quiet. 24 Damascus is waxed feeble, and turneth herself to flee, and fear hath seized on her: anguish and sorrows have taken her, as a woman in travail. 25 How is the city of praise not left, the city of my joy! 26 Therefore her young men shall fall in her streets, and all the men of war shall be cut off in that day, saith the LORD of hosts. 27 And I will kindle a fire in the wall of Damascus, and it shall consume the palaces of Ben-hadad.

Am 1:3-5   Thus saith the LORD; For three transgressions of Damascus, and for four, I will not turn away the punishment thereof; because they have threshed Gilead with threshing instruments of iron: 4 But I will send a fire into the house of Hazael, which shall devour the palaces of Ben-hadad. 5 I will break also the bar of Damascus, and cut off the inhabitant from the plain of Aven, and him that holdeth the sceptre from the house of Eden: and the people of Syria shall go into captivity unto Kir, saith the LORD.

Gog/Magog war:

In Eze 38, God tells Gog/Magog in "the latter years," to go into the land (Israel) when they are dwelling in safety "to take a spoil." Seemingly, many, perhaps most, scholars think that Magog is Russia, with Gog being the ruler of the land of Magog. Russia will be joined by Iran, Ethiopa, Libya, Gomer, Togarmah, and others, a vast army, to go and destroy Israel. God himself intervenes with pestilence, blood, hailstones, fire, and brimstone. Only one sixth of this vast invading army will survive, meaning 83 out of each 100 of this enemy army will die in the mountains of Israel. So many will die, it will take Israel seven months to bury the dead. Even the homelands of these bands will also suffer destruction to some degree. Israel and the other nations of the world will recognize this great victory as the work of God. It is not known when this war will occur, except that it is to be in the latter days when Israel is living in peace. Israel is now 72 years old as a nation, since established in 1948, and has not yet known any such peace. One possibility is when the Antichrist comes on the scene early in the Tribulation and he will make a seven-year covenant with Israel. That covenant might give the necessary peace to bring on the Gog/Magog war. At any rate this war is likely to occur before the Tribulation begins or early on after its beginning. This will be an event that will astound the entire world.

Eze 38:1-7,9-12,21-23 *And the word of the LORD came unto me, saying, 2 Son of man, set thy face against Gog, the land of Magog, the chief* prince of Meshech and Tubal, and prophesy against him, 3 And say, Thus saith the Lord GOD; Behold I am against thee, O Gog, the chief prince of Meshech and Tubal: 4 And I will turn thee back, and put hooks into thy jaws, and I will bring thee forth, and all thine army, horses and horsemen, all of them clothed with all sorts of armour, even a great company with bucklers and shields, all of them handling swords: 5 Persia, Ethiopia, and Libya with them; all of them with shield and helmet: 6 Gomer, and all his bands; the house of Togarmah of the north quarters, and all his bands: and many people with thee. 7 Be thou prepared, and prepare for thyself, thou, and all thy company that are assembled unto thee, and be thou a guard unto them. … 9 Thou shalt ascend and come like a storm, thou shalt be like a cloud to cover the land, thou, and all thy bands, and many people with thee. 10 Thus saith the Lord GOD; It shall also come to pass, that at the same time shall things come into thy mind, and thou shalt think an evil thought: 11 And thou shalt say, I will go up to the land of unwalled villages; I will go to them that are at rest, that dwell safely, all of them dwelling without walls, and having neither bars nor gates, 12 To take a spoil, and to take a prey; ... 21 And I will call for a sword against him throughout all my mountains, saith the Lord GOD: every man's sword shall be against his brother. 22 And I will plead against him with pestilence and with blood; and I will rain upon him, and upon his bands, and upon the many people that are with him, an overflowing rain, and great hailstones, fire, and brimstone. 23

Thus will I magnify myself, and sanctify myself; and I will be known in the eyes of many nations, and they shall know that I am the LORD.

Eze 39:1-4,6-7 Therefore, thou son of man, prophesy against Gog, and say, Thus saith the Lord GOD; Behold, I am against thee, O Gog, the chief prince of Meshech and Tubal: 2 And I will turn thee back, and leave but the sixth part of thee, and will cause thee to come up from the north parts, and will bring thee upon the mountains of Israel: 3 And I will smite thy bow out of thy left hand, and will cause thine arrows to fall out of thy right hand. 4 Thou shalt fall upon the mountains of Israel, thou, and all thy bands, and the people that is with thee: ... 6 And I will send a fire on Magog, and among them that dwell carelessly in the isles: and they shall know that I am the LORD. 7 So will I make my holy name known in the midst of my people Israel; and I will not let them pollute my holy name any more: and the heathen shall know that I am the LORD, the Holy One in Israel.

Antichrist coming to power, subdues three kings:

When the Antichrist is rising to power, he comes up among ten other kings in a Federation, as an eleventh person. Daniel 7 states three different times that the Antichrist plucks up three of the other kings by the roots. This is really all that we are told. The word war is not used, but it seems probable that he does defeat them in war. How much bloodshed there is, we are not told, only that he subdues those three kings. This action is probably very early in the Tribulation, and it is a key for identifying the Antichrist.

Da 7:8,20,24   *I considered the horns, and, behold, there came up among them another little horn, before whom there were three of the first horns plucked up by the roots: and, behold, in this horn were eyes like the eyes of man, and a mouth speaking great things. ... 20 And of the ten horns that were in his head, and of the other which came up, and before whom three fell; even of that horn that had eyes, and a mouth that spake very great things, whose look was more stout than his fellows. 24 And the ten horns out of this kingdom are ten kings that shall arise: and another shall rise after them; and he shall be diverse from the first, and he shall subdue three kings.*

The red horse rider with a sword:

The Red horse rider comes forth under the opening of the second seal early in the Tribulation; this is the result of the direct righteous judgment of God. People begin killing one another, peace is taken from the earth, the word war in not used here. Even so, it may be a war or a part of one of the other named wars. This is very early on in the Tribulation, is only the second of God's judgments, and there evidently is complete chaos and loss of life; it will not get better for the next seven years. That word "sword" shouts loudly "war"; we can safely assume that there is indeed war.

Rv 6:3-4   *And when he had opened the second seal, I heard the second beast say, Come and see. 4 And there went out another horse that was red: and power was given to him that sat thereon to take peace from the earth, and that they should kill one another: and there was given unto him a great sword.*

Death followed by hell:

Here only four verses later, one of the most horrific scenes in the entire Tribulation takes place, and again the word war is not used. Four causes of death are listed: sword, hunger, death, and the beasts of the earth. Sword, hunger, and death all speak loudly of war. Again, this is one of the righteous judgments of God, and one fourth of the earth's population dies, which amounts to just short of 2,000,000,000 (2 billion) people who die. And there is more to come.

Rv 6:7-8   *And when he had opened the fourth seal, I heard the voice of the fourth beast say, Come and see. 8 And I looked, and behold a pale horse: and his name that sat on him was Death, and Hell followed with him. And power was given unto them over the fourth part of the earth, to kill with sword, and with hunger, and with death, and with the beasts of the earth.*

The war in heaven:

This is clearly a war, but in heaven, not on the earth. Satan and his angels are permanently cast out of heaven to the earth, which means dreadful things for the people of the earth. At this point Satan realizes he has but a short time remaining and begins a terrible persecution, essentially a war, of the Jews and Christians.

Rv 12:7-9,12 *And there was war in heaven: Michael and his angels fought against the dragon; and the dragon fought and his angels, 8 And prevailed not; neither was their place found any more in heaven. 9 And the great dragon was cast out, that old serpent, called the Devil, and Satan, which deceiveth the whole world: he was cast out into the earth, and his angels were cast out with him. ... 12 Therefore rejoice, ye heavens, and ye that dwell in them. Woe to the inhabiters of the earth and of the sea! for the devil is come down unto you, having great wrath, because he knoweth that he hath but a short time.*

The war against God's people:
Satan hates God, Satan hates people. It is difficult to comprehend why he has such hatred. Why does he want to murder everyone? He holds a special hatred for God's people, both Jews and Christians, because they are the people of God. After the war in heaven and Satan is cast out of heaven to the earth, and knowing he has but a short time left, he will go after God's people with all of his energy, working through the Antichrist. Notice Rv 12:17 says clearly that the dragon, Satan, went to make war with the remnant of the woman's seed, Christian Jews and Gentiles. Zec 13:8 tells us that two thirds of the Jews will be slaughtered during the Tribulation. Rv 7:9-17 shows a great multitude of martyrs from out of the Great Tribulation. Scripture says no man could number (count) this multitude.

Rv 12:14,17   And to the woman were given
two wings of a great eagle, that she might fly into
the wilderness, into her place, where she is
nourished for a time, and times, and half a time,
from the face of the serpent. ... 17 And the dragon
was wroth with the woman, and went to make war
with the remnant of her seed, which keep the
commandments of God, and have the testimony of
Jesus Christ.

The war with Egypt:
Throughout Daniel 11 there is a lot of back
and forth war between the king of the north, Syria,
and the king of the south, Egypt. This continues in
history over a long period of time, from the time of
Alexander the Great, 323 BC. The vile person
mentioned in verse 21, is the Antichrist when he
first appears early in the Tribulation. In verse 40 he
responds to an attack from the king of the south,
Egypt. In this war he overthrows many countries,
but at least the southern part of Jordan escapes,
while Egypt is defeated. It is likely that part of
Jordan escapes because that is where the Jews and
Christians have fled to and are being cared for by
the Lord. The Antichrist is finally brought to his end
in verse 45, which is obviously the end of the
Tribulation, so it seems this war might be rather
late during the Tribulation.

Da 11:40-45   And at the time of the end
shall the king of the south push at him: and the
king of the north shall come against him like a
whirlwind, with chariots, and with horsemen, and
with many ships; and he shall enter into the

274

countries, and shall overflow and pass over. 41 He shall enter also into the glorious land, and many countries shall be overthrown: but these shall escape out of his hand, even Edom, and Moab, and the chief of the children of Ammon. 42 He shall stretch forth his hand also upon the countries: and the land of Egypt shall not escape. 43 But he shall have power over the treasures of gold and of silver, and over all the precious things of Egypt: and the Libyans and the Ethiopians shall be at his steps. 44 But tidings out of the east and out of the north shall trouble him: therefore he shall go forth with great fury to destroy, and utterly to make away many. 45 And he shall plant the tabernacles of his palace between the seas in the glorious holy mountain; yet he shall come to his end, and none shall help him.

The destruction of Mystery Babylon:

In Rv 17 and 18 the evil sin of Babylon is shown with the understanding that God is going to avenge his people on her. Babylon is to be destroyed completely forever. There are two Babylons, one is the actual city, the other is the spirit of Baylon, born in Babylon's beginning. All of the false religions throughout the world's history were born in Mystery Babylon. All of the evils associated with corrupt commercialism were born in Babylon the Great. Satan has given it his all throughout history. As a result, every nation and many kings have been influenced through history and now today the world is ripe for the evils of the Tribulation. The Antichrist and the ten kings that work with him support the false religions through most of the Tribulation, but toward the end, they with the Antichrist, destroy false religion as Mystery Babylon.

Rv 17:1-6,12-18   1 *And there came one of the seven angels which had the seven vials, and talked with me, saying unto me, Come hither; I will shew unto thee the judgment of the great whore that sitteth upon many waters: 2 With whom the kings of the earth have committed fornication, and the inhabitants of the earth have been made drunk with the wine of her fornication. 3 So he carried me away in the spirit into the wilderness: and I saw a woman sit upon a scarlet coloured beast, full of names of blasphemy, having seven heads and ten horns. 4 And the woman was arrayed in purple and scarlet colour, and decked with gold and precious stones and pearls, having a golden cup in her hand full of abominations and filthiness of her fornication: 5 And upon her forehead was a name written, MYSTERY, BABYLON THE GREAT, THE MOTHER OF HARLOTS AND ABOMINATIONS OF THE EARTH. 6 And I saw the woman drunken with the blood of the saints, and with the blood of the martyrs of Jesus: and when I saw her, I wondered with great admiration. ... 12 And the ten horns which thou sawest are ten kings, which have received no kingdom as yet; but receive power as kings one hour with the beast. 13 These have one mind, and shall give their power and strength unto the beast. 14 These shall make war with the Lamb, and the Lamb shall overcome them: for he is Lord of lords, and King of kings: and they that are with him are called, and chosen, and faithful. 15 And he saith unto me, The waters which thou sawest, where the whore sitteth, are peoples, and multitudes, and nations, and tongues. 16 And the ten horns which thou sawest upon the beast, these shall hate the whore, and shall make her desolate and naked, and shall eat her flesh, and burn her with fire. 17 For God hath put in their hearts to fulfil his will, and to agree, and give their kingdom unto the beast, until the words of God shall be fulfilled. 18 And the woman which thou sawest is that great city, which reigneth over the kings of the earth.*

The destruction of Babylon the Great:

Much that is said of Mystery Babylon can be said of Babylon the Great, with the understanding that the world's corrupt commercialism is associated with Babylon the Great. In this destruction of Babylon, all of false religion and all the evils of corrupt commercialism and the actual physical city of Babylon will be destroyed. This will take place as a part of the battle of Armageddon, or immediately preceding Armageddon.

Rv 18:1-5,8,23-24 *And after these things I saw another angel come down from heaven, having great power; and the earth was lightened with his glory. 2 And he cried mightily with a strong voice, saying, Babylon the great is fallen, is fallen, and is become the habitation of devils, and the hold of every foul spirit, and a cage of every unclean and hateful bird. 3 For all nations have drunk of the wine of the wrath of her fornication, and the kings of the earth have committed fornication with her, and the merchants of the earth are waxed rich through the abundance of her delicacies. 4 And I heard another voice from heaven, saying, Come out of her, my people, that ye be not partakers of her sins, and that ye receive not of her plagues. 5 For her sins have reached unto heaven, and God hath remembered her iniquities. ... 8 Therefore shall her plagues come in one day, death, and mourning, and famine; and she shall be utterly burned with fire: for strong is the Lord God who judgeth her. ... for by thy sorceries were all nations deceived. 24 And in her was found the blood of prophets, and of saints, and of all that were slain upon the earth.*

The battle of Armageddon:

In Rv 19, we see the armies of the world gathered in the name of the Antichrist and Satan to do battle against the King of Kings. When Jesus himself appears riding a white horse and is accompanied by the armies of heaven. The Antichrist and the False Prophet are taken and cast alive into the lake of fire. The Antichrist's armies are slain by the sword in the mouth of Jesus. In other words, Jesus simply speaks the words and the enemy armies are all slain. The battle of Armageddon is the best known of all battles, but really, it isn't a battle at all, just the destruction of the millions of God's enemies and the blood flows four or five feet deep for two hundred miles. That closes the Tribulation and begins the thousand years of peace, the reign of Christ. Read Joel 3, Zec 14, 2 Th 2:8 as well as Rv 19.

Rv 19:11,15-16,19-21   *And I saw heaven opened, and behold a white horse; and he that sat upon him was called Faithful and True, and in righteousness he doth judge and make war. ... 15 And out of his mouth goeth a sharp sword, that with it he should smite the nations: and he shall rule them with a rod of iron: and he treadeth the winepress of the fierceness and wrath of Almighty God. 16 And he hath on his vesture and on his thigh a name written, KING OF KINGS, AND LORD OF LORDS. ... 19 And I saw the beast, and the kings of the earth, and their armies, gathered together to make war against him that sat on the horse, and against his army. 20 And the beast was taken, and with him the false prophet that wrought miracles before him, with which he deceived them that had received the mark of the beast, and them that worshipped his image. These both were cast alive into a lake of fire burning with brimstone. 21 And the remnant were slain with the sword of him that sat upon the horse, which sword proceeded out of his mouth: and all the fowls were filled with their flesh.*

As we see the Tribulation winding down and the destruction of Mystery Babylon and Babylon the Great, let us look in more detail at the reason and finality of this destruction.

10
Mystery Babylon/ Babylon the Great

Nimrod was the builder of Babel (Babylon):

The name Babel/Babylon means confusion because it was there at the attempt to build the so-called tower of Babel, that God confused their language. Nimrod appears to have been at the center of the whole effort. It is clear from scripture that Nimrod was a rebel against God. From all that we know about it, Nimrod and Babylon both were evil from the beginning of this effort.

Ge 10:8-10   *And Cush begat Nimrod: he began to be a mighty one in the earth. 9 He was a mighty hunter before the LORD: wherefore it is said, Even as Nimrod the mighty hunter before the LORD. 10 And the beginning of his kingdom was Babel, and Erech, and Accad, and Calneh, in the land of Shinar.*

The Tower of Babel and the city of Babylon:

In the building of the tower to heaven, the people were in defiance toward God. There is also a strong element of pride; they were going to make a name for themselves and build a tower that would stand taller than any flood that God could ever bring against them in the future. They were against all that God stood for.

Ge 11:1,4,6-9 *And the whole earth was of one language, and of one speech. ... 4 And they said, Go to, let us build us a city and a tower, whose top may reach unto heaven; and let us make us a name, lest we be scattered abroad upon the face of the whole earth. ... 6 And the LORD said, Behold, the people is one, and they have all one language; and this they begin to do: and now nothing will be restrained from them, which they have imagined to do. 7 Go to, let us go down, and there confound their language, that they may not understand one another's speech. 8 So the LORD scattered them abroad from thence upon the face of all the earth: and they left off to build the city. 9 Therefore is the name of it called Babel; because the LORD did there confound the language of all the earth: ...*

Prophecies of Babylon never yet fulfilled:

Isaiah 13 clearly tells that Babylon will be destroyed in the day of the Lord, and that Babylon will be destroyed like Sodom and Gomorrah and that no Arabian shall pitch tent there nor shall it be inhabited from generation to generation. The day of the Lord is commonly understood to be speaking of the judgments of God on the wicked in the end times and it includes the time of the Tribulation. So, it seems that Babylon's complete and final destruction is yet to occur during the time of the Tribulation.

Isa 13:6,9,13,19-20   Howl ye; for the day of the LORD is at hand; it shall come as a destruction from the Almighty. … 9 Behold, the day of the LORD cometh, cruel both with wrath and fierce anger, to lay the land desolate: and he shall destroy the sinners thereof out of it. … 13 Therefore I will shake the heavens, and the earth shall remove out of her place, in the wrath of the LORD of hosts, and in the day of his fierce anger. … 19 And Babylon, the glory of kingdoms, the beauty of the Chaldees' excellency, shall be as when God overthrew Sodom and Gomorrah. 20 It shall never be inhabited, neither shall it be dwelt in from generation to generation: neither shall the Arabian pitch tent there; neither shall the shepherds make their fold there.

Jeremiah prophesied that Babylon would be destroyed utterly, nothing was to be left of her. The word utterly means Babylon was to be destroyed entirely, fully, wholly, and totally, and nothing left means nothing left. Jeremiah further prophesied that Babylon was to be inhabited no more forever nor to be dwelt in from generation to generation. Yet from generation to generation for centuries she has had inhabitants constantly.

Jer 50:25-26   … for this is the work of the Lord GOD of hosts in the land of the Chaldeans. 26 Come against her from the utmost border, open her storehouses: cast her up as heaps, and destroy her utterly: let nothing of her be left.

Further, the Lord through Jeremiah said, there will not be a stone taken from Babylon for building, yet, for centuries cities and villages have been rummaging through the ruins and carrying away stones (bricks) by the thousands, more probably millions.

Jer 51:26   *And they shall not take of thee a stone for a corner, nor a stone for foundations; but thou shalt be desolate for ever, saith the LORD.*

Concerning Babylon, none of these things have ever yet happened. Babylon is yet to be destroyed; therefore, Babylon must be rebuilt so that the above-mentioned prophecies can be fulfilled. So, there is still coming the destruction of Babylon during the terrible "day of the Lord" (Tribulation). In Isa 14:4, 22-24, Isaiah's words are much like that in chapter 13, and he added a lot of language concerning the king of Babylon and Lucifer in association with the destruction of Babylon. In verse 4, Satan is clearly labeled as the king of Babylon. It is beginning to be very clear that Babylon is evil to the core. To fix this problem, the Lord says He is going to sweep Babylon with the broom of destruction.

Isa 14:4,22-24   *That thou shalt take up this proverb against the king of Babylon, and say, How hath the oppressor ceased! the golden city ceased! ... 22 For I will rise up against them, saith the LORD of hosts, and cut off from Babylon the name, and remnant, and son, and nephew, saith the LORD. 23 I will also make it a possession for the bittern, and pools of water: and I will sweep it with the besom of destruction, saith the LORD of hosts. 24 The LORD of hosts hath sworn, saying, Surely as I have thought, so shall it come to pass; and as I have purposed, so shall it stand: ...*

Ps 137:8-9   *O daughter of Babylon, who art to be destroyed; happy shall he be, that rewardeth thee as thou hast served us. 9 Happy shall he be, that taketh and dasheth thy little ones against the stones.*

Babylon's complete destruction has never yet happened. In referencing scripture that is speaking of the things to happen in the day of the Lord, there is an abundance of scripture that speaks of Babylon as an actual city. There is also an abundance of scripture that refers to the age-old evils associated with Babylon. All of these evils are the work of Satan to defy and destroy God's people and plan. All of the evil that Satan has planned and worked toward the end of days swirls around Babylon and the spirit of Babylon. Today, there is no city of Babylon, only some ruins of the ancient city with a palace and a few other buildings that Saddam Hussein put together in an effort to restore the greatness of the ancient city. His plans failed when he was captured by American forces in Operation Red Dawn. Hussein was later executed by the Iraqi Special Tribunal for the murder of 148 Iraqis. The ruins of Babylon with Hussein's additions is surrounded by the modern city of Al Hillah, a city of some hundreds of thousands (some sources say more than a million). There are various ideas about what Babylon is, some say Babylon is Rome, others say Babylon is New York City, and there are a lot of other ideas. Babylon has been Babylon since shortly after the flood in Noah's day, with the earliest prophecies of her destruction by Isaiah being about 700 years before Christ.

Remember Isaiah's words in Isa 14:24 where the Lord said, "The LORD of hosts hath sworn, saying, Surely as I have thought, so shall it come to pass; and as I have purposed, so shall it stand: ... The Lord here was talking about the complete destruction of Babylon.

Babylon still existed in Peter's time:

From the 13th verse Chapter 5 of 1 Peter it seems quite clear that Peter spent ministry time in Babylon.

1 Pe 5:13   *The church that is at Babylon, elected together with you, saluteth you; and so doth Marcus my son.*

More prophecies of Babylon's destruction:

Isa 21:9   *And, behold, here cometh a chariot of men, with a couple of horsemen. And he answered and said, Babylon is fallen, is fallen; and all the graven images of her gods he hath broken unto the ground.*

Isa 43:14-15   *Thus saith the LORD, your redeemer, the Holy One of Israel; For your sake I have sent to Babylon, and have brought down all their nobles, and the Chaldeans, whose cry is in the ships.15 I am the LORD, your Holy One, the creator of Israel, your King.*

Rv 14:8   *And there followed another angel, saying, Babylon is fallen, is fallen, that great city, because she made all nations drink of the wine of the wrath of her fornication.*

Rv 16:17-21   And the seventh angel poured out his vial into the air; and there came a great voice out of the temple of heaven, from the throne, saying, It is done. 18 And there were voices, and thunders, and lightnings; and there was a great earthquake, such as was not since men were upon the earth, so mighty an earthquake, and so great. 19 And the great city was divided into three parts, and the cities of the nations fell: and great Babylon came in remembrance before God, to give unto her the cup of the wine of the fierceness of his wrath. 20 And every island fled away, and the mountains were not found. 21 And there fell upon men a great hail out of heaven, every stone about the weight of a talent: and men blasphemed God because of the plague of the hail; for the plague thereof was exceeding great.

Rv 18:2   And he cried mightily with a strong voice, saying, Babylon the great is fallen, is fallen, and is become the habitation of devils, and the hold of every foul spirit, and a cage of every unclean and hateful bird. ...

Jer 51:8-9   Babylon is suddenly fallen and destroyed: howl for her; take balm for her pain, if so she may be healed. 9 We would have healed Babylon, but she is not healed: forsake her, and let us go every one into his own country: for her judgment reacheth unto heaven, and is lifted up even to the skies.

Isa 47 and Rv 18 both show vivid descriptions of Babylon's destruction:

Joseph Chambers[1] shows us a verse by verse comparison of some verses of Isa 47 and Rv 18.

(Isa 47:1/Rv18:3) Isa 47:1 *Come down, and sit in the dust, O virgin daughter of Babylon, sit on the ground: there is no throne, O daughter of the Chaldeans: for thou shalt no more be called tender and delicate.* Rv 18:3 *For all nations have drunk of the wine of the wrath of her fornication, and the kings of the earth have committed fornication with her, and the merchants of the earth are waxed rich through the abundance of her delicacies. ...*

(Isa 47:8-9/Rv18:7-8) Isa 47:8-9 *Therefore hear now this, thou that art given to pleasures, that dwellest carelessly, that sayest in thine heart, I am, and none else beside me; I shall not sit as a widow, neither shall I know the loss of children: 9 But these two things shall come to thee in a moment in one day, the loss of children, and widowhood: they shall come upon thee in their perfection for the multitude of thy sorceries, and for the great abundance of thine enchantments.* Rv 18:7-8 *How much she hath glorified herself, and lived deliciously, so much torment and sorrow give her: for she saith in her heart, I sit a queen, and am no widow, and shall see no sorrow. 8 Therefore shall her plagues come in one day, death, and mourning, and famine; and she shall be utterly burned with fire: for strong is the Lord God who judgeth her.*

(Isa 47:13/Rv18:23)   Isa 47:13   *Thou art wearied in the multitude of thy counsels. Let now the astrologers, the stargazers, the monthly prognosticators, stand up, and save thee from these things that shall come upon thee.*   Rv 18:23   *And the light of a candle shall shine no more at all in thee; and the voice of the bridegroom and of the bride shall be heard no more at all in thee: for thy merchants were the great men of the earth; for by thy sorceries were all nations deceived.*

Jer 50 and 51 show the final judgment of Babylon:

Jeremiah gives a long prophecy in Jer 50 and 51 of the destruction of the great, historic, and evil city of Babylon. Verse 3 makes it clear a nation from out of the north will come against Babylon to make her desolate, then a few verses later, we are told that "an assembly of great nations from the north country" will come against Babylon. The Lord through the prophet Jeremiah tells us that it is He, God, who brings this about, and because of His wrath Babylon will not be inhabited, but will become wholly desolate. The hammer of the whole earth is to be broken and cut in two and become a waste. According to Jer 51 the Lord will raise up the Medes to bring vengeance for what Babylon has done to Zion (Israel). The Medes are the present-day Kurds, a people group found in northern Iraq and Iran and in southeastern Turkey. These countries are all a part of that great assembly of nations that will come like a plague of caterpillars, that is hordes of troops, to bring desolation on Babylon that neither man nor beast will ever live there again forever. Babylon will sink never to rise from the evil that God will bring upon her.

Jer 50:1-3,9,13-18,23-24,29-30,39-40   The word that the LORD spake against Babylon and against the land of the Chaldeans by Jeremiah the prophet. 2 Declare ye among the nations, and publish, and set up a standard; publish, and conceal not: say, Babylon is taken, Bel is confounded, Merodach is broken in pieces; her idols are confounded, her images are broken in pieces. 3 For out of the north there cometh up a nation against her, which shall make her land desolate, and none shall dwell therein: they shall remove, they shall depart, both man and beast. ... 9 For, lo, I will raise and cause to come up against Babylon an assembly of great nations from the north country: and they shall set themselves in array against her; from thence she shall be taken: their arrows shall be as of a mighty expert man; none shall return in vain. ... 13 Because of the wrath of the LORD it shall not be inhabited, but it shall be wholly desolate: every one that goeth by Babylon shall be astonished, and hiss at all her plagues. 14 Put yourselves in array against Babylon round about: all ye that bend the bow, shoot at her, spare no arrows: for she hath sinned against the LORD. 15 Shout against her round about: she hath given her hand: her foundations are fallen, her walls are thrown down: for it is the vengeance of the LORD: take vengeance upon her; as she hath done, do unto her. 16 Cut off the sower from

Babylon, and him that handleth the sickle in the time of harvest: for fear of the oppressing sword they shall turn everyone to his people, and they shall flee everyone to his own land. 17 Israel is a scattered sheep; the lions have driven him away: first the king of Assyria hath devoured him; and last this Nebuchadrezzar king of Babylon hath broken his bones. 18 Therefore thus saith the LORD of hosts, the God of Israel; Behold, I will punish the king of Babylon and his land, as I have punished the king of Assyria. ... 23 How is the hammer of the whole earth cut asunder and broken! how is Babylon become a desolation among the nations! 24 I have laid a snare for thee, and thou art also taken, O Babylon, and thou wast not aware: thou art found, and also caught, because thou hast striven against the LORD. ... 29 Call together the archers against Babylon: all ye that bend the bow, camp against it round about; let none thereof escape: recompense her according to her work; according to all that she hath done, do unto her: for she hath been proud against the LORD, against the Holy One of Israel. 30 Therefore shall her young men fall in the streets, and all her men of war shall be cut off in that day, saith the LORD. ... 39 Therefore the wild beasts of the desert with the wild beasts of the islands shall dwell there, and the owls shall dwell therein: and it shall be no more inhabited forever; neither shall it be dwelt in from generation to generation. 40 As God overthrew Sodom and Gomorrah and the neighbour cities thereof, saith the LORD; so shall no man abide there, neither shall any son of man dwell therein.

Babylon will sink never to rise:

Jer 51:1,3,7-8,11-12,24-29,37,62,64   *Thus saith the LORD; Behold, I will raise up against Babylon, and against them that dwell in the midst of them that rise up against me, a destroying wind; ... 3 ... destroy ye utterly all her host. ... 7 Babylon hath been a golden cup in the LORD's hand, that made all the earth drunken: the nations have drunken of her wine; therefore the nations are mad. 8 Babylon is suddenly fallen and destroyed: howl for her; take balm for her pain, if so she may be healed. ... 11 Make bright the arrows; gather the shields: the LORD hath raised up the spirit of the kings of the Medes: for his device is against Babylon, to destroy it; because it is the vengeance of the LORD, the vengeance of his temple. 12 Set up the standard upon the walls of Babylon, make the watch strong, set up the watchmen, prepare the ambushes: for the LORD hath both devised and done that which he spake against the inhabitants of Babylon. ... 24 And I will render unto Babylon and to all the inhabitants of Chaldea all their evil that they have done in Zion in your sight, saith the LORD. 25 Behold, I am against thee, O destroying mountain, saith the LORD, which destroyest all the earth: and I will stretch out mine hand upon thee, and roll thee down from the rocks, and will make thee a burnt mountain. 26 And they shall not take of thee a stone for a corner, nor a stone for foundations; but thou shalt be desolate forever, saith the LORD. 27 Set ye up a standard in the land, blow the trumpet among the nations, prepare the nations against her, call together against her the kingdoms of Ararat, Minni, and Ashchenaz; appoint a captain against her; cause the horses to come up as the rough caterpillers. 28 Prepare against her the nations with the kings of the Medes, the captains thereof, and all the rulers thereof, and all the land of his dominion. 29 And the land shall tremble and sorrow: for every purpose of the LORD shall be performed against Babylon, to make the land of Babylon a desolation without an inhabitant. ... 37 And Babylon shall become heaps, a dwelling place for dragons, an astonishment, and an hissing, without an inhabitant. ... 62 and say, O Jehovah, thou hast spoken concerning this place, to cut it off, that none shall dwell therein, neither man nor beast, but that it shall be desolate for ever. ... 64 And thou shalt say, Thus shall Babylon sink, and shall not rise from the evil that I will bring upon her: ...*

Babylon rebuilt:

When Medo-Persia captured Babylon in 539 BC; Babylon had reached its zenith of power and prosperity and began a long and slow but steady decline. Even so, Babylon has never been totally destroyed. Zec 5:3 tells us "this is the curse that goeth forth over the face of the whole earth:" (the curse being the Tribulation). The woman sitting in the ephah (v 8) "is wickedness", being carried to a house in Shinar (Babylon) to sit on her own base. In his book, "A Palace for the Antichrist," Joseph

Chambers[2] says, "This commercial system destined to control the whole world will be carried to Babylon by two women with the wind (speed and haste) in their wings. It will happen with great speed. The whole world systems will first focus their attention on this area (already happening) and will then swiftly move its political and military operations to be centered in the vicinity of Babylon. It will happen so fast that no one will have time to resist or even prepare an argument." Joseph Chambers is saying that Zechariah is saying that, yet in the future, the world of wickedness will be carried to Babylon. Babylon will then become the seat of Antichrist and Satan and the world center for world religions and commercialism, to then shortly thereafter be totally destroyed.

Zec 5:1-3,5-11   *Then I turned, and lifted up mine eyes, and looked, and behold a flying roll. 2 And he said unto me, What seest thou? And I answered, I see a flying roll; the length thereof is twenty cubits, and the breadth thereof ten cubits. 3 Then said he unto me, This is the curse that goeth forth over the face of the whole earth: ... 5 Then the angel that talked with me went forth, and said unto me, Lift up now thine eyes, and see what is this that goeth forth. 6 And I said, What is it? And he said, This is an ephah that goeth forth. He said moreover, This is their resemblance through all the earth. 7 And, behold, there was lifted up a talent of lead: and this is a woman that sitteth in the midst of the ephah. 8 And he said, This is wickedness. And he cast it into the midst of the ephah; and he cast the weight of lead upon the mouth thereof. 9*

*Then lifted I up mine eyes, and looked, and,
behold, there came out two women, and the wind
was in their wings; for they had wings like the
wings of a stork: and they lifted up the ephah
between the earth and the heaven. 10 Then said I
to the angel that talked with me, Whither do these
bear the ephah? 11 And he said unto me, To build
it an house in the land of Shinar: and it shall be
established, and set there upon her own base.*

Mystery Babylon is all false religion, to be destroyed:

Chambers[3] says, Of the two Babylons in Rv
17 and Rv 18, "One is mystery Babylon," false
religion, and the other is "political, commercial
Babylon." *The Great Harlot Rv* 17:1-6 Babylonian,
Mystery Religion.   Consider Isa 47 and Rev. 17
and 18 also, and Jezebel in 2 Kings 9. God is going
to do to the "whore" Baylon the same thing that
happened to the whore Jezebel. The dogs ate
Jezebel.

God calls Babylon the great whore, because
of all the evil she is guilty of, and more than that
she has led the nations of the world into that same
guilt, as well she is guilty of the blood of the saints
and the blood of the martyrs of Jesus. Like
Jeremiah 50 and 51, Revelation 17 and 18 are long
prophecies of the destruction of evil Babylon.
Jeremiah wrote his prophecies twenty-six hundred
years ago and John wrote the Revelation seven
hundred years later, yet they are much alike and
both speak of the total destruction of Babylon.
Babylon has led all of the nations and all of the

people of the earth into the abominations that she is guilty of herself. Both books, Jeremiah and The Revelation insist that the people of God come out of Babylon so as not to be partakers of her sins. No doubt the reference to coming out of Babylon is to a physical departure as well as a spiritual departure from Babylon.

Rv 17:1-6,15-18 *And there came one of the seven angels which had the seven vials, and talked with me, saying unto me, Come hither; I will shew unto thee the judgment of the great whore that sitteth upon many waters: 2 With whom the kings of the earth have committed fornication, and the inhabitants of the earth have been made drunk with the wine of her fornication. 3 So he carried me away in the spirit into the wilderness: and I saw a woman sit upon a scarlet coloured beast, full of names of blasphemy, having seven heads and ten horns. 4 And the woman was arrayed in purple and scarlet colour, and decked with gold and precious stones and pearls, having a golden cup in her hand full of abominations and filthiness of her fornication: 5 And upon her forehead was a name written, MYSTERY, BABYLON THE GREAT, THE MOTHER OF HARLOTS AND ABOMINATIONS OF THE EARTH. 6 And I saw the woman drunken with the blood of the saints, and with the blood of the martyrs of Jesus: ... 15 And he saith unto me, The waters which thou sawest, where the whore sitteth, are peoples, and multitudes, and nations, and tongues. 16 And the ten horns which thou sawest upon the beast, these shall hate the whore, and shall make her desolate and naked, and shall eat her flesh, and burn her with fire. 17 For God hath put in their hearts to fulfil his will, and to agree, and give their kingdom unto the beast, until the words of God shall be fulfilled. 18 And the woman which thou sawest is that great city, which reigneth over the kings of the earth.*

Babylon the Great: Commercial Babylon's complete destruction:

The complete destruction of Babylon is told in Rv 18. All 24 verses refer to the sudden (in one hour) and total destruction of this ancient and great city. In past ages this city has been brought near to destruction but, never to the total destruction that the prophets have spoken of. Presently very little is left of Babylon. But, very nearby the ancient ruins of Babylon there is a large city by the name of Al Hillah, population in 2020 is near 455,000 and growing. All it would take would be a name change and Babylon would be in existence again as a large city ready to take part in the last days, ready to be destroyed never to exist again forever.

Rv 18:1-3,8-13,17,20-24   *And after these things I saw another angel come down from heaven, having great power; and the earth was lightened with his glory. 2 And he cried mightily with a strong voice, saying, Babylon the great is fallen, is fallen, and is become the habitation of devils, and the hold of every foul spirit, and a cage of every unclean and hateful bird. 3 For all nations have drunk of the wine of the wrath of her fornication, and the kings of the earth have* committed fornication with her, and the merchants of the earth are waxed rich through the abundance of her delicacies. ... 8 Therefore shall her plagues come in one day, death, and mourning, and famine; and she shall be utterly burned with fire: for strong is the Lord God who judgeth her. 9 And the kings of the earth, who have committed fornication and lived deliciously with her, shall bewail her, and lament for her, when they shall see the smoke of her burning, 10 Standing afar off for the fear of her torment, saying, Alas, alas, that great city Babylon, that mighty city! for in one hour is thy judgment come. 11 And the merchants of the earth shall weep and mourn over her; for no man buyeth their merchandise any more: 12 The merchandise of gold, and silver, and precious stones, and of pearls, and fine linen, and purple, and silk, and scarlet, and all thyine wood, and all manner vessels of ivory, and all manner vessels of most precious wood, and of brass, and iron, and marble, 13 And cinnamon, and odours, and ointments, and frankincense, and wine, and oil, and fine flour, and wheat, and beasts, and sheep, and horses, and chariots, and slaves, and souls of men. ... 17 For in one hour so great riches is come to nought. ... for in one hour is she made desolate. 20 Rejoice over her, thou heaven, and ye holy apostles and prophets; for God hath avenged you on her. 21 And a mighty angel took up a stone like a great millstone, and cast it into the sea, saying, Thus with violence shall that great city Babylon be thrown down, and shall be found no more at all. 22 And the voice of harpers, and musicians, and of *pipers, and trumpeters, shall be heard no more at all in thee; and no craftsman, of whatsoever craft he be, shall be found any more in thee; and the sound of a millstone shall be heard no more at all in thee; 23 And the light of a candle shall shine no more at all in thee; and the voice of the bridegroom and of the bride shall be heard no more at all in thee: for thy merchants were the great men of the earth; for by thy sorceries were all nations deceived. 24 And in her was found the blood of prophets, and of saints, and of all that were slain upon the earth.*

Rv 18:4   *And I heard another voice from heaven, saying, Come out of her, my people, that ye be not partakers of her sins, and that ye receive not of her plagues. 5 For her sins have reached unto heaven, and God hath remembered her iniquities.*

As Jesus himself said:

Lk 21:34   *And take heed to yourselves, lest at any time your hearts be overcharged with surfeiting, and drunkenness, and cares of this life, and so that day come upon you unawares. 35 For as a snare shall it come on all them that dwell on the face of the whole earth. 36 Watch ye therefore, and pray always, that ye may be accounted worthy to escape all these things that shall come to pass, and to stand before the Son of man.*

Nearing the end of the Tribulation and having seen the destruction of Babylon we go now to look closely at the Second Coming of Jesus.

Notes:

1. Joseph R. Chambers, A Palace for the Antichrist (Green Forest, AR: New Leaf Press, 1996), p. 33-34.
2. Ibid., p. 68.
3. Ibid., p. 146.

11

The Second Coming of Jesus

There are many scriptural references to the Lord's Second Coming:

The Second Coming occurs in two phases: first, the Rapture followed by the Tribulation; then the second phase, the actual Second Coming. In the Rapture, Jesus leaves heaven, comes down to the clouds and calls us up to Him on the cloud, then we all ascend back into heaven with Him; Jn 14:3 "that where I am, there ye may be also." The Rapture is a very brief event and unseen by the world; the world will only know that something with tremendous effects has happened, because millions around the world have suddenly gone missing. There will be unexplained auto and airplane accidents, with many other kinds of mysteries. There will be a lot of people who claim to be Christians who are aware that the Rapture is coming, but they are not living in readiness and they will miss the Rapture. Many of these will very shortly realize the Rapture has occurred, and they will alert the world to what happened while making their hearts right and getting ready for the seven horrible years of the Tribulation. At the close of the unimaginable years of terror, the Lord returns in the second phase of the Second Coming. In this event, He comes to judge, to reward, to reign over the whole earth in His Millennial Reign, then continuing on in the new heaven and earth forever.

Jesus will come back for us:

There is no maybe, nor perhaps, nor if; among other witnesses, Jesus himself testified over and over that He would return.

Jn 14:2-3   *In my Father's house are many mansions: if it were not so, I would have told you. I go to prepare a place for you. 3 And if I go and prepare a place for you, I will come again, and receive you unto myself; that where I am, there ye may be also.*

Mt 25:31   *When the Son of man shall come in his glory, and all the holy angels with him, then shall he sit upon the throne of his glory:*

Mt 26:64   *Jesus saith unto him, Thou hast said: nevertheless I say unto you, Hereafter shall ye see the Son of man sitting on the right hand of power, and coming in the clouds of heaven.*

Mk 14:62   *And Jesus said, I am: and ye shall see the Son of man sitting on the right hand of power, and coming in the clouds of heaven.*

Lk 21:25-28   *And there shall be signs in the sun, and in the moon, and in the stars; and upon the earth distress of nations, with perplexity; the sea and the waves roaring; 26 Men's hearts failing them for fear, and for looking after those things which are coming on the earth: for the powers of heaven shall be shaken. 27 And then shall they see the Son of man coming in a cloud with power* and great glory. 28 And when these things begin to come to pass, then look up, and lift up your heads; for your redemption draweth nigh.

First the Rapture when He comes to save us from the wrath to come:

Rv 3:10 *Because thou hast kept the word of my patience, I also will keep thee from the hour of temptation, which shall come upon all the world, to try them that dwell upon the earth.*

1 Th 1:9-10 *For they themselves shew of us what manner of entering in we had unto you, and how ye turned to God from idols to serve the living and true God; 10 And to wait for his Son from heaven, whom he raised from the dead, even Jesus, which delivered us from the wrath to come.*

1 Co 15:51-52 *Behold, I shew you a mystery; We shall not all sleep, but we shall all be changed, 52 In a moment, in the twinkling of an eye, at the last trump: for the trumpet shall sound, and the dead shall be raised incorruptible, and we shall be changed.*

Then the Tribulation:

Both Mark and Matthew testify to the fact that all of humanity would be destroyed if the Tribulation were not shortened, but for His elect's sake He will shorten the days.

Mk 13:19-20 *For in those days shall be affliction, such as was not from the beginning of the creation which God created unto this time, neither shall be. 20 And except that the Lord had shortened those days, no flesh should be saved:*

but for the elect's sake, whom he hath chosen, he hath shortened the days.

Mt 24:21-22 *For then shall be great tribulation, such as was not since the beginning of the world to this time, no, nor ever shall be. 22 And except those days should be shortened, there should no flesh be saved: but for the elect's sake those days shall be shortened.*

Then the Second Coming, to end the Tribulation:

In the actual Second Coming, second phase, He will come bodily, personally, and visibly to the whole world. Earth's entire population will go into wailing because they see that he has come to bring extreme measures of judgment against sin and evil.

Ac 1:9-11 *And when he had spoken these things, while they beheld, he was taken up; and a cloud received him out of their sight. 10 And while they looked stedfastly toward heaven as he went up, behold, two men stood by them in white apparel; 11 Which also said, Ye men of Galilee, why stand ye gazing up into heaven? this same Jesus, which is taken up from you into heaven, shall so come in like manner as ye have seen him go into heaven.*

Rv 1:7 *Behold, he cometh with clouds; and every eye shall see him, and they also which pierced him: and all kindreds of the earth shall wail because of him. Even so, Amen.*

In three of the Gospels, Mt 24, Mk 13, and Lk 21, Jesus gives considerable attention to His return:

Jesus first mentioned that the temple would be destroyed, and that happened 40 years later in AD 70, when the Romans destroyed the temple and Jerusalem as well, and according to Josephus perhaps a million people were slain. Jesus continues by talking about last days events, saying be careful not to be deceived. He warned of wars, famines, pestilences, and earthquakes. This is only the beginning; the love for God, of many, will grow cold; the gospel will be preached in all the world, then comes the end. Jesus does not here appear to directly address the Rapture, the first phase of His Second coming, but He encourages us that all who endure to the end will be saved. He then addresses the Great Tribulation and His actual Second Coming, and final warnings again for us to be careful to not be deceived and to live in readiness and watchfulness for His coming. Mark and Luke record much the same as Matthew.

Mt 24:3–30 ... *the disciples came unto him privately, saying, Tell us, when shall these things be? and what shall be the sign of thy coming, and of the end of the world? 4 And Jesus answered and said unto them, Take heed that no man deceive you. 5 For many shall come in my name, saying, I am Christ; and shall deceive many. 6 And ye shall hear of wars and rumours of wars: see that ye be not troubled: for all these things must come to pass, but the end is not yet. 7 For nation shall rise against nation, and kingdom against kingdom: and there shall be famines, and pestilences, and earthquakes, in divers places. 8 All these are the beginning of sorrows. 9 Then shall they deliver you up to be afflicted, and shall kill you: and ye shall be hated of all nations for my name's sake. 10 And then shall many be offended, and shall betray one another, and shall hate one another. 11 And many false prophets shall rise, and shall deceive many. 12 And because iniquity shall abound, the love of many shall wax cold. 13 But he that shall endure unto the end, the same shall be saved. 14 And this gospel of the kingdom shall be preached in all the world for a witness unto all nations; and then shall the end come. 15 When ye therefore shall see the abomination of desolation, spoken of by Daniel the prophet, stand in the holy place, (whoso readeth, let him understand) 16 Then let them which be in Judaea flee into the mountains: 17 Let him which is on the housetop not come down to take any thing out of his house: 18 Neither let him which is in the field return back to take his clothes. 19 And woe unto them that are with child, and to them that give suck in those days! 20 But pray ye that your flight be not in the winter, neither on the sabbath day: 21 For then shall be great tribulation, such as was not since the beginning of the world to this time, no, nor ever shall be.22 And except those days should be shortened, there should no flesh be saved: but for the elect's sake those days shall be shortened. 23 Then if any man shall say unto you, Lo, here is Christ, or there; believe it not. 24 For there shall arise false Christs, and false prophets, and shall shew great signs and wonders; insomuch that, if it were possible, they shall deceive the very elect. 25 Behold, I have told you before. 26 Wherefore if they shall say unto you, Behold, he is in the desert; go not forth: behold, he is in the secret chambers; believe it not. 27 For as the lightning cometh out of the east, and shineth even unto the west; so shall also the coming of the Son of man be. 28 For wheresoever the carcase is, there will the eagles be gathered together. 29 Immediately after the tribulation of those days shall the sun be darkened, and the moon shall not give her light, and the stars shall fall from heaven, and the powers of the heavens shall be shaken: 30 And then shall appear the sign of the Son of man in heaven: and then shall all the tribes of the earth mourn, and they shall see the Son of man coming in the clouds of heaven with power and great glory.*

He will come to execute judgment upon sin and evil:

It is clear from all of the scripture that addresses this question concerning these judgments, that God is a very angry God. Even so, God does all that He does in righteous judgment.

Jude 1:14-15 *And Enoch also, the seventh from Adam, prophesied of these, saying, Behold, the Lord cometh with ten thousands of his saints, 15 To execute judgment upon all, and to convince all that are ungodly among them of all their ungodly deeds which they have ungodly committed, and of all their hard speeches which ungodly sinners have spoken against him.*

Mt 13:41-43 *... so shall it be in the end of this world. 41 The Son of man shall send forth his angels, and they shall gather out of his kingdom all things that offend, and them which do iniquity; 42 And shall cast them into a furnace of fire: there shall be wailing and gnashing of teeth. 43 Then shall the righteous shine forth as the sun in the kingdom of their Father.*

2 Pe 3:1-7 *This second epistle, beloved, I now write unto you; in both which I stir up your pure minds by way of remembrance: 2 That ye may be mindful of the words which were spoken before by the holy prophets, and of the commandment of us the apostles of the Lord and Saviour: 3 Knowing this first, that there shall come in the last days scoffers, walking after their own lusts, 4 And saying, Where is the promise of his coming? for since the fathers fell asleep, all things continue as they were from the beginning of the creation. 5 For this they willingly are ignorant of, that by the word of God the heavens were of old, and the earth standing out of the water and in the water: 6 Whereby the world that then was, being overflowed with water, perished: 7 But the heavens and the earth, which are now, by the same word are kept in store, reserved unto fire against the day of judgment and perdition of ungodly men.*

He comes to judge the Antichrist and his False Prophet and to make war:

In allowing the Antichrist and his False Prophet to come to earth and do all of the evil that they do, God is bringing judgment against all of the sin and evil of all ages. Then, in turn, the Lord will bring judgment on the Antichrist and his False Prophet and ultimately on Satan, the instigator of all of this evil.

2 Th 2:8 *And then shall that Wicked be revealed, whom the Lord shall consume with the spirit of his mouth, and shall destroy with the brightness of his coming: ...*

Rv 19:11-21 *And I saw heaven opened, and behold a white horse; and he that sat upon him was called Faithful and True, and in righteousness he doth judge and make war. 12 His eyes were as a flame of fire, and on his head were many crowns; and he had a name written, that no man knew, but he himself. 13 And he was clothed with a vesture dipped in blood: and his name is called The Word of God. 14 And the armies which were in heaven followed him upon white horses, clothed in fine linen, white and clean. 15 And out of his mouth goeth a sharp sword, that with it he should smite the nations: and he shall rule them with a rod of iron: and he treadeth the winepress of the fierceness and wrath of Almighty God. 16 And he hath on his vesture and on his thigh a name written, KING OF KINGS, AND LORD OF LORDS. 17 And I saw an angel standing in the sun; and he cried with a loud voice, saying to all the fowls that fly in the midst of heaven, Come and gather yourselves together unto the supper of the great God; 18 That ye may eat the flesh of kings, and the flesh of captains, and the flesh of mighty men, and the flesh of horses, and of them that sit on them, and the flesh of all men, both free and bond, both small and great. 19 And I saw the beast, and the kings of the earth, and their armies, gathered together to make war against him that sat on the horse, and against his army. 20 And the beast was taken, and with him the false prophet that wrought miracles before him, with which he deceived them that had received the mark of the beast, and them that worshipped his image. These both were cast alive into a lake of fire burning with brimstone. 21 And the remnant were slain with the sword of him that sat upon the horse, which sword proceeded out of his mouth: and all the fowls were filled with their flesh.*

He comes to put Satan in chains:

The book of Job tells how the devil viciously attacked Job in an effort to get Job to turn against God. He has done the same things, to some degree, with every person who has ever lived. God in His righteousness is going to put a stop to this in Jesus' Second Coming.

Rv 20:1-3   *And I saw an angel come down from heaven, having the key of the bottomless pit and a great chain in his hand. 2 And he laid hold on the dragon, that old serpent, which is the Devil, and Satan, and bound him a thousand years, 3 And cast him into the bottomless pit, and shut him up, and set a seal upon him, that he should deceive the nations no more, till the thousand years should be fulfilled: and after that he must be loosed a little season.*

He comes to cast the devil into the lake of fire and brimstone:

The devil has one last fling: it is a thousand years after the Second Coming, but it is his last effort. The devil is cast into hell and tormented forever and ever.

Rv 20:7-10   *And when the thousand years are expired, Satan shall be loosed out of his prison, 8 And shall go out to deceive the nations which are in the four quarters of the earth, Gog and Magog, to gather them together to battle: the number of whom is as the sand of the sea. 9 And they went up on the breadth of the earth, and compassed the camp of the saints about, and the beloved city: and fire came down from God out of heaven, and devoured them. 10 And the devil that deceived them was cast into the lake of fire and brimstone, where the beast and the false prophet are, and shall be tormented day and night for ever and ever.*

Satan was once a great and glorious being in heaven, created in holiness to serve God with a freewill, to choose to serve God or not. He chose to rebel against God and has never looked back. Isaiah spoke of this great moment when Satan will meet his doom.

Isa 14:9-12   *Hell from beneath is moved for thee to meet thee at thy coming: it stirreth up the dead for thee, even all the chief ones of the earth; it hath raised up from their thrones all the kings of the nations 10 All they shall speak and say unto thee, Art thou also become weak as we? art thou become like unto us? 11 Thy pomp is brought down to the grave, and the noise of thy viols: the worm*

is spread under thee, and the worms cover thee.
12 How art thou fallen from heaven, O Lucifer, son
of the morning!

Jesus comes to reward the faithful:

Even though the Lord judges the wicked, He does so in righteousness, and it is a blessing to His people. A greater blessing is when the Lord comes to reward His people for their godly works.

Rv 22:7,12,20   *Behold, I come quickly: blessed is he that keepeth the sayings of the prophecy this book. ... 12 And, behold, I come quickly; and my reward is with me, to give every man according as his work shall be. ... 20 He which testifieth these things saith, Surely I come quickly.*

Mt 16:27   *For the Son of man shall come in the glory of his Father with his angels; and then he shall reward every man according to his works.*

He will come to bring joy to His saints:

1 Pe 4:12-13   *Beloved, think it not strange concerning the fiery trial which is to try you, as though some strange thing happened unto you: 13 But rejoice, inasmuch as ye are partakers of Christ's sufferings; that, when his glory shall be revealed, ye may be glad also with exceeding joy.*

He is coming to bring in everlasting righteousness:

Holiness, joy, peace, and righteousness are what the millennial reign of Christ will be made up of. When this present dispensation is over, the Rapture has occurred, the Tribulation has come and gone, and the Lord has judged all of his enemies, then the Lord sets up his kingdom that lasts forever. That kingdom, the Millennial kingdom, will be unlike any other kingdom on earth. With Satan in chains and no longer able to harass anyone, peace will reign everywhere. Even the animals will be at peace with each other. All that is good will be restored, righteousness undisturbed for a thousand years. In actual fact, it will go on forever.

Da 9:24 *Seventy weeks are determined upon thy people and upon thy holy city, to finish the transgression, and to make an end of sins, and to make reconciliation for iniquity, and to bring in everlasting righteousness, and to seal up the vision and prophecy, and to anoint the most Holy.*

1 Th 3:13 *To the end he may stablish your hearts unblameable in holiness before God, even our Father, at the coming of our Lord Jesus Christ with all his saints.*

Jesus will come for the restitution of all things:

Ac 3:20-21 *And he shall send Jesus Christ, which before was preached unto you: 21 Whom the heaven must receive until the times of restitution of all things, which God hath spoken by the mouth of all his holy prophets since the world began.*

God sets up a kingdom that lasts forever:

As far back as Daniel's time in Babylon, near 600 BC, king Nebuchadnezzar dreamed and could not remember the dream. God showed Daniel the dream and gave him the meaning, which was that eventually God would set up a kingdom that would last forever and it would destroy the other kingdoms in Nebuchadnezzar's dream. This will take place at the end of the Tribulation when the Second Coming occurs. Jesus will come and establish a kingdom that will last forever, and we will work with Him as kings and priests.

Da 2:44-45   *And in the days of these kings shall the God of heaven set up a kingdom, which shall never be destroyed: and the kingdom shall not be left to other people, but it shall break in pieces and consume all these kingdoms, and it shall stand for ever. 45 Forasmuch as thou sawest that the stone was cut out of the mountain without hands, and that it brake in pieces the iron, the brass, the clay, the silver, and the gold; the great God hath made known to the king what shall come to pass hereafter: and the dream is certain, and the interpretation thereof sure.*

Da 7:9-14   *I beheld till the thrones were cast down, and the Ancient of days did sit, whose garment was white as snow, and the hair of his head like the pure wool: his throne was like the fiery flame, and his wheels as burning fire. 10 A fiery stream issued and came forth from before him: thousand thousands ministered unto him, and ten thousand times ten thousand stood before him: the judgment was set, and the books were opened. 11 I beheld then because of the voice of the great words which the horn spake: I beheld even till the beast was slain, and his body destroyed, and given to the burning flame. 12 As concerning the rest of the beasts, they had their dominion taken away: yet their lives were prolonged for a season and time. 13 I saw in the night visions, and, behold, one like the Son of man came with the clouds of heaven, and came to the Ancient of days, and they brought him near before him. 14 And there was given him dominion, and glory, and a kingdom, that all people, nations, and languages, should serve him: his dominion is an everlasting dominion, which shall not pass away, and his kingdom that which shall not be destroyed.*

The Lord Jesus Christ shall be king over all the earth forever:

Late in the Tribulation, Jerusalem is under siege; all the nations of the world are gathered to destroy Israel. This is when Jesus returns; this is when the battle of Armageddon takes place and blood flows to the depth of the horse's bridle for two hundred miles. At some point He touches down on the Mount of Olives, the same place from which He ascended to heaven; the mountain splits and fills up the valley. Jesus then walks across and enters Jerusalem through the eastern gate as King of all the earth during the Millennium and beyond that, to the new heaven and earth as King of Kings forever.

Zec 14:1-15   *Behold, the day of the LORD cometh, and thy spoil shall be divided in the midst of thee. 2 For I will gather all nations against Jerusalem to battle; and the city shall be taken, and the houses rifled, and the women ravished; and half of the city shall go forth into captivity, and* the residue of the people shall not be cut off from the city. 3 Then shall the LORD go forth, and fight against those nations, as when he fought in the day of battle. 4 And his feet shall stand in that day upon the mount of Olives, which is before Jerusalem on the east, and the mount of Olives shall cleave in the midst thereof toward the east and toward the west, and there shall be a very great valley; and half of the mountain shall remove toward the north, and half of it toward the south. ... and the LORD my God shall come, and all the saints with thee. ... 8 And it shall be in that day, that living waters shall go out from Jerusalem; half of them toward the former sea, and half of them toward the hinder sea: in summer and in winter shall it be. 9 And the LORD shall be king over all the earth: in that day shall there be one LORD, and his name one. ... 11 And men shall dwell in it, and there shall be no more utter destruction; but Jerusalem shall be safely inhabited. 12 And this shall be the plague wherewith the LORD will smite all the people that have fought against Jerusalem; Their flesh shall consume away while they stand upon their feet, and their eyes shall consume away in their holes, and their tongue shall consume away in their mouth. ... 14 And Judah also shall fight at Jerusalem; and the wealth of all the heathen round about shall be gathered together, gold, and silver, and apparel, in great abundance. 15 And so shall be the plague of the horse, of the mule, of the camel, and of the ass, and of all the beasts that shall be in these tents, as this plague.

Jesus' reign over the whole earth is forever:

All of this scripture, God's word, shows us clearly that He is setting up an eternal righteous and peaceful kingdom with Jesus as King of Kings. The Millennial reign, one thousand years, is only the beginning. Then comes the Great White Throne Judgment, the judgment of the ungodly. Then, Rv 21:1-3 tells us that God will create a new heaven and a new earth, and that God Himself will dwell with them and be their God and they will be His people, and all of this forever.

Rv 21:1-3   *And I saw a new heaven and a new earth: for the first heaven and the first earth were passed away; and there was no more sea. 2 And I John saw the holy city, new Jerusalem, coming down from God out of heaven, prepared as a bride adorned for her husband. 3 And I heard a great voice out of heaven saying, Behold, the tabernacle of God is with men, and he will dwell with them, and they shall be his people, and God himself shall be with them, and be their God.*

Rv 21 says, in the new heaven and earth that God Himself will be their God, and that does not demand a change. As Daniel and Peter both state, Jesus will go on forever being the King of Kings and Lord of Lords. God the Father appoints Jesus the Son as King of Kings; His kingdom is forever.

Da 7:13-14   *I saw in the night visions, and, behold, one like the Son of man came with the clouds of heaven, and came to the Ancient of days, and they brought him near before him. 14 And there was given him dominion, and glory, and a kingdom, that all people, nations, and languages, should serve him: his dominion is an everlasting dominion, which shall not pass away, and his kingdom that which shall not be destroyed.*

2 Pe 1:10-11   *Wherefore the rather, brethren, give diligence to make your calling and election sure: for if ye do these things, ye shall never fall: 11 For so an entrance shall be ministered unto you abundantly into the everlasting kingdom of our Lord and Saviour Jesus Christ.*

How should we live while we wait for the coming of Jesus:

2 Th 3:5   *And the Lord direct your hearts into the love of God, and into the patient waiting for Christ.*

1 Th 5:23   *And the very God of peace sanctify you wholly; and I pray God your whole spirit and soul and body be preserved blameless unto the coming of our Lord Jesus Christ.*

Jas 5:7   *Be patient therefore, brethren, unto the coming of the Lord. Behold, the husbandman waiteth for the precious fruit of the earth, and hath long patience for it, until he receive the early and latter rain.*

Php 4:5   *Let your moderation be known unto all men. The Lord is at hand.*

Mt 24:42   *Watch therefore: for ye know not what hour your Lord doth come.*

1 Co 1:7   *So that ye come behind in no gift; waiting for the coming of our Lord Jesus Christ:*

Php 3:20   For our conversation is in heaven; from whence also we look for the Saviour, the Lord Jesus Christ:

Tit 2:11-13   For the grace of God that bringeth salvation hath appeared to all men, 12 Teaching us that, denying ungodliness and worldly lusts, we should live soberly, righteously, and godly, in this present world; 13 Looking for that blessed hope, and the glorious appearing of the great God and our Saviour Jesus Christ;

Mk 8:38   Whosoever therefore shall be ashamed of me and of my words in this adulterous and sinful generation; of him also shall the Son of man be ashamed, when he cometh in the glory of his Father with the holy angels.

Da 12:1-3   And at that time shall Michael stand up, the great prince which standeth for the children of thy people: and there shall be a time of trouble, such as never was since there was a nation even to that same time: and at that time thy people shall be delivered, every one that shall be found written in the book. 2 And many of them that sleep in the dust of the earth shall awake, some to everlasting life, and some to shame and everlasting contempt. 3 And they that be wise shall shine as the brightness of the firmament; and they that turn many to righteousness as the stars for ever and ever.

Mk 13:32-37   But of that day and that hour knoweth no man, no, not the angels which are in heaven, neither the Son, but the Father. 33 Take ye heed, watch and pray: for ye know not when the time is. 34 For the Son of man is as a man taking a *far journey, who left his house, and gave authority to his servants, and to every man his work, and commanded the porter to watch. 35 Watch ye therefore: for ye know not when the master of the house cometh, at even, or at midnight, or at the cockcrowing, or in the morning: 36 Lest coming suddenly he find you sleeping. 37 And what I say unto you I say unto all, Watch.*

How to prepare for His coming:

A key to preparation for His coming is an awareness of the times, as well as an unwavering desire for Him to come and bring all of this to pass. While we are in this world let us not be drawn away from our love for the Lord.

1 Th 5:1-23   *But of the times and the seasons, brethren, ye have no need that I write unto you. 2 For yourselves know perfectly that the day of the Lord so cometh as a thief in the night. 3 For when they shall say, Peace and safety; then sudden destruction cometh upon them, as travail upon a woman with child; and they shall not escape. 4 But ye, brethren, are not in darkness, that that day should overtake you as a thief. 5 Ye are all the children of light, and the children of the day: we are not of the night, nor of darkness. 6 Therefore let us not sleep, as do others; but let us watch and be sober. 7 For they that sleep sleep in the night; and they that be drunken are drunken in the night. 8 But let us, who are of the day, be sober, putting on the breastplate of faith and love; and for an helmet, the hope of salvation. 9 For God hath not appointed us to wrath, but to obtain*

salvation by our Lord Jesus Christ, 10 Who died for us, that, whether we wake or sleep, we should live together with him. 11 Wherefore comfort yourselves together, and edify one another, even as also ye do. 12 And we beseech you, brethren, to know them which labour among you, and are over you in the Lord, and admonish you; 13 And to esteem them very highly in love for their work's sake. And be at peace among yourselves. 14 Now we exhort you, brethren, warn them that are unruly, comfort the feebleminded, support the weak, be patient toward all men. 15 See that none render evil for evil unto any man; but ever follow that which is good, both among yourselves, and to all men. 16 Rejoice evermore. 17 Pray without ceasing. 18 In every thing give thanks: for this is the will of God in Christ Jesus concerning you. 19 Quench not the Spirit. 20 Despise not prophesyings. 21 Prove all things; hold fast that which is good. 22 Abstain from all appearance of evil. 23 And the very God of peace sanctify you wholly; and I pray God your whole spirit and soul and body be preserved blameless unto the coming of our Lord Jesus Christ.

2 Pet 3:11-14   Seeing then that all these things shall be dissolved, what manner of persons ought ye to be in all holy conversation and godliness, 12 Looking for and hasting unto the coming of the day of God, wherein the heavens being on fire shall be dissolved, and the elements shall melt with fervent heat? 13 Nevertheless we, according to his promise, look for new heavens and a new earth, wherein dwelleth righteousness. 14

Wherefore, beloved, seeing that ye look for such things, be diligent that ye may be found of him in peace, without spot, and blameless.

The Lord's Second Coming has occurred and brought an end to the Tribulation and now comes His Millennial Reign over the earth.

12

The Millennial Reign
of Christ

The stone that smote the image became a great mountain:

2600 years ago, Nebuchadnezzar, king of Babylon, had a dream of a great image. Daniel gave an interpretation of that dream; the image represented four great kingdoms and a ten-nation federation through history. In the last days of these kings, God will set up a kingdom that will last forever. Jesus Christ is that stone that will strike the image and will become that kingdom that will last forever. That kingdom begins with the Millennial kingdom, then continues in the new heaven and earth forever.

Da 2:34-35   *Thou sawest till that a stone was cut out without hands, which smote the image upon his feet that were of iron and clay, and brake them to pieces. 35 Then was the iron, the clay, the brass, the silver, and the gold, broken to pieces together, and became like the chaff of the summer threshing floors; and the wind carried them away, that no place was found for them: and the stone that smote the image became a great mountain, and filled the whole earth.*

The day will come when the Tribulation is over, the Millennial Kingdom has begun, the stone has become a mountain. The Kingdom of God will last forever, beginning with the thousand years of peace. The Antichrist and False Prophet are cast into the lake of fire; Satan is bound in the bottomless pit. Jesus Christ is King of Kings and Lord of Lords, and we are kings and priests and will reign on the earth with Jesus.

Satan Bound 1000 Years, during the Millennial reign:

Rv 20:1-3 *And I saw an angel come down from heaven, having the key of the bottomless pit and a great chain in his hand. 2 And he laid hold on the dragon, that old serpent, which is the Devil, and Satan, and bound him a thousand years, 3 And cast him into the bottomless pit, and shut him up, and set a seal upon him, that he should deceive the nations no more, till the thousand years should be fulfilled: and after that he must be loosed a little season.*

The prophets tell us of the coming King:

Many of Isaiah's prophecies speak of the Millennial Kingdom. To get a better understanding of this kingdom, we need to look at some of Isaiah's prophecies, as well as those of some of the other prophets.

Ruler over Israel to come from Bethlehem:

Micah tells us that a ruler of Israel is to come out of Bethlehem. We normally associate Jesus' coming to Bethlehem as a babe with His ministry on earth and His dying on the cross. That is true, but Micah's prophecy looks further ahead and associates His coming from Bethlehem with His ruling over Israel, and for that matter over the whole world.

Mic 5:2   *But thou, Bethlehem Ephratah, though thou be little among the thousands of Judah, yet out of thee shall he come forth unto me that is to be ruler in Israel; whose goings forth have been from of old, from everlasting.*

Isaiah is in harmony with Micah and goes even further giving us names that Jesus, this King of Kings will be called: Wonderful, Counsellor, The mighty God, The everlasting Father, The Prince of Peace. Isaiah assures us again that Christ's kingdom is everlasting and worldwide.

Isa 9:6-7   *For unto us a child is born, unto us a son is given: and the government shall be upon his shoulder: and his name shall be called Wonderful, Counsellor, The mighty God, The everlasting Father, The Prince of Peace. 7 Of the increase of his government and peace there shall be no end, upon the throne of David, and upon his kingdom, to order it, and to establish it with judgment and with justice from henceforth even for ever. The zeal of the LORD of hosts will perform this.*

Isa 42:1-4   *Behold my servant, whom I uphold; mine elect, in whom my soul delighteth; I have put my spirit upon him: he shall bring forth judgment to the Gentiles. 2 He shall not cry, nor lift up, nor cause his voice to be heard in the street. 3 A bruised reed shall he not break, and the smoking flax shall he not quench: he shall bring forth judgment unto truth. 4 He shall not fail nor be discouraged, till he have set judgment in the earth: and the isles shall wait for his law.*

Reigning in righteousness:

Isaiah makes it clear that Jesus will rule with a rod of iron guided by faithfulness and righteousness:

Isa 11:1-5   *And there shall come forth a rod out of the stem of Jesse, and a Branch shall grow out of his roots: 2 And the spirit of the LORD shall rest upon him, the spirit of wisdom and understanding, the spirit of counsel and might, the spirit of knowledge and of the fear of the LORD; 3 And shall make him of quick understanding in the fear of the LORD: and he shall not judge after the sight of his eyes, neither reprove after the hearing of his ears: 4 But with righteousness shall he judge the poor, and reprove with equity for the meek of the earth: and he shall smite the earth with the rod of his mouth, and with the breath of his lips shall he slay the wicked. 5 And righteousness shall be the girdle of his loins, and faithfulness the girdle of his reins.*

Holiness unto the Lord:

Zechariah adds holiness to the nature of the Lord's reign and goes on to say that all of the nations and peoples that refuse to go up to Jerusalem to worship the Lord will receive no rain and will be smitten with a plague.

Zec 14:16-21   *And it shall come to pass, that every one that is left of all the nations which came against Jerusalem shall even go up from year to year to worship the King, the LORD of hosts, and to keep the feast of tabernacles. 17 And it shall be, that whoso will not come up of all the families of the earth unto Jerusalem to worship the King, the LORD of hosts, even upon them shall be no rain. 18 And if the family of Egypt go not up, and come not, that have no rain; there shall be the plague, wherewith the LORD will smite the heathen that come not up to keep the feast of tabernacles. 19 This shall be the punishment of Egypt, and the punishment of all nations that come not up to keep the feast of tabernacles. 20 In that day shall there be upon the bells of the horses, HOLINESS UNTO THE LORD; and the pots in the LORD's house shall be like the bowls before the altar. 21 Yea, every pot in Jerusalem and in Judah shall be holiness unto the LORD of hosts: and all they that sacrifice shall come and take of them, and seethe therein: and in that day there shall be no more the Canaanite in the house of the LORD of hosts.*

A great ingathering of Jews during Millennium:

Long ago when God brought the Israelites out of Egypt and in the centuries that followed, many of the Jews expressed disbelief in God by the lives that they lived. As a result, God scattered them into all of the nations of the world to bring them to repentance. They have remained scattered for all of those centuries until 1948 when Israel became a nation again. At that time the Jews began returning to their own land, but there are still many more of them that remain scattered than there are in the Land. Jeremiah and Isaiah both tell us that during the Millennium there will be a great ingathering of the Jews to their homeland, perhaps every Jew on earth will be brought home. Rom 11:26 says: "*so all Israel shall be saved:*"

Jer 31:1,31-34   *At the same time, saith the LORD, will I be the God of all the families of Israel, and they shall be my people. ... 31 Behold, the days come, saith the LORD, that I will make a new covenant with the house of Israel, and with the house of Judah: 32 Not according to the covenant that I made with their fathers in the day that I took them by the hand to bring them out of the land of Egypt; which my covenant they brake, although I was an husband unto them, saith the LORD: 33 But this shall be the covenant that I will make with the house of Israel; After those days, saith the LORD, I will put my law in their inward parts, and write it in their hearts; and will be their God, and they shall be my people. 34 And they shall teach no more every man his neighbour, and every man his* brother, saying, Know the LORD: for they shall all know me, from the least of them unto the greatest of them, saith the LORD; for I will forgive their iniquity, and I will remember their sin no more.

Isa 11:11-16   And it shall come to pass in that day, that the Lord shall set his hand again the second time to recover the remnant of his people, which shall be left, from Assyria, and from Egypt, and from Pathros, and from Cush, and from Elam, and from Shinar, and from Hamath, and from the islands of the sea. 12 And he shall set up an ensign for the nations, and shall assemble the outcasts of Israel, and gather together the dispersed of Judah from the four corners of the earth. 13 The envy also of Ephraim shall depart, and the adversaries of Judah shall be cut off: Ephraim shall not envy Judah, and Judah shall not vex Ephraim. 14 But they shall fly upon the shoulders of the Philistines toward the west; they shall spoil them of the east together: they shall lay their hand upon Edom and Moab; and the children of Ammon shall obey them. 15 And the LORD shall utterly destroy the tongue of the Egyptian sea; and with his mighty wind shall he shake his hand over the river, and shall smite it in the seven streams, and make men go over dryshod. 16 And there shall be an highway for the remnant of his people, which shall be left, from Assyria; like as it was to Israel in the day that he came up out of the land of Egypt.

Isa 14:1-4   For the LORD will have mercy on Jacob, and will yet choose Israel, and set them in their own land: and the strangers shall be joined with them, and they shall cleave to the house of

Jacob. 2 And the people shall take them, and bring them to their place: and the house of Israel shall possess them in the land of the LORD for servants and handmaids: and they shall take them captives, whose captives they were; and they shall rule over their oppressors. 3 And it shall come to pass in the day that the LORD shall give thee rest from thy sorrow, and from thy fear, and from the hard bondage wherein thou wast made to serve, 4 That thou shalt take up this proverb against the king of Babylon, and say, How hath the oppressor ceased! the golden city ceased!

Ro 11:12,15,26   *Now if the fall of them be the riches of the world, and the diminishing of them the riches of the Gentiles; how much more their fulness? ... 15 For if the casting away of them be the reconciling of the world, what shall the receiving of them be, but life from the dead? ... 26 And so all Israel shall be saved: as it is written, There shall come out of Sion the Deliverer, and shall turn away ungodliness from Jacob: ...*

Raptured Christians will come with Jesus to Millennium:

Jude 1:14-16   *And Enoch also, the seventh from Adam, prophesied of these, saying, Behold, the Lord cometh with ten thousands of his saints, 15 To execute judgment upon all, and to convince all that are ungodly among them of all their ungodly deeds which they have ungodly committed, and of all their hard speeches which ungodly sinners have spoken against him. 16 These are murmurers, complainers, walking after their* own lusts; and their mouth speaketh great swelling words, having men's persons in admiration because of advantage.

Faithful ones will help to govern:

Jesus told a parable of a nobleman who went on a journey; as he went, he gave his ten servants ten pounds and told them to put the money to work until he returns. When he came back, the first servant had gained ten pounds so he was put in charge of ten cities. The next servant had gained five pounds so he was put in charge of five cities. The next servant had laid his pound up in a napkin and had not gained anything; he was denounced as a wicked servant and his one pound was taken from him and given to the servant with ten pounds. Why would that be? Because, *"unto every one which hath shall be given; and from him that hath not, even that he hath shall be taken away from him."* So, we must remain occupied until He comes.

Lk 19:12-13,15-26   *He said therefore, A certain nobleman went into a far country to receive for himself a kingdom, and to return. 13 And he called his ten servants, and delivered them ten pounds, and said unto them, Occupy till I come. ... 15 And it came to pass, that when he was returned, having received the kingdom, then he commanded these servants to be called unto him, to whom he had given the money, that he might know how much every man had gained by trading. 16 Then came the first, saying, Lord, thy pound hath gained ten pounds. 17 And he said unto him,*

Well, thou good servant: because thou hast been faithful in a very little, have thou authority over ten cities. 18 And the second came, saying, Lord, thy pound hath gained five pounds. 19 And he said likewise to him, Be thou also over five cities. 20 And another came, saying, Lord, behold, here is thy pound, which I have kept laid up in a napkin: 21 For I feared thee, because thou art an austere man: thou takest up that thou layedst not down, and reapest that thou didst not sow. 22 And he saith unto him, Out of thine own mouth will I judge thee, thou wicked servant. Thou knewest that I was an austere man, taking up that I laid not down, and reaping that I did not sow: 23 Wherefore then gavest not thou my money into the bank, that at my coming I might have required mine own with usury? 24 And he said unto them that stood by, Take from him the pound, and give it to him that hath ten pounds. 25 (And they said unto him, Lord, he hath ten pounds.) 26 For I say unto you, That unto every one which hath shall be given; and from him that hath not, even that he hath shall be taken away from him.

Raptured bride to reign with Christ on the earth as kings and priests:

Rv 5:9-10   *And they sung a new song, saying, Thou art worthy to take the book, and to open the seals thereof: for thou wast slain, and hast redeemed us to God by thy blood out of every kindred, and tongue, and people, and nation; 10 And hast made us unto our God kings and priests: and we shall reign on the earth.*

The Saints will reign with Christ 1000 years, as can be seen in the following verses. The saints in this scripture location are all from the Tribulation who are beheaded by the authority of the Antichrist; they had refused his mark and refused to worship him. They, too, reign with Christ in the Millennial Kingdom.

Rv 20:4-6   *And I saw thrones, and they sat upon them, and judgment was given unto them: and I saw the souls of them that were beheaded for the witness of Jesus, and for the word of God, and which had not worshipped the beast, neither his image, neither had received his mark upon their foreheads, or in their hands; and they lived and reigned with Christ a thousand years. 5 But the rest of the dead lived not again until the thousand years were finished. This is the first resurrection. 6 Blessed and holy is he that hath part in the first resurrection: on such the second death hath no power, but they shall be priests of God and of Christ, and shall reign with him a thousand years.*

A kingdom of peace:

The kingdom is made up of peace, no more wars; the swords will be turned to plowshares, the desert will bloom as the rose, animals will be at peace with each other and with human beings. All is at rest.

Swords into plowshares:

Isa 2:1-4   *The word that Isaiah the son of Amoz saw concerning Judah and Jerusalem. 2 And it shall come to pass in the last days, that the* mountain of the LORD's house shall be established in the top of the mountains, and shall be exalted above the hills; and all nations shall flow unto it. 3 And many people shall go and say, Come ye, and let us go up to the mountain of the LORD, to the house of the God of Jacob; and he will teach us of his ways, and we will walk in his paths: for out of Zion shall go forth the law, and the word of the LORD from Jerusalem. 4 And he shall judge among the nations, and shall rebuke many people: and they shall beat their swords into plowshares, and their spears into pruninghooks: nation shall not lift up sword against nation, neither shall they learn war any more.

The desert shall blossom as the rose:

For most of the time that the Jews have been out of the land, much of the land has been a desert. During the Millennial reign, that desert will blossom as the rose. Equally as much the land will be known for peace and Holiness.

Isa 35:1-2,6-10   The wilderness and the wasteland shall be glad for them, and the desert shall rejoice and blossom as the rose; 2 It shall blossom abundantly and rejoice, even with joy and singing. The glory of Lebanon shall be given to it, the excellence of Carmel and Sharon. They shall see the glory of the LORD, The excellency of our God. ... 6 ... For waters shall burst forth in the wilderness, and streams in the desert. 7 The parched ground shall become a pool, and the thirsty land springs of water; in the habitation of jackals, where each lay, there shall be grass with reeds and rushes. 8 A highway shall be there, and a road, and it shall be called the Highway of Holiness. The unclean shall not pass over it, but it shall be for others. Whoever walks the road, although a fool, shall not go astray. 9 ... But the redeemed shall walk there, 10 and the ransomed of the LORD shall return, and come to Zion with singing, with everlasting joy on their heads. They shall obtain joy and gladness, and sorrow and sighing shall flee away.

All will be at peace including the beasts of the field:

During the Millennium all will be at peace including the animal kingdom. God's people will return to God, and He will receive Israel back as an unfaithful wife in righteousness, judgment, lovingkindness, and in mercies. "I will say to them which were not my people, Thou art my people; and they shall say, Thou art my God."

Hos 2:18-23   And in that day will I make a covenant for them with the beasts of the field, and with the fowls of heaven, and with the creeping things of the ground: and I will break the bow and the sword and the battle out of the earth, and will make them to lie down safely. 19 And I will betroth thee unto me for ever; yea, I will betroth thee unto me in righteousness, and in judgment, and in lovingkindness, and in mercies. 20 I will even betroth thee unto me in faithfulness: and thou shalt know the LORD. 21 And it shall come to pass in that day, I will hear, saith the LORD, I will hear the heavens, and they shall hear the earth; 22 And *the earth shall hear the corn, and the wine, and the oil; and they shall hear Jezreel. 23 And I will sow her unto me in the earth; and I will have mercy upon her that had not obtained mercy; and I will say to them which were not my people, Thou art my people; and they shall say, Thou art my God.*

Isa 11:6-10 The wolf also shall dwell with the lamb, and the leopard shall lie down with the kid; and the calf and the young lion and the fatling together; and a little child shall lead them. 7 And the cow and the bear shall feed; their young ones shall lie down together: and the lion shall eat straw like the ox. 8 And the sucking child shall play on the hole of the asp, and the weaned child shall put his hand on the cockatrice' den. 9 They shall not hurt nor destroy in all my holy mountain: for the earth shall be full of the knowledge of the LORD, as the waters cover the sea. 10 And in that day there shall be a root of Jesse, which shall stand for an ensign of the people; to it shall the Gentiles seek: and his rest shall be glorious.

People will live long and prosperous:

Isa 65:17-25 For, behold, I create new heavens and a new earth: and the former shall not be remembered, nor come into mind. 18 But be ye glad and rejoice for ever in that which I create: for, behold, I create Jerusalem a rejoicing, and her people a joy. 19 And I will rejoice in Jerusalem, and joy in my people: and the voice of weeping shall be no more heard in her, nor the voice of crying. 20 There shall be no more thence an infant of days, nor an old man that hath not filled his days: for the child shall die an hundred years old; but the sinner being an hundred years old shall be accursed. 21 And they shall build houses, and inhabit them; and they shall plant vineyards, and eat the fruit of them. 22 They shall not build, and another inhabit; they shall not plant, and another eat: for as the days of a tree are the days of my people, and mine elect shall long enjoy the work of their hands. 23 They shall not labour in vain, nor bring forth for trouble; for they are the seed of the blessed of the LORD, and their offspring with them. 24 And it shall come to pass, that before they call, I will answer; and while they are yet speaking, I will hear. 25 The wolf and the lamb shall feed together, and the lion shall eat straw like the bullock: and dust shall be the serpent's meat. They shall not hurt nor destroy in all my holy mountain, saith the LORD.

Satan set free; his rebellion is crushed at the end of the 1000 years:

When the Millennium is over, Satan will be released from the bottomless pit. He will go out and deceive the nations one last time. Millions of those born during the 1000 years of the millennium, who have never been tried and tested, will go for Satan's lies and will join him in surrounding "the camp" of the Christians to war against them, "and fire came down from God out of heaven, and devoured them." We can think of it as war, but it is really very one sided in the critical moment. Satan is cast into the fires of hell for eternity.

Rv 20:7-10   *And when the thousand years are expired, Satan shall be loosed out of his prison, 8 And shall go out to deceive the nations which are in the four quarters of the earth, Gog and Magog, to gather them together to battle: the number of whom is as the sand of the sea. 9 And they went up on the breadth of the earth, and compassed the camp of the saints about, and the beloved city: and fire came down from God out of heaven, and devoured them. 10 And the devil that deceived them was cast into the lake of fire and brimstone, where the beast and the false prophet are, and shall be tormented day and night for ever and ever.*

Now it is time for you to know that it is the season:

Just moments before Jesus ascended back into heaven, His apostles asked Him, "will you restore the kingdom to Israel at this time?" Jesus answered them, "It is not for you to know the times or the seasons." But after these two thousand years that have passed since then, we now know that the season is upon us.

Ac 1:6-8   *When they therefore were come together, they asked of him, saying, Lord, wilt thou at this time restore again the kingdom to Israel? 7 And he said unto them, It is not for you to know the times or the seasons, which the Father hath put in his own power. 8 But ye shall receive power, after that the Holy Ghost is come upon you: and ye shall be witnesses unto me both in Jerusalem, and in all Judaea, and in Samaria, and unto the uttermost part of the earth.*

Are you an overcomer?

Rv 2:26 *And he that overcometh, and keepeth my works unto the end, to him will I give power over the nations ...*

As the Millennial reign of Christ comes to an end the Great White Throne Judgment (judgment of sinners of all ages) is set.

13

The Righteous Judgments of Christ

God's word, has much to say about the judgment of sin and sinners:

In Lev 26:14-39, and Deut 28:15-68, the Lord talks about those who live in sin and rebellion against Him. The Lord's words in these two scripture locations were spoken directly to the nation of Israel 1400 years before the time of Christ, and they speak of punishment God will bring to sinners in this present world. We should listen, whether we be Jew or Gentile and not be too surprised to see the same sort of results in our time.

Doug Barton[1] said in a Facebook post, April 9, 2020: "... as I think of this Covid-19 virus I am convinced that it is a judgment of God, not just on America, but on the whole world. The prevalent sins in the USA are also prevalent sins north of the USA and south of the USA, as well as in Asia, Europe and the Middle East. My Old Testament professor at SNU, the late Dr. Malcom Shelton, used to remind us that "GOD'S JUDGMENTS ARE REDEMPTIVE IN PURPOSE." So, this judgment, this pandemic, is God's call to humanity to repent and turn to Him. The problem with the human race, from Genesis 3 through Revelation 22 has been its failure to repent. In chapters 2 and 3 of Revelation, the call to repent is given six times (2:5, 16, 21, 22; 3:3, 19). ... No one knows when Christ will return, but TODAY He is calling on all who are created in His image to repent because there will come the day when repentance will not be accepted!"

Two different judgments:

The Judgment Seat of Christ and the Great White Throne Judgment are two different judgments and for different purposes. The Judgment Seat of Christ is actually more for the giving of rewards for righteous works, while the Great White Throne Judgment is for unbelievers who failed, for whatever reasons, to repent, and will now face eternal separation from God.

Judgment Seat of Christ:

Mt 16:27   *For the Son of man shall come in the glory of his Father with his angels; and then he shall reward every man according to his works.*

Ro 14:10-12   *But why dost thou judge thy brother? or why dost thou set at nought thy brother? for we shall all stand before the judgment seat of Christ. 11 For it is written, As I live, saith the Lord, every knee shall bow to me, and every tongue shall confess to God. 12 So then every one of us shall give account of himself to God.*

2 Co 5:8-10   *We are confident, I say, and willing rather to be absent from the body, and to be present with the Lord. 9 Wherefore we labour, that,*

whether present or absent, we may be accepted of him. 10 For we must all appear before the judgment seat of Christ; that every one may receive the things done in his body, according to that he hath done, whether it be good or bad.

It goes without saying that Jesus Christ will be the judge at the Judgment Seat of Christ, which will occur in heaven, sometime after the Rapture, for faithful believers. Only truly born-again Christians will be there to give an account to God for actions done in fulfilling their calling and ministry. There will be no condemnation, only gain or loss of reward for actions done in their service to the Lord.

Jn 5:22,28-29   *For the Father judgeth no man, but hath committed all judgment unto the Son: ... 28 Marvel not at this: for the hour is coming, in the which all that are in the graves shall hear his voice, 29 And shall come forth; they that have done good, unto the resurrection of life; and they that have done evil, unto the resurrection of damnation.*

The following scripture helps us to understand part of what the Judgment Seat of Christ is about.

Jas 1:12   *Blessed is the man that endureth temptation: for when he is tried, he shall receive the crown of life, which the Lord hath promised to them that love him.*

1 Co 3:10-4:5 speaks of a number of things that help us to understand more about what the Christian person should expect at the Judgment seat of Christ. Notice specifically in verses 13-15,

which tell us that God will test our works to see if they are good or bad; if our works abide we will be rewarded, but if our works are burned, we will but suffer loss, yet we will be saved.

1 Cor 3:13-15 *Every man's work shall be made manifest: for the day shall declare it, because it shall be revealed by fire; and the fire shall try every man's work of what sort it is. 14 If any man's work abide which he hath built thereupon, he shall receive a reward. 15 If any man's work shall be burned, he shall suffer loss: but he himself shall be saved; yet so as by fire.*

This judgment has nothing to do with determining our salvation, that was made possible when Jesus died on the cross. Our salvation became effective when we repented and called on the Lord to be our Savior (See John 3:16, Rom 8:1, and 1 John 2:2). The Judgment Seat of Christ has to do with our faithfulness after repentance as we serve Christ. Have we been victorious over sin? (Rom 6:1-4); have we sought earnestly to fulfill the great commission? (Matt 28:18); have we been faithful? (1 Cor 9:4-27; 2 Tim 2:5); have we been careful with our words? (Jas 3:1-9). Beside any other rewards we might receive, we will receive crowns.

There will be crowns received:

In addition to all other rewards, believers will also receive crowns.

1 Co 9:24-25 *Know ye not that they which run in a race run all, but one receiveth the prize? So run, that ye may obtain. 25 And every man that*

striveth for the mastery is temperate in all things. Now they do it to obtain a corruptible crown; but we an incorruptible.

2 Ti 2:5   And if a man also strive for masteries, yet is he not crowned, except he strive lawfully.

There will be different crowns:

2 Ti 4:5-8   But watch thou in all things, endure afflictions, do the work of an evangelist, make full proof of thy ministry. 6 For I am now ready to be offered, and the time of my departure is at hand. 7 I have fought a good fight, I have finished my course, I have kept the faith: 8 Henceforth there is laid up for me a crown of righteousness, which the Lord, the righteous judge, shall give me at that day: and not to me only, but unto all them also that love his appearing.

1 Pe 5:4   And when the chief Shepherd shall appear, ye shall receive a crown of glory that fadeth not away.

Rv 2:10   Fear none of those things which thou shalt suffer: behold, the devil shall cast some of you into prison, that ye may be tried; and ye shall have tribulation ten days: be thou faithful unto death, and I will give thee a crown of life.

Judgment Seat of Christ, righteous receive rewards for their works:

In writing to Timothy, Paul encourages us to work hard for the Lord. Few will be able to measure up to Paul's standard, but the things mentioned here by Paul and others are the things we should strive for, and the unbelievable rewards which our works bring when our works are done as to the Lord.

Ro 8:1-6,16-18   *There is therefore now no condemnation to them which are in Christ Jesus, who walk not after the flesh, but after the Spirit. 2 For the law of the Spirit of life in Christ Jesus hath made me free from the law of sin and death. 3 For what the law could not do, in that it was weak through the flesh, God sending his own Son in the likeness of sinful flesh, and for sin, condemned sin in the flesh: 4 That the righteousness of the law might be fulfilled in us, who walk not after the flesh, but after the Spirit. 5 For they that are after the flesh do mind the things of the flesh; but they that are after the Spirit the things of the Spirit. 6 For to be carnally minded is death; but to be spiritually minded is life and peace. ... 16 The Spirit itself beareth witness with our spirit, that we are the children of God: 17 And if children, then heirs; heirs of God, and joint-heirs with Christ; if so be that we suffer with him, that we may be also glorified together. 18 For I reckon that the sufferings of this present time are not worthy to be compared with the glory which shall be revealed in us.*

1 Pe 5:2-3   *Feed the flock of God which is among you, taking the oversight thereof, not by constraint, but willingly; not for filthy lucre, but of a ready mind; 3 Neither as being lords over God's heritage, but being ensamples to the flock.*

Rv 2:10   *Fear none of those things which thou shalt suffer: behold, the devil shall cast some* of you into prison, that ye may be tried; and ye shall have tribulation ten days: be thou faithful unto death, and I will give thee a crown of life.

Rv 3:4-5,11-12   Thou hast a few names even in Sardis which have not defiled their garments; and they shall walk with me in white: for they are worthy. 5 He that overcometh, the same shall be clothed in white raiment; and I will not blot out his name out of the book of life, but I will confess his name before my Father, and before his angels. ... 11 Behold, I come quickly: hold that fast which thou hast, that no man take thy crown. 12 Him that overcometh will I make a pillar in the temple of my God, and he shall go no more out: and I will write upon him the name of my God, and the name of the city of my God, which is new Jerusalem, which cometh down out of heaven from my God: and I will write upon him my new name.

Rv 4:4   And round about the throne were four and twenty seats: and upon the seats I saw four and twenty elders sitting, clothed in white raiment; and they had on their heads crowns of gold.

Rv 22:12   And, behold, I come quickly; and my reward is with me, to give every man according as his work shall be.

Rv 6:9-11   I saw under the altar the souls of them that were slain for the word of God, and for the testimony which they held: 10 And they cried with a loud voice, saying, How long, O Lord, holy and true, dost thou not judge and avenge our blood on them that dwell on the earth? 11 And white robes were given unto every one of them;

and it was said unto them, that they should rest yet for a little season, until their fellowservants also and their brethren, that should be killed as they were, should be fulfilled.

Rv 7:13-17   And one of the elders answered, saying unto me, What are these which are arrayed in white robes? and whence came they? 14 And I said unto him, Sir, thou knowest. And he said to me, These are they which came out of great tribulation, and have washed their robes, and made them white in the blood of the Lamb. 15 Therefore are they before the throne of God, and serve him day and night in his temple: and he that sitteth on the throne shall dwell among them. 16 They shall hunger no more, neither thirst any more; neither shall the sun light on them, nor any heat. 17 For the Lamb which is in the midst of the throne shall feed them, and shall lead them unto living fountains of waters: and God shall wipe away all tears from their eyes.

Rv 21:2-4   And I John saw the holy city, new Jerusalem, coming down from God out of heaven, prepared as a bride adorned for her husband. 3 And I heard a great voice out of heaven saying, Behold, the tabernacle of God is with men, and he will dwell with them, and they shall be his people, and God himself shall be with them, and be their God. 4 And God shall wipe away all tears from their eyes; and there shall be no more death, neither sorrow, nor crying, neither shall there be any more pain: for the former things are passed away.

Rv 22:12   *And, behold, I come quickly; and my reward is with me, to give every man according as his work shall be.*

The day of the Lord GOD of hosts, a day of vengeance:

The word vengeance is mentioned in both Old and New Testaments and many times in direct relationship with God. The word carries the idea of judgment, punishment, and recompence.

Ro 12:19   *Dearly beloved, avenge not yourselves, but rather give place unto wrath: for it is written, Vengeance is mine; I will repay, saith the Lord.*

2 Th 1:7-8   *And to you who are troubled rest with us, when the Lord Jesus shall be revealed from heaven with his mighty angels, 8 In flaming fire taking vengeance on them that know not God, and that obey not the gospel of our Lord Jesus Christ: ...*

Heb 10:30   *For we know him that hath said, Vengeance belongeth unto me, I will recompense, saith the Lord. And again, The Lord shall judge his people.*

Great White Throne Judgment, the unrighteous are sentenced to eternal damnation in the lake of fire:

Rv 20:11-15   *And I saw a great white throne, and him that sat on it, from whose face the earth and the heaven fled away; and there was found no place for them. 12 And I saw the dead, small and great, stand before God; and the books were opened: and another book was opened, which is the book of life: and the dead were judged out of those things which were written in the books, according to their works. 13 And the sea gave up the dead which were in it; and death and hell delivered up the dead which were in them: and they were judged every man according to their works. 14 And death and hell were cast into the lake of fire. This is the second death. 15 And whosoever was not found written in the book of life was cast into the lake of fire.*

Heb 9:27   *And as it is appointed unto men once to die, but after this the judgment.*

In the Great White Throne Judgment, Jesus Christ is the judge, the same as in the Judgment Seat of Christ. The Great White Throne Judgment has other things that are different: it is a thousand years later, after the Millennium, and it is for unbelievers. This judgment will bring all unbelievers to an accounting for their unforgiven sins, of which the main one is the rejection of the Lord Jesus Christ as the God sent Savior of the world. This is not a trial to discover innocence or guilt, there is no appeal. The time for appeal is now. No one going to this judgment will get off without guilt or punishment, although there will be various degrees of guilt and punishment. Rv 20:15, above, tells us *"whosoever was not found written in the book of life was cast into the lake of fire."* Add to the fire, shame, hopelessness, the knowledge that your own choices put you there, plus an awareness that you are excluded from God's presence for eternity, and you have an awful and overwhelming situation in hell (the lake of fire), which is the outcome for all unbelievers at the Great White Throne Judgment, and it is forever. All of this will be done in fairness and according to the righteous judgments of God.

Mk 9:42-48 *And whosoever shall offend one of these little ones that believe in me, it is better for him that a millstone were hanged about his neck, and he were cast into the sea. 43 And if thy hand offend thee, cut it off: it is better for thee to enter into life maimed, than having two hands to go into hell, into the fire that never shall be quenched: 44 Where their worm dieth not, and the fire is not quenched. 45 And if thy foot offend thee, cut it off: it is better for thee to enter halt into life, than having two feet to be cast into hell, into the fire that never shall be quenched: 46 Where their worm dieth not, and the fire is not quenched. 47 And if thine eye offend thee, pluck it out: it is better for thee to enter into the kingdom of God with one eye, than having two eyes to be cast into hell fire: 48 Where their worm dieth not, and the fire is not quenched.*

1 Co 6:9-10 *Know ye not that the unrighteous shall not inherit the kingdom of God? Be not deceived: neither fornicators, nor idolaters, nor adulterers, nor effeminate, nor abusers of themselves with mankind, 10 Nor thieves, nor covetous, nor drunkards, nor revilers, nor extortioners, shall inherit the kingdom of God.*

Gal 5:19-21 *Now the works of the flesh are manifest, which are these; Adultery, fornication, uncleanness, lasciviousness, 20 Idolatry,* witchcraft, hatred, variance, emulations, wrath, strife, seditions, heresies, 21 Envyings, murders, drunkenness, revellings, and such like: of the which I tell you before, as I have also told you in time past, that they which do such things shall not inherit the kingdom of God.

2 Pe 3:7   But the heavens and the earth, which are now, by the same word are kept in store, reserved unto fire against the day of judgment and perdition of ungodly men.

Mt 10:7-8,14-15   And as ye go, preach, saying, The kingdom of heaven is at hand. 8 Heal the sick, cleanse the lepers, raise the dead, cast out devils: freely ye have received, freely give. ... 14 And whosoever shall not receive you, nor hear your words, when ye depart out of that house or city, shake off the dust of your feet. 15 Verily I say unto you, It shall be more tolerable for the land of Sodom and Gomorrha in the day of judgment, than for that city.

Jude 1:7   Even as Sodom and Gomorrha, and the cities about them in like manner, giving themselves over to fornication, and going after strange flesh, are set forth for an example, suffering the vengeance of eternal fire.

Mt 12:41-42   The men of Nineveh shall rise in judgment with this generation, and shall condemn it: because they repented at the preaching of Jonas; and, behold, a greater than Jonas is here. 42 The queen of the south shall rise up in the judgment with this generation, and shall condemn it: for she came from the uttermost parts

352

of the earth to hear the wisdom of Solomon; and, behold, a greater than Solomon is here.

Scripture for both Great White Throne and Judgment Seat of Christ:

Mt 12:35-37   *A good man out of the good treasure of the heart bringeth forth good things: and an evil man out of the evil treasure bringeth forth evil things. 36 But I say unto you, That every idle word that men shall speak, they shall give account thereof in the day of judgment. 37 For by thy words thou shalt be justified, and by thy words thou shalt be condemned.*

Pr 11:21   *Though hand join in hand, the wicked shall not be unpunished: but the seed of the righteous shall be delivered.*

Lk 12:42-48   *And the Lord said, Who then is that faithful and wise steward, whom his lord shall make ruler over his household, to give them their portion of meat in due season? 43 Blessed is that servant, whom his lord when he cometh shall find so doing. 44 Of a truth I say unto you, that he will make him ruler over all that he hath. 45 But and if that servant say in his heart, My lord delayeth his coming; and shall begin to beat the menservants and maidens, and to eat and drink, and to be drunken; 46 The lord of that servant will come in a day when he looketh not for him, and at an hour when he is not aware, and will cut him in sunder, and will appoint him his portion with the unbelievers. 47 And that servant, which knew his lord's will, and prepared not himself, neither did according to his will, shall be beaten with many stripes. 48 But he that knew not, and did commit things worthy of stripes, shall be beaten with few stripes. For unto whomsoever much is given, of him shall be much required: and to whom men have committed much, of him they will ask the more.*

Ro 2:1-9,12-13   Therefore thou art inexcusable, O man, whosoever thou art that judgest: for wherein thou judgest another, thou condemnest thyself; for thou that judgest doest the same things. 2 But we are sure that the judgment of God is according to truth against them which commit such things. 3 And thinkest thou this, O man, that judgest them which do such things, and doest the same, that thou shalt escape the judgment of God? 4 Or despisest thou the riches of his goodness and forbearance and longsuffering; not knowing that the goodness of God leadeth thee to repentance? 5 But after thy hardness and impenitent heart treasurest up unto thyself wrath against the day of wrath and revelation of the righteous judgment of God; 6 Who will render to every man according to his deeds: 7 To them who by patient continuance in well doing seek for glory and honour and immortality, eternal life: 8 But unto them that are contentious, and do not obey the truth, but obey unrighteousness, indignation and wrath, 9 Tribulation and anguish, upon every soul of man that doeth evil, of the Jew first, and also of the Gentile. ...   12 For as many as have sinned without law shall also perish without law: and as many as have sinned in the law shall be judged by the law; 13 (For not the hearers of the law are just before God, but the doers of the law shall be justified.

Jn 3:16-18   For God so loved the world, that he gave his only begotten Son, that whosoever believeth in him should not perish, but have everlasting life. 17 For God sent not his Son into the world to condemn the world; but that the world through him might be saved. 18 He that believeth on him is not condemned: but he that believeth not is condemned already, because he hath not believed in the name of the only begotten Son of God.

2 Th 1:7-10   And to you who are troubled rest with us, when the Lord Jesus shall be revealed from heaven with his mighty angels, 8 In flaming fire taking vengeance on them that know not God, and that obey not the gospel of our Lord Jesus Christ: 9 Who shall be punished with everlasting destruction from the presence of the Lord, and from the glory of his power; 10 When he shall come to be glorified in his saints, and to be admired in all them that believe (because our testimony among you was believed) in that day.

Rv 21:7-8,27   He that overcometh shall inherit all things; and I will be his God, and he shall be my son. 8 But the fearful, and unbelieving, and the abominable, and murderers, and whoremongers, and sorcerers, and idolaters, and all liars, shall have their part in the lake which burneth with fire and brimstone: which is the second death. ... 27 And there shall in no wise enter into it any thing that defileth, neither whatsoever worketh abomination, or maketh a lie: but they which are written in the Lamb's book of life.

Mt 13:41-43   The Son of man shall send forth his angels, and they shall gather out of his kingdom all things that offend, and them which do iniquity; 42 And shall cast them into a furnace of fire: there shall be wailing and gnashing of teeth. 43 Then shall the righteous shine forth as the sun in the kingdom of their Father. ...

Judgment both then and now:

There is ample scripture that shows that we will go before the Lord Jesus in judgment both at the Judgment Seat of Christ or at the Great White Throne Judgment. There is also ample Scripture to show there are times in this life when the Lord chooses to bring judgment in the here and now. Jude 5 mentions the time when Israel was punished after they came out of Egypt. God had shown them His miracles many times, yet they refused to believe Him, so He judged (destroyed) them. Rv 20:7-9 speaks of a time in the future when God will bring a strong judgment at the time of the sin committed.

Jude 1:5   I will therefore put you in remembrance, though ye once knew this, how that the Lord, having saved the people out of the land of Egypt, afterward destroyed them that believed not.

Rv 20:7-9   And when the thousand years are expired, Satan shall be loosed out of his prison, 8 And shall go out to deceive the nations which are in the four quarters of the earth, Gog and Magog, to gather them together to battle: the number of whom is as the sand of the sea. 9 And they went up on the breadth of the earth, and compassed the camp of the saints about, and the beloved city: and fire came down from God out of heaven, and devoured them.

There is also the example of Sodom and Gomorrah; the story is told in Gen 19:1-25. For further examples of judgment in our lifetimes see the following scripture locations: Isa 26:21, Ps 37:38, Isa 13:11, Am 3:14, Zep 1:12, 1 Th 4:6, Mt 25:31-46.

So, we should all live and serve the Lord with clean hands and a pure heart, as the Psalmist says,:

Ps 24:3-5 *Who shall ascend into the hill of the LORD? or who shall stand in his holy place? 4 He that hath clean hands, and a pure heart; who hath not lifted up his soul unto vanity, nor sworn deceitfully. 5 He shall receive the blessing from the LORD, and righteousness from the God of his salvation.*

With the judgment of godless sinners behind us, let us take a look at the new heaven and earth that is coming.

Notes:
1. Doug Barton, Facebook post, 4-9-2020. Link: https://www.facebook.com/douglas.barton.73

14

A New Heaven and Earth

A new heaven and earth:

800 years before John wrote the Revelation, Isaiah told us there will be a new heaven and a new earth.

Isa 65:17-18 *For, behold, I create new heavens and a new earth: and the former shall not be remembered, nor come into mind. 18 But be ye glad and rejoice for ever in that which I create: for, behold, I create Jerusalem a rejoicing, and her people a joy.*

Isa 66:22 *For as the new heavens and the new earth, which I will make, shall remain before me, saith the LORD, so shall your seed and your name remain.*

John the Apostle tells us he saw a new heaven and a new earth, for the first heaven and earth were passed away.

Rv 21:1 *And I saw a new heaven and a new earth: for the first heaven and the first earth were passed away; and there was no more sea.*

Some scholars teach that this new heaven and earth will just be renewed rather than actually a new heaven and earth. Pastor David Jeremiah[1], no doubt a great man of God and respected scholar, is one who says it will be a renewal and a purifying and a renovation, rather than a newly created earth. Dr. Jeremiah refers to 2 Pet 3:5-12 and says that according to older manuscripts the words "burned up" really say "cleansed", and the word "new" really means "renewal" rather than a new creation. If this is correct there will be a cleansing and renewal for this present earth.

In his book, "The Second Coming of Jesus," G. F. Taylor[2] says the earth will be renewed, rather than destroyed, and another created. His reasoning is partly because of some of God's promises to Abraham and others. According to scripture the promises of the land of Canaan being given to Abraham and his seed was to be forever.

Ge 13:14-15   *And the LORD said unto Abram, after that Lot was separated from him, Lift up now thine eyes, and look from the place where thou art northward, and southward, and eastward, and westward: 15 For all the land which thou seest, to thee will I give it, and to thy seed for ever.*

Ps 105:8-11   *He hath remembered his covenant for ever, the word which he commanded to a thousand generations. 9 Which covenant he made with Abraham, and his oath unto Isaac; 10 And confirmed the same unto Jacob for a law, and to Israel for an everlasting covenant: 11 Saying, Unto thee will I give the land of Canaan, ...*

Taylor also referred to other scripture that declares that the earth abides forever, saying that unless the earth abides forever the Lord cannot keep His promises to the patriarchs.

Ps 104:5   *Who laid the foundations of the earth, that it should not be removed for ever.*

Ecc 1:4   *One generation passeth away, and another generation cometh: but the earth abideth for ever.*

These arguments seem to strongly show that the earth will indeed be cleansed and renewed.

If it proves to be what the King James Version seems to be saying, "the first heaven and earth are passed away", there will indeed be a new heaven and earth. In this new (or renewed) heaven and earth there will be no more sea; that alone will be a big difference. Some other differences that can be seen by reading Revelation 21 and 22: no more pain nor death, the holy city, New Jerusalem, is made of pure gold, no need for the sun, no night there for the city is lightened by the glory of God, no more sin only righteousness. That new heaven and earth and the New Jerusalem will all be glorious beyond comprehension and it will all be eternal. The Lord Jesus told John:

Rv 22:14   *Blessed are they that do his commandments, that they may have right to the tree of life, and may enter in through the gates into the city.*

Peter adds his testimony to that of Isaiah and John, going even further and describing for us the passing or renewal of the present earth and heavens: it is going to be burned up. In speaking of the heavens, it is not clear if he means what we think of as heaven or simply the earth's atmosphere along with the present physical earth. He further declares there will be new heavens and a new earth. Peter concludes his remarks by encouraging us to be diligently striving to be found without spot and blameless.

2 Pe 3:10-14   *But the day of the Lord will come as a thief in the night; in the which the heavens shall pass away with a great noise, and the elements shall melt with fervent heat, the earth also and the works that are therein shall be burned up. 11 Seeing then that all these things shall be dissolved, what manner of persons ought ye to be in all holy conversation and godliness, 12 Looking for and hasting unto the coming of the day of God, wherein the heavens being on fire shall be dissolved, and the elements shall melt with fervent heat? 13 Nevertheless we, according to his promise, look for new heavens and a new earth, wherein dwelleth righteousness. 14 Wherefore, beloved, seeing that ye look for such things, be diligent that ye may be found of him in peace, without spot, and blameless.*

And again, in his first epistle, John tells us that this first world is passing away:

1 John 2:17   *And the world is passing away along with its desires, but whoever does the will of God abides forever.*

Last, but far from least, Jesus himself tells us the He is going away to prepare for us a place.

Jn 14:2-3   *In my Father's house are many mansions: if it were not so, I would have told you. I go to prepare a place for you. 3 And if I go and prepare a place for you, I will come again, and receive you unto myself; that where I am, there ye may be also.*

New Jerusalem:

John's next words are: there is a New Jerusalem descending from God out of heaven, and that God will dwell with men. Abraham looked for this city. Every Christian on earth and living in the end times should be greatly encouraged and excited, and like Abraham, looking for that city.

Heb 11:8-10,13-16   *By faith Abraham, when he was called to go out into a place which he should after receive for an inheritance, obeyed; and he went out, not knowing whither he went. 9 By faith he sojourned in the land of promise, as in a strange country, dwelling in tabernacles with Isaac and Jacob, the heirs with him of the same promise: 10 For he looked for a city which hath foundations, whose builder and maker is God. ... 13 These all died in faith, not having received the promises, but having seen them afar off, and were persuaded of them, and embraced them, and confessed that they were strangers and pilgrims on the earth. 14 For they that say such things declare plainly that they seek a country. 15 And truly, if they had been mindful of that country from whence they came out, they might have had opportunity to have returned. 16 But now they desire a better country, that is, an heavenly: wherefore God is not ashamed to be called their God: for he hath prepared for them a city.*

Rv 21:2-5   *And I John saw the holy city, new Jerusalem, coming down from God out of heaven, prepared as a bride adorned for her husband. 3 And I heard a great voice out of heaven saying, Behold, the tabernacle of God is*

363

with men, and he will dwell with them, and they shall be his people, and God himself shall be with them, and be their God. 4 And God shall wipe away all tears from their eyes; and there shall be no more death, neither sorrow, nor crying, neither shall there be any more pain: for the former things are passed away. 5 And he that sat upon the throne said, Behold, I make all things new. And he said unto me, Write: for these words are true and faithful.

Jesus told the Philadelphian church through the apostle John that there is a New Jerusalem coming down out of heaven from God.

Rv 3:12 *Him that overcometh will I make a pillar in the temple of my God, and he shall go no more out: and I will write upon him the name of my God, and the name of the city of my God, which is new Jerusalem, which cometh down out of heaven from my God: and I will write upon him my new name.*

The Glory of the Holy city the New Jerusalem:

This beautiful city descends to the new earth out of heaven from God. Whether this great city settles onto the new earth or suspends in the air above the new earth is not made clear to us. At any rate it is magnificent and beautiful.

Rv 21:9-14 *And there came unto me one of the seven angels which had the seven vials full of the seven last plagues, and talked with me, saying, Come hither, I will shew thee the bride, the Lamb's wife. 10 And he carried me away in the spirit to a* great and high mountain, and shewed me that great city, the holy Jerusalem, descending out of heaven from God, 11 Having the glory of God: and her light was like unto a stone most precious, even like a jasper stone, clear as crystal; 12 And had a wall great and high, and had twelve gates, and at the gates twelve angels, and names written thereon, which are the names of the twelve tribes of the children of Israel: 13 On the east three gates; on the north three gates; on the south three gates; and on the west three gates. 14 And the wall of the city had twelve foundations, and in them the names of the twelve apostles of the Lamb.

A city of gold measuring 1500 miles, long, wide, and high:

This new Jerusalem, in a manner of speaking is unbelievable. The city itself, as well as the streets, are pure gold; it has twelve gates of pearl and twelve foundations of precious stones. It is 12,000 furlongs square. A furlong is one eighth of a mile, meaning this city is 1500 miles square. If this city were set down on the United States, it would occupy much of the space from Canada to Mexico, and from the Mississippi River to the west coast.

Rv 21:15-21 And he that talked with me had a golden reed to measure the city, and the gates thereof, and the wall thereof. 16 And the city lieth foursquare, and the length is as large as the breadth: and he measured the city with the reed, twelve thousand furlongs. The length and the breadth and the height of it are equal. 17 And he measured the wall thereof, an hundred and forty and four cubits, according to the measure of a man, that is, of the angel. 18 And the building of the wall of it was of jasper: and the city was pure gold, like unto clear glass. 19 And the foundations of the wall of the city were garnished with all manner of precious stones. The first foundation was jasper; the second, sapphire; the third, a chalcedony; the fourth, an emerald; 20 The fifth, sardonyx; the sixth, sardius; the seventh, chrysolite; the eighth, beryl; the ninth, a topaz; the tenth, a chrysoprasus; the eleventh, a jacinth; the twelfth, an amethyst. 21 And the twelve gates were twelve pearls; every several gate was of one pearl: and the street of the city was pure gold, as it were transparent glass.

The Lord God Almighty and the Lamb are the Temple:

The glory of God and the Lamb will be the light of this great city, with no need for the sun or moon. There will be no night there. The nations of that new world will bring their glory into that city. Nothing evil will ever be found there, no further contamination of sin forever; only those whose names are written in the Lamb's book of life will be there.

Rv 21:22-27   And I saw no temple therein: for the Lord God Almighty and the Lamb are the temple of it. 23 And the city had no need of the sun, neither of the moon, to shine in it: for the glory of God did lighten it, and the Lamb is the light thereof. 24 And the nations of them which are saved shall walk in the light of it: and the kings of

the earth do bring their glory and honour into it.
25 And the gates of it shall not be shut at all by
day: for there shall be no night there. 26 And they
shall bring the glory and honour of the nations into
it. 27 And there shall in no wise enter into it any
thing that defileth, neither whatsoever worketh
abomination, or maketh a lie: but they which are
written in the Lamb's book of life.

Satan is absent in the new world:

One thing that is very different and very
wonderful: Satan will have no part at all in this new
world. He had access to the first world and every
human being who ever was born into the world.
But in the new world he will have no part; he will
never even see it. He was created by God in
righteousness as a freewill being and he chose to
defy God in disobedience and has troubled mankind
ever since; his first victims were Adam and Eve.
His time will be over after the Tribulation and
another brief time after the Millennium, but then no
more. He will be thrown into the lake of fire
forever.

Rv 20:7-10   *And when the thousand years*
are expired, Satan shall be loosed out of his prison,
8 And shall go out to deceive the nations which are
in the four quarters of the earth, Gog and Magog,
to gather them together to battle: the number of
whom is as the sand of the sea. 9 And they went
up on the breadth of the earth, and compassed the
camp of the saints about, and the beloved city: and
fire came down from God out of heaven and
devoured them. 10 And the devil that deceived

them was cast into the lake of fire and brimstone, where the beast and the false prophet are, and shall be tormented day and night for ever and ever.

The tree of life is there:

Not only is the tree of life there, but also the river of the water of life. Besides that, there is no curse, and there is no night as God gives the light. *"and his servants shall serve him: ... and they shall reign for ever and ever."* Blessing is pronounced on all who go there.

Rv 22:1-7,11-13   *And he shewed me a pure river of water of life, clear as crystal, proceeding out of the throne of God and of the Lamb. 2 In the midst of the street of it, and on either side of the river, was there the tree of life, which bare twelve manner of fruits, and yielded her fruit every month: and the leaves of the tree were for the healing of the nations. 3 And there shall be no more curse: but the throne of God and of the Lamb shall be in it; and his servants shall serve him: 4 And they shall see his face; and his name shall be in their foreheads. 5 And there shall be no night there; and they need no candle, neither light of the sun; for the Lord God giveth them light: and they shall reign for ever and ever. 6 And he said unto me, These sayings are faithful and true: and the Lord God of the holy prophets sent his angel to shew unto his servants the things which must shortly be done. 7 Behold, I come quickly: blessed is he that keepeth the sayings of the prophecy of this book. ... 11 He that is unjust, let him be unjust still: and he which is filthy, let him be filthy still:*

and he that is righteous, let him be righteous still: and he that is holy, let him be holy still. 12 And, behold, I come quickly; and my reward is with me, to give every man according as his work shall be. 13 I am Alpha and Omega, the beginning and the end, the first and the last.

Conclusion:

This brings our look at "The End of the Days" to an end. We have arrived in the new heaven and earth, living in the golden city, New Jerusalem.

Rv 22:3-5 ... *the throne of God and of the Lamb shall be in it; and **his servants shall serve him**: 4 And they shall see his face; and his name shall be in their foreheads. 5 ... **and they shall reign for ever and ever.***

This is not the end, but a continuation, with a new, beautiful, and blessed beginning, with all of eternity out there before us.

Notes:

1. David Jeremiah, Turning Point, online sermons. Link: https://www.lightsource.com/ministry/turning-point/the-new-heaven-and-the-new-earth-836299.html
2. G. F. Taylor, The Second Coming of Jesus (Franklin Springs, GA: Pentecostal Holiness Church Publishing House, 1950), p. 116.

Made in the USA
Middletown, DE
25 October 2021